Advisory Board

Albrecht Classen, University of Arizona
Everett U. Crosby, University of Virginia
Jean Dufournet, Université de Paris III, Sorbonne
Leonardas V. Gerulaitis, Oakland University
Ulrich Goebel, Texas Tech University
Karl Heinz Göller, Universität Regensburg
Ann Tukey Harrison, Michigan State University
William E. Jackson, University of Virginia
Sibylle Jefferis, University of Pennsylvania
J. Daniel Kinney, University of Virginia
William Magee, University of North Carolina Greensboro
Guy R. Mermier, University of Michigan
Ulrich Müller, Universität Salzburg
Perri Lee Roberts, University of Miami Coral Gables
Graham A. Runnalls, University of Edinburgh
Barbara N. Sargent-Baur, University of Pittsburgh
Joseph T. Snow, Michigan State University
Jean Subrenat, Université de Provence
Jane H. M. Taylor, Collingwood College (University of Durham)
Steven M. Taylor, Marquette University
Arjo Vanderjagt, University of Groningen
Carlos A. Vega, Wellesley College
Martin Walsh, University of Michigan

Founder: Edelgard E. DuBruck

Consulting Editor: William C. McDonald

Fifteenth-Century Studies

Volume 30

Edited by
Edelgard E. DuBruck
and
Barbara I. Gusick

CAMDEN HOUSE

Copyright © 2005 the Contributors
All Rights Reserved. Except as permitted under current legislation,
no part of this work may be photocopied, stored in a retrieval system,
published, performed in public, adapted, broadcast, transmitted,
recorded, or reproduced in any form or by any means,
without the prior permission of the copyright owner.

ISSN: 0164–0933

ISBN: 1–57113–309–7

First published 2005
by Camden House
Camden House is an imprint of Boydell & Brewer Inc.
668 Mt. Hope Avenue, Rochester, N.Y. 14620–2731 USA
and of Boydell & Brewer Limited
PO Box 9, Woodbridge, Suffolk IP12 3DF, U.K.

This publication is printed on acid-free paper.

Printed in the United States of America.

Fifteenth-Century Studies appears annually. Please send orders
and inquiries to Boydell & Brewer at the above address.

For editorial correspondence and manuscript submissions, write to:
Prof. Edelgard E. DuBruck
29451 Halsted Road, Apt. 141
Farmington Hills, Michigan 48331 USA
Articles and book reviews submitted for publication
may be edited to conform to *FCS* style.

Submit books for review to:
Peter Meister
Foreign Languages
University of Alabama
Huntsville, AL 35899 USA

Information on membership in the Fifteenth-Century Society,
which entitles the member to a copy of each issue of *Fifteenth-Century Studies*,
is available from Prof. Edelgard E. DuBruck, 29451 Halsted Road, Apt. 141,
Farmington Hills, MI 48331 USA

Contents

Essays

The Current State of Research on Late-Medieval Drama: 2002–2004.
Survey, Bibliography, and Reviews   1
   Edelgard E. DuBruck

Gestural Communication in French Religious Drama and Art of
the Late Middle Ages: The *Passion Isabeau* and Its Miniatures   39
   Edelgard E. DuBruck

Some Renaissance Views about Madness and Genius:
Reading Ficino and Paracelsus   58
   Leonardas Vytautas Gerulaitis

Christ's Transformation of Zacchaeus in the
York Cycle's *Entry into Jerusalem*   68
   Barbara I. Gusick

Bibliographie des Miracles et Mystères français   95
   Graham A. Runnalls et Jesse Hurlbut

The Cleveland *St. John the Baptist,* Attributed to Petrus Christus, and
Philip the Good's Triumphal Entry into Bruges (1440)   162
   Mark Trowbridge

Book Reviews

Ashley, Kathleen, and Pamela Sheingorn, ed. *Interpreting
   Cultural Symbols: Saint Anne in the Late-Medieval Society.*
   Athens and London: The University of Georgia Press,
   1990 (Jefferis).   190

Baraz, Daniel. *Medieval Cruelty: Changing Perceptions,
   Late Antiquity to the Early Modern Period.*
   Ithaca: Cornell University Press, 2003 (DuBruck).   197

Brown, Cynthia J., ed. Pierre Gringore. *Oeuvres polémiques
   rédigées sous le règne de Louis XII.*
   Geneva: Droz, 2003 (Hochner).   199

Di Stefano, Giuseppe, ed. *Boccace, 'Decameron,' traduction
   (1411–1414) de Laurent de Premierfait.*
   Montréal: Éditions CERES, 1998–1999 (Duhl).   202

Duval, Frédéric, and S. Hériché-Pradeau, ed. *Guillaume Tardif: Les Facecies de Poge, traduction du 'Liber facetiarum' de Poggio Bracciolini.* Geneva: Droz, 2003 (DuBruck).   206

Findlen, Paula, Michelle M. Fontaine, and Duane J. Osheim, ed. *Beyond Florence: The Contours of Medieval and Early Modern Italy.* Stanford: Stanford University Press, 2003 (Even).   207

Hope, Geoffrey, ed. *Le Violier des histoires rommaines.* Geneva: Droz, 2002 (Diller).   210

Jankrift, Kay Peter. *Krankheit und Heilkunde im Mittelalter.* Darmstadt: Wissenschaftliche Buchgesellschaft, 2003 (Gerulaitis).   212

Séris, Émilie. *Les Étoiles de Némesis: La rhétorique de la mémoire dans la poésie d'Ange Politien (1454–1494).* Geneva: Droz, 2002 (Saslow).   213

Wolfegg, Christoph Graf zu Waldburg. *Venus and Mars: The World of the Medieval Housebook.* Munich: Prestel, 1998 (DuBruck).   215

The Current State of Research on Late-Medieval Drama: 2002–2004. Survey, Bibliography, and Reviews

Edelgard E. DuBruck

This article is a regular feature of Fifteenth-Century Studies. *Our intent is to catalogue, survey, and assess scholarship on the staging and textual configuration of dramatic presentations in the late Middle Ages. Like all such dated material this assessment remains incomplete. We shall therefore include 2004 again in the next listing [vol. 31]. Our readers are encouraged to bring new items to our attention, including their own work. Monographs and collections selected for detailed review will appear in the third section of this article and will be marked by an asterisk in the pages below.*

During the time span 2002–2004 English drama generated less scholarly inquiry than that devoted to French theater or European drama generally. Therefore, we begin by investigating collections focusing upon European studies.

The *European Medieval Drama* series (henceforth: *EMD*) published its fourth volume under the combined editorship of André Lascombes* and Sydney Higgins. The mix of articles here is discernibly well balanced, in that medieval drama from a variety of European countries is reflected. A distinguishing theme for 02–04 is gestures which complement and enhance play texts: Clifford Davidson* published *Gesture in Medieval Drama and Art*; Charles Reginald Dodwell researched Anglo-Saxon body motions as compared to those of the Roman stage, where Forcefulness, Restraint, Belligerence, Compliance, Dissent, Agreement, Puzzlement, Love, Fear, Grief, Supplication, Amazement, and Reflection are shown to have been easily *readable* in medieval Terence codices. The gestures of classical theater were also the subject of John McKinnell's article in *Leeds Studies in English*; further, monographs and collections on general themes were offered by Hindley, Hüsken/Schoell, Eisenbichler/Hüsken, Pietrini, Tydeman, Gusick/DuBruck, Duhl, and Bordier.

Alan Hindley* edited *Drama and Community: People and Plays in Medieval Europe*, while Sandra Pietrini wrote *Spettacoli e immaginario teatrale nel Medioevo* and William Tydeman published *The Medieval European Stage, 500–1550*. Wim Hüsken* and Konrad Schoell edited *Farce and Farcical Elements*, containing an uneven mix of countries (with six essays on English drama alone!), while Konrad Eisenbichler* and Hüsken collected *Carnival and the Carnivalesque: The Fool, the Reformer, the Wildman, and Others in Early Modern Theatre* (representing many European countries). Yumi Dohi* researched holy communion on the European stage, an enlightening (if somewhat technical) enterprise, which centered on communion theology. Barbara I. Gusick and Edelgard E. DuBruck collected *New Approaches to European Theater of the Middle Ages: An Ontology*, whereas Jean-Pierre Bordier* published three general series on this subject: *Le Jeu théâtral, ses marges, ses frontières*; *Langues, codes et conventions de l'ancien théâtre européen*; and *L'Économie du dialogue dans l'ancien théâtre européen*.

Concerning England, the plays of York, Croxton, Coventry, N-Town, and Towneley were investigated. Olga Horner wrote on the Old Testament Covenant performed on the York moving stages, while Barbara I. Gusick reviewed York's Millennium production of the mysteries in a superb article, which also comprises previous York plays in 1992 (modernized) and 1998 (authentic). The 2000 venue (the York Minster) was enhanced by lighting and music; thirteen color photos (permission of Kippa Matthews) are a special bonus, complementing Gusick's essay. For Croxton, Leanne Groenveld and Heather Hill-Vasquez wrote on Christ's image and body in the *Play of the Sacrament*. Pamela M. King and Clifford Davidson published *The Coventry Corpus Christi Plays* — a cycle *in absentia*, since only two plays survive; the text of this monograph, as well as its Appendix, contain material from previous publications by both authors. Charivaris in the N-Town cycle was Richard J. Moll's topic, with special emphasis placed on the *Trial of Mary and Joseph*, wherein Mary's pregnancy is doubly suspicious to Joseph and the community, eliciting such questions as: was she unfaithful? did she break her vow of chastity? Towneley's *Second Shepherds' Play* came under Karen E. Sawyer's scrutiny, specifically regarding six saints (among them Saint Nicolas) associated with Advent or Christmas. A reference to Jean Bodel's *Jeu de saint Nicolas* (twelfth century) would have assisted the argument (26). Victor Scherb published a monograph on the staging of Faith in East Anglian drama.

Timing theatrical action was Philip Butterworth's topic, whereas Lawrence M. Clopper wrote on the London Clerkenwell plays, as yet little known at this point, and penned a monograph on English festive culture in dramas, plays, and games. Peter Greenfield published a census of drama productions, while Lynn Forest-Hill viewed transgressive language in a monograph, and Richard Rastall examined a speaking tube for God in religious performances. Finally, Alan J. Fletcher investigated drama (early Gaelic traditions) in pre-Cromwellian Ireland. The stance on anti-theatrical matters (*Tretise of Miraclis Pleyinge*) occupied Pietrini, Clopper, and Hill-Vasquez, whereas articles on French drama as compared to certain English plays were penned by Robert L. Clark, Peter Happé, and Peter Meredith. We regret that Clifford Davidson's *Early Drama, Art, and Music Review* has ceased production as of 2003.

The French profane stage received much attention. Besides Marie Bouhaïk-Gironès's article on Parisian clerks and law students as authors, we have Andrew Cowell's* monograph *At Play in the Tavern*, a study of comico-realistic plays and the metageneric symbiose of tavern and theater. Here, signs, coins, and bodies were exchanged in festivals of ambiguity and profit (*Jeu de saint Nicolas, Courtois d'Arras, le Jeu de la Feuillée*, and others — except for the *Roman de Renart*). Olga Anna Duhl's* collection of articles contains mostly profane plays, and her title *Théâtre français des années 1450–1550* is therefore inconclusive. Farces were researched by Boucquey, Mazouer, Faivre, Koopmans, Romagnoli, and Schoell. Thierry Boucquey translated six farces; Charles Mazouer compared farces to Renaissance comedies, and studied *badin* and Christian eschatology in farces. Bernard Faivre investigated farce gestures and language concerning their rhythmical features; Jelle Koopmans wrote on the status of the homeless as reflected in farces, and, with Paul Verhuyck, penned an article on metaphors; Koopmans also investigated two short plays intercalated by an inadvertent editor (Gustave Cohen), and studied the Parisian farce theater. Konrad Schoell researched farce actors, scenes, and audiences, and pondered the semiotics of performances, while, in *EMD*, he compared farce humor to that evidenced in German carnival plays. There are still other essays on farces, of which we mention only Bruno Roy's examination of *Maître Pathelin*.

Four authors studied the *sottie* (a satirical play by witty buffoons): Nicole Hochner discussed the political significance of Gringore's *Jeu du Prince des Sotz*; Pierre Romagnoli interpreted the *sottie* of the *Gens nouveaux* (contrast between old and new, and the nostalgia of some for a Golden Age past); Jelle Koopmans examined farce elements in *sotties*; and Stéphanie Robert viewed poetic forms and versification of a *sottie* by André de la Vigne.

The mystery plays predominated within research on French theater. Pierre Kunstmann proposed an electronic edition of religious theater, while Mario Longtin pondered the *Mystère de sainte Barbe* and Guy Borgnet the *Passion de Maastricht*. George Tuaillon examined *L'Histoire de Monseigneur Saint Sébastien* and two *Dioclétiane* mysteries (Savoy); Jean-Pierre Perrot and J.-J. Nonot edited a *Jour du Jugement*, whereas C. Lucken treated the devil's kitchen and St. Bernard's hospice in the *Mystère de Saint Bernard de Menthon* (Savoy). Stéphanie Le Briz-Orgeur investigated Arnoul Gréban's *Passion* (dialogues; and monologues of hesitation). Graham A. Runnalls studied civic drama in Burgundy; mysteries in imprint*; he published (with Jesse Hurlbut) a "Bibliography of French Miracle and Mystery Plays"; Runnalls also investigated the *Mystère de l'Assomption* from the viewpoint of marketing; and gestures along with language of the *Mystère de s. Laurent*. Alan E. Knight* edited the *Pentateuch* and *De Josué à David* of the *Mystères de la Procession de Lille*, and Edelgard E. DuBruck examined Lazarus's vision of hell in passion plays. The feminine figures in mysteries were Sharon M. Loewald's* topic, while James D. Wilkins studied the body as currency in religious drama, and Véronique Dominguez discussed the body's theology. Jean Subrenat showcased daily life of the lower classes in passion plays, and the *Mistere du Siege d'Orleans* was edited by Vicki L. Hamblin.

The French moralities were Jonathan Beck's subject, and Jean-Pierre Bordier studied the *Moralité du jour saint Antoine* (1427), as well as a *Moralité de l'Envie des frères*. Miracle plays or themes were examined by Marla Carlson, Pierre Kunstmann, Pascale Dumont, and Gérard Gros. Carol Symes contributed an eloquent plea for the study of early vernacular French plays from the viewpoint of New Philology, which examines manuscripts within their surroundings (codex) before editing texts.

Other countries' productions were researched by Alan Hindley* (the Netherlands); A. Robert Lauer and Juan Carlos Garrot (Spain); Sharon M. Carnicke (Puerto Rico); and Hans-Jürgen Linke and Katja Scheel (Germany). Two recent studies by Cobie Kuné should be mentioned here: one on "The Prague Last Supper," and the other on a Lüben Easter fragment (a Silesian witness). We had to abbreviate our account, often giving only names and topics; the full references will be found in our bibliography. As substantiated by the breadth and volume of scholarly publications focusing upon the medieval theater, it is obvious that interest in and research of the medieval stage are growing, to which we respond: bravo!

Bibliography

Beck, Jonathan. "La place de la moralité de *Bien Avisé Mal Avisé* dans le théâtre en France du moyen âge." In *Le Théâtre français des années 1450–1550. État actuel des recherches*, edited by Olga Anna Duhl, 15–24. Dijon: Centre de Recherches Le Texte et l'Édition, Université de Dijon, 2002. Henceforth: Duhl.

———. "Sur la moralité de *Bien Avisé Mal Avisé*. Codes et conventions (d'autrefois et d'aujourd'hui) du langage des anciens textes dramatiques." In *Langues, codes et conventions de l'ancien théâtre européen*, edited by Jean-Pierre Bordier, 45–54. Paris: Champion, 2002.

Beckwith, Sarah. *Signifying God: Social Relation and Symbolic Act in the York Corpus Christi Plays*. Chicago: University of Chicago Press, 2001.

Bordier, Jean-Pierre, ed. *L'Économie du dialogue dans l'ancien théâtre européen*. Paris: Champion, 1999.

———, ed. *Le Jeu théâtral, ses marges, ses frontières*. Paris: Champion, 1999. Henceforth: Bordier, *Jeu*.

———, ed. *Langues, codes et conventions de l'ancien théâtre européen* (see above). Henceforth: Bordier, *Langues*.

—. "Magis mouent exempla quam uerba: une définition du jeu théâtral dans la *Moralité du jour saint Antoine* (1427)." In Bordier, *Jeu*, 91–104.

—. "*La Moralité de l'Envie des frères*, conventions théâtrales et codes herméneutiques." In Bordier, *Langues*, 191–209.

—. "Le rôle de Jean-Baptiste chez Arnoul Gréban et Jean Michel." In *Jean-Baptiste le Précurseur au Moyen Âge*, edited by Chantal Connochie-Bourgne, 43–59. Aix-en-Provence: Publications de l'Université de Provence CUER-MA (*Senefiance* 48), 2002.

Borgnet, Guy. "Réflexions sur la *Passion de Maastricht*: autorité de la parole, parole de l'autorité." In Bordier, *Jeu,* 105–14.

Boucquet, Thierry, tr. *Six Medieval French Farces*. Lewiston: Mellen, 1999.

Bouhaïk-Gironès, Marie. "Les Clercs et les écoliers, auteurs de théâtre profane à Paris à la fin du XVe siècle et au début du XVIe siècle." In Duhl, 29–36.

Butterworth, Philip. "Discipline, Dignity, and Beauty: The Wakefield Mystery Plays, Bretton Hall, 1958." *Leeds Studies in English*, n.s. 32 (2001): 49–80.

—. "Timing Theatrical Action in the English Medieval Theatre." *Early Theatre* 4 (2001): 87–100.

Carlson, Marla. "Spectator Response to an Image of Violence: Seeing Apollonia." *Fifteenth-Century Studies* 27 (2002): 7–20.

Carnicke, Sharon Marie. "Medieval Theatre Revisited in Juana Diaz, Puerto Rico." *Gestos* 32 (2001): 127–40.

Clark, Robert L. "Othered Bodies and Racial Cross-Dressing in the *Mystère de la Sainte Hostie* and the *Croxton Play of the Sacrament*." *Journal of Medieval and Early Modern Studies* 29 (1999): 61–87.

Clopper, Lawrence M. "London and the Problem of the Clerkenwell Plays." *Comparative Drama* 34 (2000): 291–304.

Cowell, Andrew. *At Play in the Tavern: Signs, Coins, and Bodies in the Middle Ages*. Ann Arbor: University of Michigan Press, 1999.

Davidson, Clifford, ed. *Gesture in Medieval Drama and Art*. Kalamazoo: MIP, 2001.

Dodwell, Charles Reginald. *Anglo-Saxon Gestures and the Roman Stage*. Cambridge: Cambridge University Press, 2000.

Dohi, Yumi. *Das Abendmahl im spätmittelalterlichen Drama*. Frankfurt am Main: Lang, 2000.

Dominguez, Véronique. *Le Corps dans les 'Mystères de la Passion' français: discours théologique et esthétique théâtrale*. Diss. Université de Paris IV, 1999.

—. "Voir l'invisible au théâtre: les mystères de la foi dans quelques *Mystères de la Passion*." In *Par la vue et par l'ouïe. Littérature du Moyen Âge et de la Renaissance*, edited by M. Gally and M. Jourde, 111–34. Fontenay-aux-Roses: Éditions ENS, 1999.

DuBruck, Edelgard E. "The Current State of Research on Late-Medieval Drama 1997–98. Survey, Bibliography, and Reviews." *Fifteenth-Century Studies* 27 (2002): 1–20. 1998–2000, *FCS* 28 (2003): 1–36.

—. "Lazarus's Vision of Hell: A Significant Passage in Late-Medieval Passion Plays." *Fifteenth-Century Studies* 27 (2002): 44–55.

Duhl, Olga Anna, ed. *Le Théâtre français des années 1450–1550. État actuel des recherches*. Dijon: Université de Bourgogne, Centre de Recherches Le Texte et l'Édition, 2002.

Eisenbichler, Konrad, and Wim Hüsken, ed. *Carnival and the Carnivalesque: The Fool, the Reformer, the Wildman, and Others in Early Modern Theatre*. Amsterdam: Rodopi, 1999.

Faivre, Bernard. "Le dit et le joué." In Bordier, *Jeu*, 193–99.

—. "Les Rhythmes de la farce ou les gestes et les mots." In *L'Économie du dialogue*, edited by Jean-Pierre Bordier, 33–39. Paris: Champion, 1999.

—. "'Je veux que tu me dises à qui tu parles quand tu dis cela' ou le spectateur partenaire du farceur." In Bordier, *Langues*, 135–47.

Fletcher, Alan J. *Drama, Performance and Polity in Pre-Cromwellian Ireland*. Toronto: University of Toronto Press, 2000.

Forest-Hill, Lynn. *Transgressive Language in Medieval English Drama: Signs of Challenge and Change*. Burlington, Vermont: Ashgate, 2000.

Greenfield, Peter. "Census of Medieval Drama Productions." *Research Opportunities in Renaissance Drama* 40 (2001): 197–206.

Groeneveld, Leanne. "Christ as Image in the *Croxton Play of the Sacrament.*" *Research Opportunities in Renaissance Drama* 40 (2001): 177–95.

Gros, Gérard. "L'Avocate et sa vocation: Étude sur la dramatisation d'une propriété mariale dans *l'Advocacie Nostre Dame.*" In Bordier, *Jeu*, 125–40.

Gusick, Barbara I., and Edelgard E. DuBruck, ed. *New Approaches to European Theater of the Middle Ages: An Ontology.* New York: Peter Lang, 2004.

Gusick, Barbara I. "A Review of the York Millennium Mystery Plays." *Research Opportunities in Renaissance Drama* 40 (2001): 111–32.

Hamblin, Vicki L., ed. *Le Mistere du Siege d'Orleans.* Geneva: Droz, 2002.

—. "Lire les didascalies du *Siege d'Orleans*: conventions théâtrales ou tradition commémorative?" In Bordier, *Langues*, 93–100.

Happé, Peter. "The Management of Narrative in the Performance of Cycle Plays: The *Cornish Ordinalia*, *La Passion d'Auvergne*, and N-Town." *EDAMR* 24 (Spring, 2002): 105–21.

—. "Performing Passion Plays in France and England." *EMD* 4 (2000): 57–76.

Hill-Vasquez, Heather. "'The precious body of crist that they tretyn in ther hondis': 'Miraclis Pleyinge' and the *Croxton Play of the Sacrament.*" *Early Theatre* 4 (2001): 73–86.

Hindley, Alan, ed. *Drama and Community: People and Plays in Medieval Europe.* Turnhout: Brepols, 1999.

—, and G. Small. "Théâtre et Réforme aux anciens Pays-Bas à la fin du moyen âge: une découverte aux Archives départementales du Nord [une moralité intitulée *le Jeu du Grand Dominé et du Petit*]." In *Liber Amicorum Claude Lannette* [hors série]: Commission Historique du Nord, 2001: 159–71.

Hochner, Nicole. "Pierre Gringore: une satire à la solde du pouvoir?" [*Jeu du Prince des sotz*]. *Fifteenth-Century Studies* 26 (2001): 102–20.

Horner, Olga. "Biblical and Medieval Covenant in the York OT Plays." *Leeds Studies in English*, n.s. 32 (2001): 129–50.

Hüsken, Wim, and Konrad Schoell, ed. *Farce and Farcical Elements.* Amsterdam: Rodopi, 2002.

King, Pamela M., and Clifford Davidson. *The Coventry Corpus Christi Plays*. Kalamazoo: MIP, 2000.

—. "'He pleyeth Herodes upon a scaffold hye'?" *Leeds Studies in English*, n.s. 32 (2001): 211–28.

Knight, Alan E., ed. *Les Mystères de la Procession de Lille*, 5 vols. planned. I: *le Pentateuque*. Geneva: Droz, 2001; II: *De Josué à David*. Geneva: Droz, 2003.

Koopmans, Jelle. "Les démunis en scène: satire ou utopie, répression ou contestation?" In *Les Niveaux de vie au moyen âge*, edited by Jean-Pierre Sossons, 123–39. Louvain-la-Neuve: Academia Bruyland, 1999.

—. "Les Éléments farcesques de la sottie française." In *Farce and Farcical Elements*, edited by Wim Hüsken and K. Schoell, 121–41. Amsterdam: Rodopi, 2002.

—. "Théâtre du monde et monde du théâtre." In Bordier, *Jeu*, 17–34.

—. "*La vente d'Amourettes (en gros et en détail)* et *Adam Fier des Couilles*. Un texte pour deux farces." In Duhl, 51–62.

—. "'Vous aurez de ceci, c'est remède contre cela': la langue et les langages dramatiques de la farce." In Bordier, *Langues*, 33–43.

Koopmans, Jelle, and Paul Verhuyck. "Les Mots et la chose, ou la métaphore comme spectacle. Nouvelle étude sur la représentation scénique de l'acte sexuel dans les farces." *Versants* 38 (2000): 31–51.

Kuné, Cobie, ed. "Das Prager Abendmahlsspiel." *Zeitschrift für deutsches Altertum und deutsche Literatur* 128 (1999): 414–24.

—, ed. "Das Lübener Osterspielfragment." *Zeitschrift für deutsches Altertum und deutsche Literatur* 131 (2002): 346–54.

Kunstmann, Pierre. "Édition électronique: le cas des *Miracles de Nostre Dame par personnages*." *Le Moyen Français: le Traitement du texte*, edited by C. Buridant, 115–22. Strasbourg: Presse Universitaire, 2000.

—. "Édition électronique: le cas du théâtre religieux." In Duhl, 63–69.

Lascombes, André, and Sydney Higgins, ed. *European Medieval Drama* 4 (2000).

Lauer, A. Robert. "*La Celestina* (teatro). Producción de Departamento de Teatro y Danza de la Universidad Nacional de México." *Celestinesca* 24 (2000): 181–90.

Le Briz-Orgeur, Stéphanie. "Les Monologues d'hésitation dans la *Passion* d'Arnoul Gréban." In Bordier, *Langues*, 149–66.

——. "Le *Mystère de la Passion* d'Arnoul Gréban: un atelier du dialogue." In *La Recherche: bilan et perspective*, edited by Giuseppe Di Stefano and R. Bidler, 327–46. *Le Moyen Français*. Montréal: Éditions CERES, 1999.

Linke, Hansjürgen. *Die deutschen Weltgerichtspiele des späten Mittelalters*. Bern: Francke, 2002.

Loewald, Sharon M. *Les Figures féminines dans certains Mystères de la Passion en France au Moyen Âge*. Villeneuve d'Ascq: Presses Universitaires du Septentrion, 2001.

Longtin, Mario. "Conventions de lecture: l'exemple de la *pausa* dans le *Mystère de sainte Barbe en cinq journées*." In Bordier, *Langues*, 83–92.

Lucken, C. "La Cuisine du diable et l'hospice du saint: Le *Mystère de Saint Bernard de Menthon*." In *Scrivere il Medioevo: lo spazio, la santità, il cibo*, edited by Bruno Laurioux and L. Moulinier-Brogi, 277–91. Rome: Viella, 2001.

Mazouer, Charles. "Le *badin* au XVIe siècle." In Bordier, *Langues*, 167–76.

——. "La Comédie de la Renaissance contre la farce médiévale." In Duhl, 3–14.

——. "L'eschatologie chrétienne dans le théâtre médiéval." In *La Fin des temps*, II. *Eidôlon* 58 (2001): 43–52.

——. "La Prédication populaire et le théâtre au début du XVIe siècle: le cas de Michel Menot." In Bordier, *Jeu*, 79–88.

McKinnell, John. "Significant Gestures: Two Medieval Illustrations of Classical Theatre." *Leeds Studies in English*, n.s. 32 (2001): 289–320.

Meredith, Peter. "Carved and Spoken Words: the Angelic Salutation, the *Mary Play* and South Walsham Church." *Leeds Studies in English*, n.s. 32 (2001): 369–98.

Moll, Richard J. "Staging Disorder: Charivari in the N-Town Cycle." *Comparative Drama* 35 (2001): 145–61.

Perrot, Jean-Pierre, and J.-J. Nonot, ed. *Le Jour du Jugement, mystère du XIVe siècle*. Chambéry: Éditions Comp'Act, 2000–2001.

Pettitt, Thomas. "The Living Text: The Play, the Players, and Folk Tradition." *Leeds Studies in English*, n.s. 32 (2001): 413–29.

Pietrini, Sandra. "Medieval Ideas of the Ancient Actor and Roman Theater." *EDAMR* 24 (2001): 1–21.

——. *Spettacoli e immaginario teatrale nel Medioevo*. Rome: Bulzoni, 2001.

Portillo, Rafael. "Impersonating Spirits: Ghosts and Souls on the Medieval Stage." *Leeds Studies in English*, n.s. 32 (2001): 431–38.

Rastall, Richard. "The Construction of a Speaking Tube for Late Medieval Drama." *EMD* 4 (2000): 231–44.

Robert, Stéphanie. "Formes poétiques et versification dans la *Sotise à huit personnages* d'André de la Vigne." In Bordier, *Langues*, 55–66.

Romagnoli, Pierre. "Faims du monde: figures de la nouveauté dans la sotie." *Versants* 38 (2000): 11–29.

Roy, Bruno. "*La Farce de Maître Pathelin*: récapitulation 1979–99." In Duhl, 65–78.

——. "La Liturgie et l'édition des farces: le cas de *Frère Guillebert*." In Bordier, *Jeu*, 65–77.

Runnalls, Graham A. "Civic Drama in the Burgundian Territories in the Later Middle Ages." *Revue Belge de Philologie et d'Histoire* 78 (2000): 409–22.

——. "Le Commerce des mystères imprimés: le cas du *Mystère de l'Assomption*." In Bordier, *Jeu*, 175–90.

——. "Langage de la parole ou langage du geste? Le *Mystère de s. Laurent*." In Bordier, *Langues*, 121–34.

——. *Les Mystères français imprimés*. Paris: Champion, 1999.

——. "Religious Drama and the Printed Book in France during the Late Fifteenth and Sixteenth Centuries." In *The Sixteenth Century French Religious Book*, edited by Andrew Pettegree, P. Nelles, and P. Conner, 18–37. Aldershot, U.K.: Ashgate, 2001.

Runnalls, Graham A., and Jesse Hurlbut. *Bibliographie des miracles et mystères français* available at www.byu.edu/~hurlbut/fmddp/bmmf (2003–).

Sawyer, Karen E. "Saints in the *Second Shepherds' Play*." *EDAMR* 24 (2001): 22–33.

Scheel, Katja. "Le Jeu de Carnaval comme élément des coutumes carnavalesques. Rôle et fonction des jeux de carnaval au sein des processus de socialisation dans la bourgeoisie urbaine." In Bordier, *Langues*, 211–29.

Scherb, Victor I. *Staging Faith: East Anglian Drama in the Later Middle Ages*. Madison: Fairleigh Dickinson University Press, 2001.

Schoell, Konrad. "Actor, Scene, and Audience of the Fifteenth-Century French Farce: the Farce in the Light of the Semiotics of Performance." *Fifteenth-Century Studies* 26 (2001): 158–68.

––. "Humour in Farce and *Fastnachtspiel*." *EMD* 4 (2000): 9–22.

Subrenat, Jean. "La Vie quotidienne des petites gens et sa représentation dans les *Passions* du XVe siècle." In *Les Niveaux de vie au moyen âge*, edited by Jean-Pierre Sossons et al., 317–39. Louvain-la-Neuve: Academia Bruylant, 1999.

Symes, Carol. "The Appearance of Early Vernacular Plays: Forms, Functions, and the Future of Medieval Theater." *Speculum* 77 (2002): 778–831.

Tuaillon, Gaston. "Saint Sébastien dans le théâtre religieux de Maurienne et de la vallée de Suse." In *Le Théâtre populaire dans les Alpes Occidentales*, 101–16. Vallée d'Aoste: Bureau . . . l'Éthnologie et la Linguistique, 1999.

––. "Le Théâtre religieux en Maurienne et dans le val de Suse: *L'Histoire de Monseigneur Saint Sébastien*, la *Dioclétiane de Lanslevillard* et *la Dioclétiane de Chaumont*." In *Mémoires de l'Académie de Savoie*, tome I (2000): 239–59.

Tydeman, William. *The Medieval European Stage, 500–1550*. Cambridge: Cambridge University Press, 2001.

Wilkins, James D. "Corps et biens: The Body as Currency in Fifteenth-Century *Mystères de la Passion*." *Fifteenth-Century Studies* 24 (1998): 254–72.

Reviews

Bordier, Jean-Pierre, ed. *Le Jeu théâtral, ses marges, ses frontières* (Paris: Champion, 1999). Pp. 208.

In these proceedings of the Second Meeting on Old European Theater held in Tours (1997), a group of scholars discussed the marginal areas of the medieval stage, as well as its limits. The twelve conference papers consider theater from all angles: the liturgical stage, farces, passion plays, moralities, ceremonies, miracle plays, dramatizations of historical and fictional topics — mostly in France. The premise is that thespian activities bordering on theatricality will be considered in this volume especially: jongleurs mime and dialogue with one another, liturgical singing and actions become liturgical drama, and preachers illustrate their sermons by their own (theatrical) presentations. There exist *tableaux vivants*, festive ceremonial processions, and tournaments, all of which are shown to an audience — activities existing within the margins of theater.

Jelle Koopmans, in "Théâtre du monde et monde du théâtre," shows that there were in fact three worlds of theater in France: one with Guillaume Crétin and the *Rhétoriqueurs*, one in Parisian subcultures, and lastly the Lyonese world of François Girault and Jean d'Abondance. Koopmans hopes that further studies will highlight these three areas, especially the thespian rivalries existing among the civic groups in Paris. Bruno Roy ("La Liturgie et l'édition des farces: le cas de *Frère Guillebert*") explains that in farce ceremonies, the most evident liturgical allusions refer to the mass (e.g., *Pathelin*, vv. 23–27). He then shows the use of church Latin in the text of *Frère Guillebert* (Tissier, vol. 6), a corrupted Latin shown mostly for the purposes of comedy, uncovering a parody of genres (farce, confession, liturgy); as lover, Brother Guillebert manifests almost a husband's fears of impotence and death. Here, as elsewhere, medieval texts, especially unedited pieces, lend themselves to multiple interpretations because of their textual ambiguities. Often, the text is "naked," having no punctuation; we must therefore ask: when is a phrase a question? Are the lines faulty by transmission or on purpose? What gestures accompanied them? The scenic play was much richer than the text, of course, even unbridled, and all written passages should be considered mere attempts at transcription.

In "La Prédication populaire et le théâtre au début du XVIe siècle: Michel Menot," Charles Mazouer points out that mendicant preachers abandoned composure in their sermons. His example is Menot (d. 1518), a minorite and itinerant monk, who interacted with his audience, putting on a theatrical show in public places, using the Bible, the apocrypha, and legends; his favorite topics were the Prodigal Son and the Sacrifice of Isaac. Bordier showcases the *Moralité du Jour Saint Antoine* (1427), explaining that morality plays (as yet ill-defined as a genre) are a powerful ancillary to sermons and art, which speak to a fairly intelligent audience who knows how to decode allegories. This *moralité* has five personages: the Doctor, God, the Devil, Man, and Sin (who is a woman).

The *Passion of Maastricht* (fourteenth century), a fragmented text, is the subject of Guy Borgnet's contribution. The play (the first to feature the Process of Paradise) reflects confidence in humankind and exalts the Pope's authority, especially in this century of the schism. Christ's death is explained according to the "satisfaction" theory (reparation for human sins) and thus makes Justice (one of God's four daughters) acquiesce; emphasis on Mary Magdalene shows that conversion remains possible, thus enforcing the role of the preaching Church. Elisabeth Lalou reflects upon ceremonies and processions as theatrical activities, while Gérard Gros considers the *Advocacie Nostre Dame* as an example of genre migration marking an early fourteenth-c. miracle text transformed into a mystery.

Denis Hüe proves that *l'Estoire de Griseldis* (edited by Mario Roques in 1957) could have been staged, as miniatures seem to indicate. According to Vicky L. Hamblin, *le Siege d'Orleans*, a mystery describing the events of 1428–29, grew out of a procession and is indeed theatrical, although the text may never have been presented in front of an audience. Of 180 mystery texts, forty have been preserved in printed form, according to Graham A. Runnalls, who (in "Le Commerce des mystères imprimés: le cas du *Mystère de l'Assomption*") highlights the problems with prints, when the first editions of plays are lost. The second edition of this *Mystère* (1512–19) was done by Jean Janot, probably together with the widow of the famous Trepperel, in a run of about 500 copies, of which 400 remained after Janot's death and were sold in France until 1535. Most of such editions were meant to be read, and for staging reconverted into manuscripts. Finally, Bernard Faivre considers the famous farce *Frère Guillebert* (see above) as a playtext, a scatological *sermon joyeux* acted out.

Our short review highlights all parts of this interesting collection by Bordier, the sixth volume of a series published by the Centre d'Études Supérieures de la Renaissance de Tours. The book is welcome to all theater specialists, as well as beneficial to students and teachers of the late Middle Ages.

Bordier, Jean-Pierre, ed. *Langues, codes et conventions de l'ancien théâtre européen* (Paris: Champion, 2002). Pp. 252.

This volume, the eighth of the Tours collection of conference papers, covers seven centuries of dramatic productions; we chose the essays devoted to the fifteenth and sixteenth centuries for review. Most articles treat French theater (three on farces, two on morality plays, one on a *sotie*, four on *mystères*); there are two essays on German drama, one on Spanish and one on early Latin plays. Despite this imbalance, the collection as a whole brings new research and insights; in his introduction the editor emphasizes that this small compendium is meant not to be exhaustive, but rather to show the long tradition and the variety of thespian events in western Europe. All articles are in French.

Jelle Koopmans chose the dramatic idioms of the French farces for discussion. By idioms he means not only the economy of dialogues, syncopated by ambiguities and metaphors (especially for sexual matters), but also dances, costumes, accessories, and colors — all of which signify in these *allégories inversées*. Bernard Faivre ("'Je veux que tu me dises à qui tu parles quand tu dis cela,' ou le spectateur partenaire du farceur") discusses monologues and asides on the stage, by which the listener may become an intimate partner of the actor. Some *apartés* are strategies to avoid addressing another character directly; medieval dramaturgy relies much on soliloquies: to tell actions happening before or during playtime (off-stage), for example, or in order to voice the feelings of a person. In the farces monologues often begin and/or end the plays, provide transitions, and organize scenic spaces.

Charles Mazouer's "Le *Badin* au XVIe siècle" introduces a farce convention, a character who appears stupid in order to make the audience laugh. His face is whitened by flour (like Marcel Marceau's); he is an acrobat, master of many gestures, is agitated and petulant, playing continually on words. Young, sensual, often hungry or drunk, he uses ruses and deceits, blundering on his path through a farce; during the sixteenth century the *badin* becomes more ambiguous and less dumb. It would have been appropriate for M. to allude at least to André Tissier's treatment of the character on pp. 21–25 of his vol. 4 in *Recueil des farces 1450–1550* (Geneva: Droz, 1989).

André de la Vigne's *Sotise à huit personnages* is the topic of Stéphanie Robert's contribution. Robert studies poetic forms and versification in this *Sotise* which stages two allegorical characters (World and Abuse) and six *sots*: *Sot dissolu l'Église, Sot corrompu la Justice, Sot glorieux les gens d'armes, Sot trompeur les marchands, Sot ignorant le peuple,* and *Sotte Folle* (femininity and folly). Katja Scheel writes about the social function of the German carnival plays, and, according to her interpretation, the comedies of this world upside-down are to reinforce the existing social order by offering a socialization of young people. Fortunately, Scheel also mentions the *humor* of these pieces and their function as entertainment (224).

"Sur la moralité de *Bien avisé mal avisé*. Codes et conventions (d'autrefois et d'aujourd'hui) du langage des anciens textes dramatiques" was written by Jonathan Beck, who compares its manuscript with the imprint of this morality play. He finds the usual variances in morphology and spelling: often, the copyist transcribes the same phrases differently at various junctions within the text, or he omits certain characters or episodes present in one version while absent from another. A modern editor must therefore strive above all to preserve what seems to be the authentic version, and to avoid copyists' mistakes. (For the contents of the *moralité*, please see my review of Beck's article appearing in Duhl's collection, below.)

Bordier's "*La Moralité de l'Envie des frères*: conventions théâtrales et codes herméneutiques" is based on the OT story of Joseph envied by his brothers, a text treated in the *Mystère du Viel Testament* and in another morality play, *la Vendition de Joseph*. Among allegorical characters, Envy takes the initiative here, while Hatred of the father (Jacob) is another important figure. In "Lire les didascalies du *Siege d'Orleans*: conventions théâtrales ou tradition commémorative?" Vicki L. Hamblin asks whether certain episodes of this mystery (1465) were staged at historical sites of the siege (during 1428–29) and reveals that in fact a theater for the play's performance was built near the Tourelles, where the decisive battle (under leadership of Jeanne d'Arc) had taken place.

Graham A. Runnalls investigates the fifteenth-c. *Mystère de Saint Laurent*, which had a fairly mediocre text; characters repeat literally what they have been told to do (in a previous scene); then they perform this action, accompanied by movements and gestures, while describing it (once more!). "Les Monologues d'hésitation dans la *Passion* d'Arnoul Gréban" is the topic of Stéphanie Le Briz-Orgeur's excellent article: monologues of hesitation are a *new* instrument in Gréban's mystery (i.e., not used before, and not researched by anyone). The dramatist's text shows a certain development in these soliloquies, a complexity which at times prepares the next phase or reflects upon the previous moments of the play. Le Briz-Orgeur studies especially Marie-Madeleine's monologue before she applies the salve to Christ's face; the soliloquy of Judas as he meets *Désespérance*; and that of the Virgin, reflecting upon a dialogue with Jesus (the four questions and answers, stemming from the *Passion Isabeau*, 1398).

Bordier's collection is another rich contribution to the growing corpus of research on the medieval stage and its language. Since all articles are in French, the number of Anglo–Saxon readers will be limited; despite this drawback, the volume should be acquired by all university libraries.

Boucquey, Thierry, trans. *Six Medieval French Farces* (Lewiston: Mellen, 1999). Pp. 247.

In his introduction, the author makes a case for his translation by recalling how few of some seventy French comedies of the late Middle Ages have ever been rendered into English; yet, in order to have the plays read and performed in the anglophone world, translations are indispensable. He discusses the different collections of edited farces, the origin of the word *farce* (=stuffing, interpolation into liturgy), the farce as Shrovetide entertainment, its late-medieval actors (students, clerics, artisans, sons of bourgeois), its audiences from all social classes, and the (simple) stage.

Written in octosyllabic couplets, the surviving pieces (which influenced Molière) are for the greatest part early sixteenth-c. copies. Research in farce production, texts, and their history dates from the second half of the twentieth century, with outstanding scholarship provided by Barbara Bowen, Halina Lewicka, André Tissier (who edited twelve volumes of farces), and Bernadette Rey-Flaud, who characterized the pieces as *machines à rire*. The leitmotifs are "questioning of authority, conquest of married women, and the duping of the duper" (5), and the plays' comic devices are "hiding, disguise, jargon, literalization of proverbs or idioms" (ibid.). B. neglected to mention situation comedy, a stock-device used frequently in this world upside-down, and he also omitted the stratagem of comic misunderstandings. Each of the six farces chosen is preceded by the translator's brief introduction.

The "Farce of the Miller" (Tissier edition, vol. 4), inserted in the *Mystère de Saint Martin*, was written by the latter's author, André de La Vigne, in 1496, and performed in Seurre. De La Vigne used Rutebeuf's *fabliau* "Le Pet au villain," according to which a common man's soul does not go to paradise after death, but straight to hell, this feature being an interesting social comment. What is worse, the villain's soul does not leave the body by the mouth, but by the nether end, and since the devils are soon offended by the stench, they refuse hell *tout court* to the poor man. In the farce, social satire is even more pointed when the dying man is made a miller, believed dishonest in medieval tradition. In addition, the play has many other facets of comedy: 1) a rivalry between man and wife for domestic authority; 2) a husband cuckolded by a priest; 3) food and drink offered to a woman's lover (a metaphor for sexual hospitality); 4) scatology; 5) disguises: the priest appears as cousin, in order to approach the miller's wife freely in the presence of her husband; the *cousin* then becomes a priest again, to hear the miller's confession; and 6) the confession, another technique of social satire, here for disclosing the miller's cheating everyone. The play is furthermore unique, as it links earth and hell and uses the devils of the *Mystère de Saint Martin* (the same actors!) to catch the filthy soul of social enemy number one. Incidentally, the Paris Parliament finally stepped in to prevent further persecution of millers, if unjust (note of the reviewer).

The "Farce of Calbain" (Tissier, vol. 3), dated during the second half of the fifteenth century, seems to be influenced by "Maître Pathelin," and originated probably in the Île-de-France. Singing cobblers are stock-figures in French farces; here, Calbain's songs are the only reply to his wife's demands for better clothing and more attention. Upon the advice of a friend (*le galland*), she gives her husband a soporific and steals his purse; awake, Calbain misses the latter but gets no response from the wife, as she now sings in her turn — a new version of the *trompeur trompé*, as borne out at the very end of the farce in an elaborate play on the root *tromp-*, its morphological variants and multiple meanings, in the French source text. B. has given an equivalent of this play on a word as follows:

He who is deceived sounds the *trumpet* from afar.	(*trompette* in French;
Deceivers are deceived by deceptions.	the French meaning of
Deceivers, sound the trumpet for the deceived!	*tromper* has survived in
Man is deceived.	English "trumped-up"
Good-bye deceivers, good-bye gentlemen,	and "trumpery"
Excuse the deceiver and his wife (99).	— the reviewer)

The "Farce of the Bonnet" (Tissier, vol. 10) was featured for the first time in the *Histoire du théâtre français, depuis son origine jusqu'à présent* by the brothers Parfaict (1745), where this copy of a lost manuscript was appended to a *Mystère*. Both texts, the *mystère* and the farce, ended in the words "Fin sans fin" typical for writings by Jean d'Abondance, a lawyer (or just a clerc) of the *basoche* and royal notary of Pont Saint Esprit (Avignon). Dated 1535, the farce appeared in various later copies; the crux of the play is a misunderstanding that celebrates feminine ruse. A young wife deceives her elderly husband "right and left" with the help of her valet Finet, and her spouse's two nephews complain to one another about her disorderly conduct. She in turn tells her man about these complaints, using the pronoun *elle* but referring it to his bonnet (*la cornette*), which is not up to snuff, turning right and left; her husband throws the nephews out of the house. B. has not acknowledged here the symbolic identification of *cornette* (French for bonnet, close to *cornu*=cuckold) and (the name of) Jean d'Abondance (a pseudonym reminding of cornucopia — which is affirmed at the end of the farce by the devise "Fin sans fin").

In the "Farce of the Kettlemaker" (Tissier, vol. 3), a quarrel and beating between man and wife end in a wager as to which of the two would be able to keep silent the longest. A kettlemaker arrives and, finding the two mute, is first puzzled and then begins to make verbal and even manual passes at the woman, ending the silence all at once: the kettlemaker gets a beating, and the couple go for a drink. Both origin and date of this piece are uncertain; the date is of course prior to the first edition (c.1550). B. has annotated "Saint Coquibault" (line 142) and thus improved upon the Tissier edition; his equivalent is "Saint Cucklebeau" (close enough to "cuckold").

The "Farce of the Chimney Sweep" (Tissier, vol. 4) dates from the first quarter of the sixteenth century. In contrast to other comedies, no intrigue exists here: the dialogues, between the chimney sweep and his helper, or husband and wife, disclose the man's inability to sweep efficiently, because he is too old. The audience is soon aware of ambiguity, having almost expected it: the husband's failure is not only professional but also erotic: the use of "sweeping" as sexual metaphor was known and enjoyed traditionally, appearing in other texts as well, and B.'s translation manages this ambiguity with finesse and discretion. The piece voices a sexual *carpe diem* linguistically, as it uses an everyday manual activity and its metaphors; this farce is also an eloquent commentary on aging.

The "Farce of the Gentleman and Naudet" (Tissier, vol. 1), dated between 1542 and 1549, may be based on a story of the *Cent Nouvelles Nouvelles* (1462). Naudet has the function of a fool (*badin*): he is a peasant whose wife is courted by a nobleman trying to get Naudet out of the house, in order better to enjoy the wife's favors. The clever clodhopper, however, knows exactly what is going on, steals and dons the gentleman's clothing, and presents himself to the latter's wife with the intention of acting out in every respect what her husband is doing with Naudet's wife — an activity not unpleasing to the gentlewoman. Here, the hierarchy of social class relations is certainly upside down.

Boucquet's translations are satisfactory; once in a while, his English is not perfect, but this circumstance is hardly a serious flaw. However, the volume shows neglect: note numbers are missing or are wrong in the text; typos and misspellings are disturbing, and the references in the notes appear incomplete or faulty, as does the bibliography. For the purpose of performance this translation is quite adequate.

Cowell, Andrew. *At Play in the Tavern: Signs, Coins, and Bodies in the Middle Ages* (Ann Arbor: University of Michigan Press, 1999). Pp. 270.

Cowell's monograph distinguishes two basic viewpoints in medieval thought and literature. Taking as his specific fields of research the taverns, inns, and brothels of the twelfth and thirteenth centuries, the author opposes a new *comico–realist* literary tradition (emanating from these milieus) to the earlier heuristic Neoplatonism and its centuries-old ecclesiastical model of life and writings. Said in a nutshell, he confronts the Church and its charities with commercial economics, whose literary production often contradicts and satirizes *high* interpretations. Signs (language, coins, and bodies) cease to be symbolic and become reified instead.

In the first of four chapters, "Charity, Hospitality, and Profit," Cowell highlights the Church's view of taverns extending hospitality for profit in transgression of sacred hermeneutics and vocabulary (a tavern is the "church of the devil"). In inns, dice playing is comparable to the economic practice of usury, the charging of interest subject to fortune and unquantifiable conditions — familiar to merchants. In the hands of the middle class, the new profit economy is based on money and writing, and may be socially disruptive. Both gifts and ritual disappear in tavern traffic, and with them the high literary genres of epic, hagiography, and moral and didactic works, making way for secular comico-realism, as studied here in several French medieval plays.

"Le *Jeu de Saint Nicolas* and the Poetics of the Tavern" (chapter two) shows the literature of the tavern to be proto-novelistic (Bakhtin) and mirroring many facets of medieval life. Jean Bodel's play refigures Church views of profit and usury ironically; dicing becomes here an economic, linguistic, and semiotic practice (*compter/mescompter/conter/mesconter*) comparable to gaining interest. Invaluable for a study of medieval dicing and of thieves' slang (as in Villon's poetry), the *Jeu de Saint Nicolas* showcases an old man (lone survivor of a battle between pagans and Christians) invoking aid before an image of the saint. Consequently, the oldster is imprisoned, and the pagan king tests the image by exposing his treasures in front of it: if they are not stolen, the *vieillard* shall go free. Three thieves in the tavern decide to steal the money and precious objects, whereupon Saint Nicolas appears in person, calling upon the robbers to restore the treasure: they comply, the Saracens and their king convert, and the old man is freed. Here, a saint's image needed to come alive to bring about not a miracle, but restoration of money by persuasion, funds — as it were — to purchase the old man's life. Thus, hagiography is replaced by commercialism.

In Picard dialect and octosyllabic rhymed couplets, the play was presented in 1200 by an Arras *confrérie* for the saint's day; Bodel exposed in this *jeu* a realistic view of the life and wealth of Arras, combining a crusade topic, hagiographic detail, and a comedic setting. That linguistics (semiotics) has the volubility to change meanings (as coins can vary their value) is the pivot of Bodel's work — and of Cowell's book. On page 105, the author makes an important point, for which we have been waiting, namely: the *just prices* for goods may be changing (according to market conditions), and merchants often performed some labor *meriting* a profit, as recognized by canonists.

Chapter three, "The Moral Economy of the Tavern," discusses *Courtois d'Arras*, a remake of the Prodigal Son parable (first quarter of the thirteenth century). Here, Cowell showcases a brothel, where the female body challenges masculine authority and intentionality, as Courtois identifies himself with his purse (=money, scrotum, and testicles), which is "robbed" by the prostitutes. An economic deal is handled in a language of multiple *entendres* by a set of comico-realist figures.

In chapter four we realize anew that any monolithic approach is beset with dangers. To narrow in on Rutebeuf's realistic and "autobiographical" poetry from the viewpoint of the tavern and its linguistic monetary exchanges is to cast aside the poet's philosophy, Augustinian religiosity (*le Miracle de Théophile*, c.1260), political and social criticism. Likewise reduced to the tavern scene (=theater) by Cowell, *le Jeu de la Feuillée* (c.1276) loses the valuable insight and the multiple personalities of Adam de la Halle (shown by Alfred Adler, Jean Dufournet, and myself), features which not only delineate the limits of autobiography but also show a certain (admirable) restraint of Adam, the author, in handling the story of his own life.

Cowell has taken advantage of his predecessors (Dufournet, Rousse, Bordier, Aubailly), while combining their findings in a new context. Disturbing, however, are grammatical uncertainties (especially split infinitives, incorrect spellings, as on pages 8 and 151, Huizinga's name consistently misspelled as "Huizenga," and a lack of colons before inset quotations). The author's translations are perfect, and so is his knowledge of ancient and medieval writers.

Davidson, Clifford, ed. *Gesture in Medieval Drama and Art* (Kalamazoo: Medieval Institute Publications, 2001). Pp. xii; 239; 48 illustrations in black/white.

As with many books printed by this publisher, the volume's title is general, even though the text is almost entirely based on English evidence (five articles), while Italy and France are treated in only one essay each, and all but one article study sacred drama. In spite of these limitations, the volume is successful: it examines gestures, drawing careful conclusions mostly from iconography, but also from rhetoric and rubrics.

Jody Enders, who inspired this latest book in the Early Drama, Art, and Music Series, introduced the subject of gesture in "Of Miming and Signing: The Dramatic Rhetoric of Gesture" (1–25). Her research is based on insight into Roman rhetoric gained while formulating her *Rhetoric and the Origins of Medieval Drama* (Ithaca: Cornell University Press, 1992); in addition, this article has been formed in conjunction with more recent research on gesture and mimicry. According to E., gesture is indispensible for medieval drama, not as an accompaniment, but as complementary to speech and even sometimes as explicatory component. In liturgical drama gestures "translated," as it were, the Latin no longer understood by the *menu peuple*; in mysteries, gestures helped comprehension (or simplification) of theoretical passages, we might add, also in situations where the audience was too distant from the stage to hear the spoken words. Enders's style is admirable in its clarity and precision.

In his "Gesture and Characterization in the Liturgical Drama" (26–47), Dunbar H. Ogden detects the first signs of dynamic dramaturgy beyond ritualistic presentation. With the help of rubrics in selected plays he singles out three gestural elements: a formal gesture with added emotion or feeling (expression of grief by Mary Magdalene), an informal gesture, and an informal gesture having an emotional or poetic quality (Herod's raging when he hears of the newborn king). A long list of gesture-related rubric vocabulary from Walther Lipphardt's texts (*Lateinische Osterfeiern und Osterspiele*, 9 vols. [Berlin: de Gruyter, 1975–90]) concludes the article. Janet Schrunk Ericksen examines a scene in MS Junius 11:

"Offering the Forbidden Fruit" (48-65), and comes to the conclusion that the dramatic emphasis on making careful choices in this Anglo-Saxon *Genesis B* is not matched elsewhere. The focus on the enticing object, the apple, together with the serpent's gestures of temptation and the initial refusal by Adam, as well as eager acceptance by Eve, are read by Ericksen as being repeated emphases on the moment of enticement and the possibility of choice, played out in the text and several miniatures.

In "Gesture in Medieval British Drama" (66-111), Clifford Davidson attempts some educated conjectures about gestures on the stage. While his sources are rubrics, contemporary iconography, typological commonplaces, actual records, miniatures, classical rhetoric, and monastic sign language, the important influence of narrative passion tracts, such as the *Meditationes Vitae Christi* and its vernacular "translations" (some with miniatures), must not be neglected in providing and explaining gestures (note of the reviewer). Nor should the continental mystery plays — not mentioned once in D.'s article — be left undiscussed here, as some parallels to English findings are obvious to students and teachers of medieval religious drama in Europe. The aspects treated by D. are: the Nativity, the *Mactacio Abel* (Wakefield Master), Judas's Kiss of Betrayal, the Doomsday plays (influenced by courts of law), the Raising of Lazarus, the Suffering Christ, and the Flagellation (all from N-Town), the Crucifixion, and the Ascension. A list of hand-movements taken from Roman theatrical gestures is given on page 107.

Barbara D. Palmer's "Gestures of Greeting: Annunciations, Sacred and Secular" (128-57) is an adept contribution on announcements, sudden appearances, welcomes, and ironic or parodic reversal greetings. Palmer begins with the "Annunciation to Mary" (especially in N-Town), and the Virgin's astonishment with her hands held out in surprise, and further on views greetings in the "Harrowing of Hell." Another category is salutations (Entry into Jerusalem, comparable to princes' entries into their cities), with kisses of greeting, later reversed by Judas's kiss of betrayal. In "The Body in Motion in the York *Adam and Eve in Eden*" (158-77), Natalie Crohn Schmitt studies the actors' movements: blocking, postures, and gestures. By 1350, English manuscript illumination had become very similar to its continental counterparts; within iconography, however, some limitations are inevitable, as static pictures must come alive on the stage. During skillful scenic effects, the audience experienced the "terrible loss" of Eden; pointing (in warning or demonstration), kneeling, and the Gothic bend of female bodies are noticeable.

Beth A. Mulvaney's "Gesture and Audience: The Passion and Duccio's *Maestà*" (178-220) is a long treatment of the fourteenth-c. Italian painter's work, in which M. tries to draw parallels between iconographic gestures and drama. Unfortunately, she does not reference dramas but interprets gestures solely in Duccio, specifically on the reverse side of the *Maestà*, which shows

Christ's passion in fourteen panels. Almost certainly, some Duccio scenes used conventional iconography: this article shows some of the dangers of conjecture. The last contribution to this volume, Jesse Hurlbut's "Body Language in *Jeu de Robin et Marion*: the Aix Witness" (221–29), brings some evidence of body language in a French manuscript with 132 miniatures, a considerable number for a thirteenth-c. text of only eleven folios. In the illuminations, the gestures are carefully articulated and even exaggerated (such as dance movements). Davidson's collection is welcome to students and teachers of drama, especially for modern productions; we appreciate having had access to the volume.

Dohi, Yumi. *Das Abendmahl im spätmittelalterlichen Drama* (Frankfurt am Main: Peter Lang, 2000). Pp. 399.

In this monograph, Holy Communion as enacted in late-medieval English mystery cycles is compared to the ceremony staged in French and German biblical dramas. Dohi, who also includes non-dramatic evidence in her study, is aware of the value of spectacles as a form of communication between *orantes* and *laborantes*, and of the overwhelming manifestation of biblical plays on the continent. Nevertheless, English works remain predominant in this volume. Also, Dohi's emphasis on questions of theoretical theology and the minute variations of communion phases depicted from one play to another strike us as perhaps unnecessary in a work of this nature (we found the same insistence on doctrine in the otherwise excellent work by Jean-Pierre Bordier, reviewed in vol. 28).

These remarks made upfront by us, we pay heed to the rich texture of aspects in Dohi's book as handled adeptly throughout; namely, development of communion theology and piety; communion liturgy; biblical accounts of the sacrament in dramas, narratives (including the *Passion Isabeau*, 1398), and poetry; communion in the N-Town cycle (by phases): preparation for the Last Supper and associated activities; the assemblage of the council of high priests and doctors; the supper itself, including Mary Magdalene's anointment of Christ; the announcement of Judas's betrayal; the betrayal proper; the distribution of the Eucharist; Jesus' washing of the disciples' feet; and so forth.

As an historical text, the communion stems both from the Bible and apocryphal sources. *Fatistes* were creative and altered the events *ad libitum*, following non-dramatic accounts as well, above all the *Meditationes Vitae Christi* (henceforth: *MVC*). To make the plays realistic for the here-and-now moments of presentation, phases of the ritual might be withheld or added by the play director; for example, a communion with bread only (*Passion des Jongleurs*) was common in liturgical services of some late-medieval regions. Again, the *MVC* helped to adapt communion scenes to contemporary life and emotions, especially by the humanization of Jesus and Mary, likewise found in the vernacular account by Heinrich von St. Gallen and in the *Passion Isabeau*. The dialogue of the four requests and answers between Mary and Jesus can be found in the *Passion Isabeau*, in the passions of Brixen, Augsburg, Gréban, Michel, Eger, and Lucerne — but not in England.

As for dogmatic theology, the tendency to exclude all non-orthodox teachings was common to all late-medieval communion scenes. Bread (and wine) were identified with Christ's body, and the Latin words for this part of the ceremony were retained. Another important theme was the identification of Judas as betrayer, who was excluded from the communion eventually; furthermore, the ritual signified the priesthood of the apostles, with the prime role of St. Peter made manifest. For Towneley and Hans Sachs's *Gantz Passio* (sixteenth-c. Protestant), St. John was the prominent disciple — although many other passages had references to the Gospel of John. Liturgy and verses in Latin can be found in many German and French dramatic (and some non-dramatic) passion texts (mostly for significant Bible quotations); on the stage, Jesus spoke and acted as a priest: the scene was paraliturgical. In most presentations, including N-Town and Lucerne, Jesus referred to the supper as Passover festivity, based on the Jewish custom; Chester, Towneley, Tirol, and Ahlsfeld, however, do not show such a reference, either because of Protestant or anti-Judaic influence.

In conclusion, Dohi's book gives a good introduction to the communion topic portrayed in passion texts; the scholar of medieval drama will nevertheless miss the inclusion of a number of details, such as costumes, lighting, audience participation (in a modern staging of *Jesus Christ, Superstar*, the New York audience partook of communion!) and reactions, fragrances, music, and (of course) the influence of art on the communion scene. An article by Ann Eljenholm Nichols, "The Bread of Heaven: Foretaste or Foresight?" 40–68 in *The Iconography of Heaven*, ed. Clifford Davidson (Kalamazoo: MIP, 1994), should have been included in the bibliography (371–99).

Duhl, Olga Anna, ed. *Le Théâtre français des années 1450–1550. État actuel des recherches* (Dijon: Centre de Recherches Le Texte et l'Édition, Université de Bourgogne, 2002). Pp. xvii; 95.

This collection, the result of a 1999 colloquium at the Université de Bourgogne, is devoted to the French comic stage during the transition between the Middle Ages and the Renaissance: farces, *sotties*, and certain morality plays. In "La Comédie de la Renaissance contre la farce médiévale?" Charles Mazouer explains that farces were rejected by Pléiade authors because of these plays' vulgarity and formlessness, their amorality and ludicrousness. Farces were a mirror of daily life in countryside and rural towns and provided insight into certain social groups; but this image was deformed, grotesque. In contrast, Renaissance comedies showed the urban middle class and individuals (often typical figures resembling those of the *commedia dell'arte*); these were plays emphasizing a moral life and a moneyed economy; in short, the texts followed Horace's precept to provide both pleasurable and useful elements to one's audience.

Jonathan Beck's "La Place de la moralité de *Bien Avisé Mal Avisé* dans le théâtre en France au moyen âge" proves that *Well Advised Badly Advised* (1439?) is a typical morality play having allegorical personifications of virtues and vices, as well as professional and religious abstractions (a peasant; Penitence). Moralities may be long or short, literary, theatrical, or edifying. These plays advise rather than amuse, becoming political during the Renaissance; to understand fully a medieval morality play, one must recognize its epistemological and moral ingredients. *Bien Avisé Mal Avisé* considers life a path between good and evil, a narrow thoroughfare between humility and presumptuousness.

Marie Bouhaïk-Gironès ("Les Clercs et les écoliers, auteurs de théâtre profane à Paris à la fin du XVe et au début du XVIe siècle") examines the *Basoche*, a juridical corporation for clerks who become lawyers. The organization is self-administered and has a hierarchy comparable to that of a kingdom; we distinguish the B. of Parliament, of the Châtelet, and that of the Chambre des Comptes (Audit Office?). Naturally, fictive lawsuits (for young lawyers in order to learn the trade) lend themselves easily to profane theater and also influence college drama. Historical sources are sparse, but fake letters of remission give clues on subjects and the dating of plays; as yet it is necessary to establish a precise repertory of *Basoche* theater. Bruno Roy, in "La *Farce de Maître Pathelin*, récapitulation 1979–1999," surveys existing editions, translations, and studies of this masterful play; he proposes a new hypothesis on this farce's origin in Anjou/Provence, dated 1450, instead of 1460 (in Paris/Normandy).

Jelle Koopmans, in turn, shows the insufficiency and haste affecting farces printed at the beginning of the sixteenth century. He is currently editing the plays of the *Recueil de Florence* (*Recueil Cohen*), the errors of which were reprinted by Gustave Cohen, not having availed himself of critical research (1949). As an example of this superficiality, Koopmans has taken apart a farce which hides, in fact, *two* plays, the *Vente d'Amourettes (en gros et en détail)* and *Adam Fier des Couilles*, pieces intercalated by a printer or a binder. Thus, a play about marketing was joined intimately (but without good reason) to a household incident, a quarrel between husband and wife.

Pierre Kunstmann proves that a computerized version of the *Miracle de l'enfant donné au diable* (end of fourteenth century) allows us to view all versions of this miracle play at once, by hypertextual links. Finally, Madeleine Lazard shows that the differences between medieval and Renaissance theater are theoretical rather than practical, especially for the first generation of Pléiade authors. Farce techniques have a long-lasting influence even as demonstrated on the modern comedy stage. In sum, Duhl's collection is a valuable contribution to the study of medieval comedic theater, because the articles touch all essential problems of farce research, as well as present questions about early (hasty?) print quality.

Eisenbichler, Konrad, and Wim Hüsken, ed. *Carnival and the Carnivalesque: The Fool, the Reformer, the Wildman, and Others in Early Modern Theatre* (Amsterdam: Rodopi, 1999). Pp. 281.

Fortunately, collections of research on European medieval theater have begun to proliferate; the present edition showcases thirteen essays of excellent quality which include some para-dramatic studies. Peter H. Greenfield writes about Robin Hood games and king ales in England, while Roberta Mullini has found carnivalesque features in John Heywood's plays. Samuel Kinser ("Why Is Carnival So Wild?" 43–87) devotes considerable space to the Nürnberg *Schembartlauf* (a masked procession since 1449), an activity sometimes banned because of its excesses. Carnival as a world upside-down allows indeed for comical confrontations of civilization and wildness, but Kinser also tests some underlying associations in which the wildman appears as a forceful primitive, a rascal in Italy (*Decameron* IV, 2), and a humanoid beast-devil in German carnivals (under the uneasy eyes of municipalities), a figure who sports obscene and grotesque clothing, a metaphor in fact for carnival itself. "Fictions, Realities, and the Fifteenth-Century Nuremberg *Fastnachtspiel*," 89–116, by James Erb, investigates the special climate and some political considerations which made the Nuremberg carnival comedies possible. By destabilizing cognitive categories (nonsense verses) and making illicit love affairs and desires the subjects of comedy, the plays barely escape official censure.

In "The Judgement of Paris: Three Late Medieval *Fastnachtspiele* from Northern Europe" (117–27), Leif Søndergaard traces the ancient legend in three popular shrovetide plays of the fifteenth century, but in its pragmatic, bourgeois form. Two pieces are German: *das fasnacht spill Troya* (1463) and *das vasnacht spill mit den dreyen nacketten gottin von Troya* (1468), both published by Schnorr von Carolsfeld in 1874; the second play is more *risqué*, since the three women (played by men) must undress. A Danish *Paris' dom* survived in an Odense manuscript from 1531. Guy Borgnet, in "Jeu de Carnaval et Antisémitisme: Pureté Théologique et Pureté Éthnique chez Hans Folz" (129–45), examines three Nürnberg carnival plays treating the Jews in comparison with Christians: Keller 1, K 106, and K 20. K 1 is a debate between Church and Synagogue, where the Church ridicules the latter, ending with the conversion of a Jew; in K 106, Pope Sylvester debates with the Jews, and at the end a rabbi converts; K 20 demonstrates (with the help of a Wheel of Fortune) that the Jewish Messiah is deemed to fall. Why has Folz, a gifted *Meistersinger*, chosen these subjects? He did indeed want to renew the contents of carnival plays by including polemic themes of the moment, mostly to please the Nürnberg patricians and the town council (while his other comedies are addressed to a rural audience). Nevertheless, these three plays remain a stain on Folz's reputation.

"La Satire Sociale dans le Répertoire de la Mère Folle de Dijon" (147–63) by Juliette Valcke showcases a theater group in Dijon (called *Mère Folle*), its origin, and the aims of its satire. Three strands of sources are noticeable: the fools of the Dukes of Burgundy, rural associations of young people performing, and the *Basochiens* of the Parisian courts of justice (*sociétés joyeuses*). The texts of the Dijon players are bilingual (Parisian French and Burgundian) and persiflage certain personalities of high standing because of their marital conducts, mis-managements of their jobs, and other abuses. Also, the plays castigate vestimentary extravagance (luxury) and the lubricity of women. Note 23 is missing in this article, and the work by Olga Anna Dull (now Duhl) *Folie et rhétorique dans la sottie* (Geneva: Droz, 1994) should have been mentioned.

In "Approche du Comique Carnavalesque dans le Théâtre Populaire Catalan de Source Médiévale" (243–61), Josep M. Martorell Coca proves that a medieval drama tradition is alive and well in the Catalan area. He discusses two popular plays, one a Christmas piece, and another for the feast of St. Thecla in Tarragona. Thomas Pettitt concludes the volume with a follow-up of European medieval drama in the new world. While not all essays of this collection are in fact on theater, the contributions as a whole are well prepared and printed, with comparatively few spelling errors in French and German words.

Hindley, Alan, ed. *Drama and Community: People and Plays in Medieval Europe* (Turnhout: Brepols, 1999). Pp. xi; 294.

The editor of this collection defines community involvement in drama as activities helping to maintain collectively the "multimediality" of theater (ii). A variety of essays offered here, with some overlaps and contradictions, is to invite (require!) further research; while due attention is given to various European regions, still five out of sixteen articles treat English theater, hence, almost one third of the book, an amount seeming out of proportion.

Lynette Muir ("European Communities and Medieval Drama," 1–17) cites the Italian *disciplinati*, the Dutch *Rederijkers*, guilds, and the French *Basoche* as originators and supporters of dramatic activities. Significantly, Muir warns that true community drama ceases to exist when commercialism takes over. "Drama and Community in Late Medieval Paris" (18–33) by Graham A. Runnalls showcases varieties of religious drama in the French capital, and the support by guilds (the goldsmiths) and the *Confrérie de la Passion*. In

"Community Versus Subject in Late Medieval French Confraternity Drama and Ritual" (34–56), Robert L. A. Clark explains the importance of confraternity theater. Comparable to Van Gennep's *rites of passage*, miracle plays present transgressions resolved eventually by Marian intervention; the performances raise the spirituality of their audiences and the social standing of confraternity members.

Frederick W. Langley ("Community Drama and Community Politics in Thirteenth-Century Arras: Adam de la Halle's *Jeu de la Feuillée*," 57–77) discusses Adam's attitude toward local and topical issues of the community (*clercs bigames*, local power struggles, etc.). A real-life citizen of Arras, Adam talks not only "of the illusions of love" (60) but also, above all, of old age (note of the reviewer). References to important research on *Feuillée* have been omitted, unfortunately, in this somewhat monolithic article. Also, Langley seems to confuse Robert le Clerc with Hélinant (71: in 1269 Robert *imitated* the illustrious Hélinand's *Vers de la Mort*, penned in 1194–97 — note of the reviewer). Hindley's "Acting Companies in Late-Medieval France: Triboulet and His Troupe" (78–98) views a "micro-community" of French entertainers, who wrote the satirical *sotties* in the *Recueil Trepperel*, and discusses the company of the *farceur* Triboulet. Women began to join the troupes, and musical expertise was welcome.

Alan E. Knight writes on "Processional Theatre and the Rituals of Social Unity in Lille" (99–109) and calls the plays "controlled town events" promoting civic pride; Knight discovered seventy-two Lille plays of the fifteenth century in Wolfenbüttel, Germany. During the processions, mysteries as well as *tableaux vivants* were shown (see a description of the first two volumes below). The Dutch Chambers of Rhetoric are treated by Wim Hüsken (110–25) and Elsa Strietman (126–47), both scholars discussing community involvement. Hüsken omits valuable bibliographic references when mentioning the world of the taverns (114 — in *Maria Hoedeken*, by Cornelis Everaert, 1509); also, he is too ready to equate Dutch farces with the French and German profane genres: the latter were certainly not meant to reflect "a highly stylized literary culture" of the educated classes (124), except in some isolated cases. Strietman shows that the *Retorikers* dramatized contemporary preoccupations, influenced public opinion, and provoked debates; she also highlights the gradual disappearance of Chambers of Rhetoric and their plays during the influx of reformed religions.

John Tailby ("Drama and Community in South Tyrol," 148–60) examines the area South of the Brenner Pass (German-speaking) for its religious plays in a collection by Benedikt Debs and Vigil Raber (1510–38). Plays for Passion and Easter, for Ascension Day, and Corpus Christi are extant, and archival records attest to community involvement; Raber's Sterzing collection contains twenty-five secular pieces. "Individual and Social Affiliation in the Nuremberg Shrovetide Plays" (161–78) by Konrad Schoell repeats much information known already; however, the author successfully individualizes some farce characters who (by their self-awareness) transcend the role dictated by their social group.

Performances in medieval Ireland have been neglected in theater research, according to Alan J. Fletcher who examines three ethnic communities: ancient Gaelic, post-Norman invasion, and the Anglo-Irish (179–99). By the early fifteenth century, imported English *harpeurs* and *piperes* were organized into guilds; in medieval Dublin, a network of performed drama secured corporate morale as well as recreational outlets. As for England, the biblical narratives in the York cycle are aesthetical, social, topical, and political, as Pamela King shows in "Contemporary Cultural Models for the Trial Plays" (200–216), and the jury trial practices on the stage reflect actual forensic proceedings. Chris Humphrey, on the other hand, studies Coventry and "paratheatrical" activity, but his attention is focused on customs of vegetation gathering, not on drama (217–30). Philip Butterworth then discusses "Prompting in Full View of the Audience" during English plays (231–47) and inserts valuable photographic evidence. The last two articles, by Alexandra F. Johnston and Jane Oakshott (her name is omitted in the Table of Contents!), concern sixteenth-c. and modern stagings. Hindley's collection is very informative and well proofread throughout, a welcome addition to late-medieval drama studies (in spite of the reservations mentioned above).

Knight, Alan E., ed. *Les Mystères de la Procession de Lille*, 5 vols. planned
I: *Le Pentateuque*. (Geneva: Droz, 2001). Pp. 630. II: *De Josué à David*. (Geneva: Droz: 2003). Pp. 668.

The *Pentateuque*, containing twelve short mystery plays, is the first partial edition of the seventy-two fifteenth-c. plays in the Guelf.9 Blankenburg Codex, discovered by K. in the Herzog August Bibliothek Wolfenbüttel. Each mystery is preceded by a miniature (not necessarily a scenic reproduction), and it is regrettable that the format did not allow inclusion of these images. As K. explains in the introduction (127 pages), the codex's paper stems from Troyes (Briquet), and the work was written by two scribes in a cursive hand. The ownership of the codex (bound in parchment and created between 1485 and 1490) is not traceable before the eighteenth century, when it belonged to Pieter van der Aa, a printer/bookdealer in Leyden (successor of the Elzevirs), while the codex was then called *Histoire de la Bible en poésie* and sold to Duke Ludwig of Braunschweig-Wolfenbüttel.

The seventy-two mysteries are mostly biblical (forty-three of the OT, twenty-one of the NT); four pieces of Roman history and four of Christian legends are appended. The Lille procession started in 1270, on Sunday after Trinity; civic as well as ecclesiastic, the event featured all the crafts and military orders, and celebrated miracles by the Virgin Mary (her statue, called "Notre Dame de la Treille," is located in the Collegiate Church of Saint Peter in Lille). Containing mysteries and *tableaux vivants*, the procession was first managed by youth groups but later taken over by the city government (to maintain order). During the fifteenth century, the municipality contributed to the cost for prizes (*fleurs de lis* in silver) bestowed upon the winners of what had become a contest for the best plays. The magistrate further paid for wine and travel expenses, when the actors had to repeat parts of the processional program in neighboring cities.

In the competition, the "Fools' Bishop" (who organized the contest), or the *fatiste* of a winning group, received the prize. Each unit had to present a mystery and a farce (the farces are all lost now) in front of the town hall; after some unruliness, the Fools' Bishops were replaced by the magistrate. Passion episodes followed in outline and sequence the order established by Arnoul Gréban (1452). Naturally, during the sixteenth century, these activities ceased eventually because of the Reformation, the "crime of the Lutheran heresy" (62). Source of the mysteries was the Vulgate Bible, whose episodes were translated into rhymed French by the play directors, who also created the dialogues. The Bible text was glossed at the margins with commentaries by the Church Fathers, annotations which were believed to be as important as the biblical text and provided typological comparisons. Often, the *Postilla* of the Franciscan Nicolas de Lyre was consulted also, as was Pierre Comestor and other authorities (Knight did not mention the *MVC* and their vernacular versions). The Lille mysteries had several anonymous authors, who also played parts in the performances; staging directions do not exist, and the verses are sprinkled with Picardisms.

The twelve mysteries in this edition are each preceded by the editor's one-page introduction pointing out salient features. Texts (in rhymed couplets mostly) are: The Creation of Adam and Eve, Abraham and His Three Celestial Visitors, Abraham's Sacrifice, The Marriage of Isaac and Rebecca, Isaac's Benediction, Jacob's Ladder, The Rape of Dinah, Joseph Sold by His Brothers, Joseph and His Wheat, Manna from Heaven, Victory over Amalek, and The Tables of Law. The introduction to "Adam and Eve," for example, highlights the text's differences from the twelfth-c. *Jeu d'Adam* by amplification and a poetic lamentation after the Fall; both characters are well developed and nuanced, and the miniature presents the three events of the story in shortened form. A concise bibliography, a list of characters, two indexes (of proper names and of proverbs), and a good glossary (thirty pages) conclude Knight's volume. Since we have not seen the manuscript, all we can do is praise the clear transcription and the easy legibility of the edition; it would have been worthwhile for the editor to reproduce at least one manuscript facsimile page. We hope to receive the remaining volumes as soon as possible.

II: *De Josué à David* contains critical editions of sixteen plays, two of which treat episodes in the history of Joshua, and two other pieces deal with the wars of Saul against his enemies. There is also the story of Gideon and the fleece, as well as that of the marriage of Ruth and Boaz. The volume ends with a series of nine plays staging events in the life and reign of David.

Drama 13, "The Destruction of the City Aï," shows very few dialogues. The author invented dramatic scenes based on the commentary of Nicolas de Lyre (and probably also on the *Meditationes Vitae Christi* — the reviewer). Knight suggests that the miniaturist had not read the piece, but simply showed a city, soldiers, and the king of Aï killed by an arrow (the same fifteenth-c. illustrations — often from chronicles — served for several texts [note of the reviewer]). As in all the Lille drama manuscripts, the versification becomes most complicated, when the scenes show movement and emotions.

Drama 14, "Joshua goes to help Gabaōn," brings a military battle ending with the hanging of five kings — an example (for the spectators) of royal justice. The miniature capitalizes on this execution: the more spectacular the events depicted are, the more chances the playwrights had to be awarded prizes by the chambers of rhetoric. Play 15, "Gideon and the Fleece" (a title given by Knight — for lack of a heading in the manuscript), shows again vivid battle scenes, with a miniature in two parts. To the left is Gideon, kneeling in front of the fleece, while on the right he surprises the Madianites, who kill one another while fleeing. Piece 16, "The Marriage of Boaz and Ruth," is not striking in action but shows lyrical and pastoral themes: medieval society valued fidelity and family ties. On the left of the miniature, Ruth gathers the ears of grain, while, on the right side, Boaz obtains purchasing rights (for land) from a relative (in simple rhymes: aabb).

Play 17, "The Philistines Take the Ark (of the Covenant)," is divided into three parts: a prologue, the introduction of young Samuel, and the war between Israelites and Philistines. Knight surmises the delight of fifteenth-c. spectators at seeing a young child selected by God — after a military disaster. The eighteenth spectacle in this series describes the "Anointing of Saul," with the help of Nicolas de Lyre and Hugues de St. Cher. The author enlarges a fifteen-line section of Samuel's first book to almost 900 verses, in order to show the prince's prowess in battle: the audience liked scenes of war. On the left of the miniature, the Israelites fight the Ammonites, where Saul distinguishes himself by bravery, while the future king is anointed on the right. Play 19 features "Saul's War against Amaleq," with the result that the city is destroyed by the king; remarkably, the author arouses the spectators' sympathy for the defeated: the scenes of child murders echo the Massacre of the Innocents.

Play 20 brings "Saul's Attack of David," the warrior, musician, and friend of Jonathan, but also the object of Saul's hatred. Yet, Saul's children help to save David, allowing him (in a comical scene!) to escape through a window, while a "statue" is left in a bed (another Maître Pathelin=David seeming sick) — a development seen in the illustration. "David and Jonathan" is the subject of chapter 21, where the two become loving friends, as the miniature shows (to the left), while on the other side a game of archery reminds onlookers of their favorite fifteenth-c. pastime. Knight points out that the author is one of the most skilled poets of the collection, his versification being admirable throughout.

Play 22, "David and Abigaïl," shows the king's preparations for combat against Nabal (a cruel rich man), whose wife Abigaïl averts the attack; eventually, she becomes David's spouse. Play 23, "Joab and Abner," is again influenced by Nicolas de Lyre and the Vulgate. Written by learned clerks, the play was staged by laymen, showing Abner murdered by Joab, and Saul's son Hisboseth killed by bandits, so that justice prevails upon villainy — as citizens would expect in the Duchy of Burgundy. The miniature is not related to the contents of the play. "David and Bethsabée" (24) presents the love affair of the protagonists as cause of the woman's husband's (Uriah's) murder by David's men. The characters of David and his victim are well described: adultery versus fidelity and courage.

Play 25 features the rape of Tamar by her half-brother Amnon and the latter's death by the hand of her brother Absalon, the piece serving the spectators as a reminder to avoid "disorderly love." Play 26, "Absalon's War against David," shows the treachery of David's son against his (compassionate) father. The audience is advised to beware of presumptuousness, as Absalon hangs in a tree (on the miniature). Play 27, "Sheba's Revolt against David," brings the assassination of Amasa by Joab, the siege of a city, and Queen Sheba's execution. Play 28, "The Census of Israel," shows that the unethical attitude of a people may influence its ruler; David orders the census, and God's wrath is enflamed against the Israelites, to whom he sends the plague. The illustration preceding the text presents David kneeling before God and asking that his people be spared.

We are pleased that the editor has drawn conclusions about audiences' presumed reactions to the plays. Fifteenth-c. people certainly appreciated battle scenes, love, and comments on moral behavior; and the playwrights apparently knew (and catered to) the onlookers' emotions and expectations. Each play is followed by Knight's notes.

Lascombes, André, and Sydney Higgins, ed. *European Medieval Drama* 4 (2000). Pp. xi; 244.

This fourth volume of the series provides a well-balanced mix of European medieval plays; except for Croatian drama, the thespian activities of the East are not mentioned. Danielle Buschinger ("La Réception du *Décaméron* dans les *Jeux de Carnaval* de Hans Sachs") shows that Sachs's use and dramatization of Boccaccio's tales was not direct. The German playwright read translations by Heinrich Steinhöwel and Heinrich Schlüsselfelder (Arigo), who had amplified their source texts, and one result is, for example, Sachs's *Faßnachtspiel mit fünf Personen, die listig bulerin genandt* (vol. 17, 17–28, in the Keller/Goetze edition). Sachs, however, individualized his personages, emphasizing their social stations; he amplified the story even more than the translators had done, including allusions to contemporary German and Nürnberg politics. Unfortunately, this article is marred by errors in spelling; apparently, the printer had only handwritten copy, and neither it nor the printed version were proofread.

Konrad Schoell examines the humor of farces, *sotties*, and carnival plays, distinguishing different forms of wit according to country. It is difficult to gauge just how a medieval audience reacted to humor, to the comedy of bodily functions, grotesque deformation of language (even *rhetoriqueur* mannerisms), and names. On the stage, humor was mostly aimed at peasants and women. While this study is interesting, it is somewhat myopic and lists almost no references to recent scholarship on the three genres of plays.

Manuela Carvalho's "Shepherds and Social Satire in Gil Vicente" demonstrates that several aspects of the Portuguese writer's work are comparable to those of the Chester *Shepherds' Play* and the Towneley *Prima* and *Secunda Pastorum*, but C. does not offer reasons for these similarities. Staging biblical Nativity scenes, the English plays and those by Vicente (1470?–1536?) also feature social criticisms and concerns. Profane elements stand side by side with religious matters, and some titles are: *Auto dos Reis Magos, Auto da Sibila Cassandra, Auto dos Quatro Tempos, Auto da Fé*. Vicente's later plays are comparable to Elizabethan drama.

"La Sacra rappresentazione croata tra Oriente e Occidente" by Barbara Lomagistro explains that Croatian drama was influenced by eastern orthodox tradition (liturgy and hagiography) and the western Roman Catholic Church, especially in the *laudas* (the Italian *laudas drammaticas*). Peter Happé's "Performing Passion Plays in France and England" brings little that is new, but matters of performance are indeed in the foreground of Happé's discussion — as the author perceives staging to have been handled, without his providing documented proof. Adverbs such as "undoubtedly" and "presumably" are employed frequently in this article, and the relationship between processions and drama remains quite unclear here.

"The Leuven Ommegang and Leuven City Archives: Report on Work in Progress" by Meg Twycross is an enthusiastic essay on Leuven processions (without texts) since 1413, not on drama in the strict sense of the term. Therefore, Lascombes's remark in the book's introduction is certainly inappropriate, as this editor calls the processions "the most prolific and promising forms of

European drama" (ix). In "Armies of God: Procession and Pageant in Florentine Religious Drama," Nerida Newbigin examines a range of plays with kings, retinues, and armies — popular in spite of the fact that real kings were unknown in Tuscany. The valuable book by James W. Cook and Barbara C. Cook (*Antonia Pulci. Florentine Drama for Convent and Festival* [Chicago: University of Chicago Press, 1996]) was not mentioned here.

Leif Søndergaard's "Prologues and Epilogues of *Fastnachtspiele*: Their Functions in the Socio-Cultural Context" is a good summary on a theme treated already in other studies not listed here. Prologues establish initial contact of the players with the audience, clarify performance conditions, and introduce the actors, while epilogues lead the audience back to reality and invite spectators to drink and/or dance. The printing quality of this essay is poor: no proofreading, some titles in bold print, others not, incomplete references, etc. The Croxton *Play of the Sacrament* has been questionable in doctrine and aesthetics since its creation, and Janette Dillon discusses the play's focus on the body and its materiality. Jonathas the Jew pays a merchant to steal the host from the church, in order to test the truth of Eucharistic doctrine; a juxtaposition of consecrated and ordinary bread appears as problematic. Moreover, the violation of the bread provides the thrill of taboo, Dillon continues, whereas a cauldron overflowing with blood is clearly an excessive gesture.

Pamela King's "Corpus Christi: Valencia" has little to do with medieval theater, since this modern celebration includes many folkloric elements added to the religious festival, with the host carried inside the virginal pomegranate. "The Serpent with a Matron's Face: Medieval Iconography of Satan in the Garden of Eden," by Frances Gussenhoven, is an excellent piece of work which sheds light on the possibilities of performing the Eden scene on the stage, with the serpent depicted not as man, boy, or maiden, but as a knowledgeable matron. Finally, Richard Rastall suggests the use of a speaking tube for the voice of God, who remains invisible.

The material brought in volume four of *European Medieval Drama* is rich, varied, and valuable for research concerning the European medieval stage. Not all of these studies are on a professional level, however, and it is regrettable that the volume is marred by errors due to inadequate proofreading.

Loewald, Sharon M. *Les Figures féminines dans certains Mystères de la Passion en France au Moyen Âge* (Villeneuve d'Ascq: Presses Universitaires du Septentrion, 2001). Pp. 408.

The field of research chosen by Madame Loewald for her monograph is interesting: a homogeneous corpus of passion mysteries (c.1350–1500), in which she investigates womankind, complementing numerous studies already published on medieval females and the analyses of the fifteenth century by Johan Huizinga and his successors. At the same time, this work shows the subtle interplay between features permanent from one text to another and the small variations and modifications in the portraits of women by each successive generation of authors.

The neatness of her method is sometimes a bit laboured: complete inventories and rigorous recapitulations support general statistics on women. She ponders some facts; for example, the number of women in Gréban's work is not exceptionally high but comparable to that in other passions, while less so in *Semur* (21%) and Jean Michel (26%). Loewald's enumerations are thoroughly classified; however, the virtues of women might have been grouped differently. She views females in their relationships to other figures: Jesus, men in general, other women, and children. As shown by Philippe Ariès, medieval women seem to lack an understanding of youngsters and their forms of affection (*L'Enfant et la vie familiale sous l'Ancien Régime* [Paris: Le Seuil {third edition}, 1975]): Loewald agrees. Women in passion plays fall into two groups: those who act and those who witness (see France Quéré, *Les Femmes de l'Évangile* [Paris: Le Seuil, 1982]); further varieties are the daughters of Mary and those of Eve, etc.

Seen from this vantage point, we sometimes regret that L. does not classify her discoveries when tracing the origins of feminine names: those from the Bible, from antiquity, from medieval literature; also, the name of the blacksmith's wife, Maragonde, seems to stem from a well-known *chanson de geste* (*Fierabras*). We are grateful for L.'s excellent documentation and thorough summaries of all details on women, for her presenting each person's (fictional) biography and portrait, and for showing how she influences the dramatic action. Studying the intricacies of rewriting from one author to another, she focuses on five important figures: Eve, Mary Magdalene, Herodias (and her daughter), the mother of the man born blind, and the blacksmith's wife. L.'s careful and very readable work showcases women expected within the *landscape* of a passion mystery (the Virgin, Mary Magdalene) and those — more original — , such as the mother of the man born blind, and Pilate's and the blacksmith's wives. At the same time, Loewald characterizes less-known passion dramas, such as *Semur* and its extended use of liturgical hymns (217), as well as songs profane or fantastic in Hebrew (218).

On the other hand, L. lists creative variations (glimpses), for example the knife wielded by Herodias against the Baptist's head (*Passion d'Arras* — 336); the Virgin called "Lady Mary" in the *Passion d'Amboise*; and the realistic lyricism of pain in *Sainte-Geneviève*, the *Livre de la Passion, Isabeau*, and *Autun-Biard* (225). Some of these variations should perhaps have been researched more thoroughly: Jean Michel, for example, has the tendency to give complete biographies to his personages; or else, they receive several roles: thus, Hedroit (here wife of the blacksmith) forges the three nails for the crucifixion; she brings a lantern to the soldiers arresting Christ by night; as concierge for the highpriest Annas, she recognizes Peter as Christ's disciple.

We question, in turn: are the shepherdesses of *Semur* and *Troyes* identical? The former are derived from the pastoral tradition (*Jeu de Robin et Marion*), whereas the Troyes shepherdesses hail from anticurial literature and Franc Gontier's free style of living (a reference to Villon's poem). In contrast to Gréban, Michel does not accentuate the comical aspect of the man born blind, but rather the extraordinary miracle performed by Christ. Finally, it would have been worthwhile to devote more space to questions raised incidentally; for example, who played women's roles? Men did. And how? How does the language of women differ from men's discourse? Or: does Mary Magdalene ever stray from her preoccupation with perfumes in Michel (see Jean-Pierre Albert, *Odeurs de sainteté, la mythologie chrétienne des aromates* [Paris: Éditions de l'École des Hautes Études en Sciences Sociales, 1990])? Should we not instead emphasize her sensuality based on all five senses? Speaking of lyric poetry on death, the author should not have stopped with Philippe Ariès (*L'Homme devant la mort* [Paris: Le Seuil, 1977]), and should instead have mentioned the works by Edelgard E. DuBruck (*The Theme of Death in French Poetry of the Middle Ages and the Renaissance* [La Haye: Mouton, 1964]) and Christine Martineau–Genièys (*Le Thème de la mort dans la poésie française de 1450 à 1550* [Paris: Champion, 1978]), as well as such fifteenth-c. poets as Georges Chastellain and Villon. The motifs of despair and welcoming death in Gréban and Michel were left unnoticed by L., and the diabolic language of the Canaanite woman might have been compared to Maître Pathelin's delirium (in the farce of his name), to medieval nonsense poetry (*fatrasies*), and to the idioms upside-down of carnival.

Nevertheless, these reservations are minor compared to the problems raised and debated by Loewald in this suggestive and rich monograph, which places at our fingertips many facts to interpret yet within other analyses of women in late-medieval studies. We congratulate the author for having prepared this excellent doctoral thesis with tenacity, passion, and intelligence. (A review by Jean Dufournet as translated by DuBruck: see vol. 29, 230–32.)

Runnalls, Graham A. *Les Mystères français imprimés* (Paris: Champion, 1999). Pp. 198.

Divided into two parts, this latest monograph by the renowned scholar of medieval French drama presents a study of the relationship between religious theater and the printing industry, as well as a repertory of mysteries in print at the end of the Middle Ages. In his introduction, R. reminds us that the extant manuscripts of mysteries (230 French religious dramas) are but a small part of a vast corpus of texts, most of which have disappeared or were destroyed. Printing started in 1470 in Paris, at the moment when French medieval theater had reached its apogee. How did the new industry influence the circulation of texts and representations and even help the plays to survive? While mysteries were soon out of fashion in Paris, they flourished elsewhere in France until the seventeenth century. Of 181 plays, thirty-six were printed, while the remainder still exist in manuscript form; a list of the prints can be found in R.'s repertory.

A study of the manuscripts reveals that most mysteries survived in just a single document — but the diversity of these handwritten copies is enormous. All were to serve theatrical representations, and R. gives a typology of seven different (possible) manuscripts of a play, six of which were composed *before* the performance: author's copy, basic manuscript, actors' roles, revised basic manuscript, stage manager's copy, second revised copy of the basic manuscript, and a commissioned luxury copy, done *after* the performance. A typographer worked from a copy of the basic manuscript, which was destroyed during his composing of print characters; the printer was at first not able to duplicate this first print; to obtain a copy, one had to reprint. We must distinguish between printer, printer/bookseller, and the bookseller who decided to publish an edition and took steps to do so; for a voluminous work (e.g., *Le Viel Testament*), several booksellers joined. The Parisian Trepperels and the Janot family were booksellers *and* printers. As to how printers acquired an expensive manuscript (which was as a rule unique), we have no information, especially for provincial establishments. The printing industry was concentrated in Paris and Lyon, and supply along with financial benefits was its aim (not matters of faith, for example). The fifteenth-c. *Catalogue du Libraire de Tours* exists, and eight of its mysteries are related to that city or to western France; many of the Tours prints (not just mysteries) were identical with titles published in Paris by Vérard (1485–1512).

Runnalls gives two tabulations for the number of general editions and mysteries published by each printer in Paris and elsewhere in France. Of ninety Parisian editions, seventy-six were mysteries; of 120 provincial editions, twenty-five were mysteries. Chronologically, between 1484 and the mid-sixteenth century, about 100 mystery editions were published, anywhere from eleven to twenty-six in a decade. After 1550, however, the frequency of new mystery editions diminished in favor of saints' lives; most edited mysteries were either in quarto or octavo format; the in-folio works were more luxurious and costly. Some books had lovely woodcuts, for example the 1493–94 edition of the *Mystère de la Passion* by Jean Michel. Vérard published *la Destruction de Troyes* in-folio (1498), as well as *la Vengeance* (1493), later reprinted by Jean Trepperel.

As for the number of books printed from one edition, those most in demand varied from 300 to 2,250; 600 sheets might be drawn from one page composed in half a day. It is interesting to peruse the list of books left at the death of a printer/bookseller; the value of the books varied according to the amount of pages (for sale, one multiplied by four or five). Book prices can be verified easily by looking at the collection of Fernando Colombus (son of the explorer), books bought between 1531 and 1536 and stored in Seville. This bibliophile entered the price into each new book he acquired (he had 270 French books); in view of the cost of living, the prices were not high.

The circulation of passions was larger than that of hagiographic mysteries, at least in the fifteenth century; many manuscripts circulated from one city to another, or from one bookseller to another in the same town. Sometimes, a manuscript copy was made from a printed edition; the latter was destined mostly for reading, while manuscripts continued to be used for representations. The spread of literacy was surprising, mostly within the upper classes of municipalities; devout bourgeois read mysteries — while the humanists despised these works. With so many printed copies available, it is astonishing that actors did not receive a copy per person; sometimes, editions were reworked after the performances.

Runnalls's chapter fourteen delineates the end of mystery playing, first in cities, then in provincial towns. His repertory of printed mysteries also contains a list of provenances of manuscripts and editions and is followed by a bibliography of eight pages. There is no doubt that this precious monograph will be indispensable for university libraries, specialists of late-medieval religious theater, and historians of printing.

[The reviewer decided to append here a recent note received from Runnalls about documents hitherto lost, but rediscovered now, in a private fund.]

Vers la fin du XIXe siècle, Florimond Truchet publia deux études consacrées au théâtre religieux en Savoie à la fin du moyen âge. Celles-ci étaient fondées dans une grande mesure sur des manuscrits de mystères que Truchet lui-même avait pour ainsi dire exhumés dans son pays natal, la Maurienne: "Le *Mystère de la Passion* à Saint-Jean-de-Maurienne et la *Dioclétiane* à Lanslevillard," lecture faite au premier Congrès des Sociétés Savantes de la Savoie (Saint-Jean-de-Maurienne, Vulliermet, 1878); et "*Le Mystère de l'Antéchrist et du Jugement,*" communication faite au Congrès des Sociétés Savantes de la Savoie à La Roche-sur-Foron (La Roche: Imprimerie Typographique, 1895).

Mais, en 1966, lorsque Jacques Chocheyras, l'historien des mystères alpins, faisait les recherches qui devaient être publiées dans son *Théâtre Religieux en Savoie au XVIe siècle* (Geneva: Droz, 1971), ces manuscrits avaient disparus. Tout récemment, ils ont été retrouvés, faisant partie maintenant d'un fonds privé, nommé le Fonds Florimond Truchet, dont le propriétaire habite la Maurienne. Celui-ci a eu la gentillesse de nous prêter des microfilms et quelques photocopies de ces manuscrits.

Essentiellement, les manuscrits conservent, en entier ou en partie, les textes suivants: *Le Mystère de l'Antéchrist et du Jugement de Dieu* (deux versions, l'une complète en trois journées de 20,000 vers; de l'autre version les seconde et troisième journées seulement); *La Dioclétiane* (texte de 14,000 vers, mélange d'une tragédie et d'un mystère, datant de la fin du XVIe siècle); *Le Mystère de Saint Sébastien* (des fragments du même mystère que celui qui se trouve à la BNF); *Le Mystère de la Passion de Jésus en deux journées* (remaniement de la *Passion* de Jean Michel); *Le Mystère de la Passion* (fragment de la troisième journée — remaniement différent de Michel); de plus, on y trouve le *Registre des Affaires* concernant la représentation d'un *Mystère de la Passion* à Saint-Jean-de-Maurienne en 1573.

Il va de soi que la (re-)découverte de cet ensemble de documents est de la plus grande importance pour l'histoire du théâtre français, et en particulier pour celle des mystères. Cependant, ces documents exigent beaucoup de travail. Gaston Tuaillon est en train de procurer une édition critique de *La Dioclétiane*; pour la part de M. Runnalls, il travaille sur les deux *Passions* et sur le *Registre*. Si l'un des mystérophiles est attiré par la possibilité de faire des recherches (une édition critique?) sur l'*Antéchrist* (un travail sans doute de longue haleine) ou *Saint Sébastien*, Runnalls le prie de le contacter. Il compte publier aussi rapidement que possible un article décrivant ces manuscrits en plus de détail.

Marygrove College

Gestural Communication in French Religious Drama and Art of the Late Middle Ages: The 'Passion Isabeau' and Its Miniatures

Edelgard E. DuBruck

> [To the praise of God, the sovereign Virgin, and all saints (men and women), and upon the request of the very excellent and famous lady and powerful princess Ysabel de Bavière, through God's grace queen of France, I have translated this Passion of Jesus Our Savior from Latin into French, without adding moralities, stories, *exempla* or figures (of speech), in 1398, beginning with the resuscitation of Lazarus, because this miracle and previous wonders gave occasion to the false, felonious Jews to contrive Jesus' death and passion] (DuBruck, ed. *La Passion Isabeau* [New York: Peter Lang, 1990], 61).

The passage above (in my translation) presents the incipit of the *Passion Isabeau* (1398 — hereafter: *PI*), a narrative text leading readers and listeners through Holy Week, a sacred period fraught with potential for gestural expression (e.g., ritualistic, experiential, theatrical). When viewing the illuminated scenes of this text, one is struck by the intriguing gestic language used by the persons depicted, attesting to the miniaturists' skill while, at the same time, evoking the *tableaux vivants* of paradramatic stagings.[1] What is interesting about gestures is that the bodily movements of the persons captured on canvas or elsewhere are frozen in time but come to life on stage. In art or theater, gestures are prompted bodily reactions, and sometimes a cognitive disconnect is involved, especially if movements do *not* achieve the response which they are intended to elicit — for example, acceptance or approval.[2] While there are many variables (some of them indistinct) operating simultaneously to produce a gesture, within the present essay gestural communication is seen as unambiguous, having predictable outcomes.

Gestures in miniatures participate in a much wider discourse accessible to all. Modern dramatists use gestures, certainly, in their contemporizing of medieval religious plays. These gestures are culled from a variety of sources: rubrics in the text, contemporary iconography, typological commonplaces, official records, miniatures, classical rhetoric, and monastic sign language. Conventional passion iconography certainly conveys the characters' hand and arm movements, their facial expressions, and such voluntary and involuntary actions as a kiss or bodily movements, planned or seemingly spontaneous — for expressing grief, joy, astonishment, fear, awe, and explicit or implied actual relationships between individuals. All these gestures illustrate and parallel words spoken as dramatic dialogue, as borne out in lines of text which are often lost in crowds of thousands of spectators who, being too distant from the stage, cannot hear the speakers.[3]

Gestures (even involuntary movements) are forms of communication, instances of transmitting information from source to receptor. The stage, a locus of communication, allows viewers to receive messages from religious or secular sources by multiple means: language, song, mimicry, actions, and gestures performed by initiated actors and decoded through a common system of symbols, signs, or behavior. Miniatures, in turn, communicate by means of pictorial subjects, again on the basis of decodable images or symbols. It should be understood that these communications transcend the spoken word and include life-like reactions; religious drama and iconography do communicate spirituality and lead to meditation.

Thus far, communication by gestures in French religious drama and art of the Middle Ages has not received the critical attention this aspect deserves, despite some enlightening probes by Enders, Palmer, Roeder, and Schmitt.[4] The present study attempts to fill the gap by examining the miniatures of the *PI*, a choice determined by the need to show the many forms of gestural communication in the images of a French passion narrative become seminal for subsequent theatrical stagings and pictorial elucidations of Holy Week.[5]

The first decisive moment of the *PI* is the story of Lazarus's Resurrection (see figure 1, MS 978 BNF), which sets the events of Holy Week into motion, urging the Pharisees and doctors to persecute Jesus; the resuscitation also prefigures Christ's own resurrection and redemption.[6] This episode starts the *PI*, while the narrative ends with the deposition of Christ in the sepulcher of Joseph of Arimathea. The grisaille miniature shows Lazarus sitting up in his coffer tomb (as in the *Biblia Pauperum*[7]), surrounded by the Marys and Martha, as Christ is pointing at the resuscitated man, blessing him with the index of his right hand, while Jesus' left arm gathers the folds of his garment. Next to him appears the Virgin, who has folded her hands in prayer; behind her can be seen Judas with his money pouch; and other persons stand by, awed by the miracle. On the right side, in the background, a spade attests to the digging done to place the coffer tomb into the ground, a spade which is the symbol of labor and of the Fall from Paradise, of sin and mortality since the first father, Adam. Lazarus has folded his hands in prayer, still traumatized by the pains of hell he has just witnessed and is going to describe at the table of Simon the Leper at Bethany, the night before Palm Sunday.

In dramatic performances Lazarus's report from hell, an apocryphal story, was very meaningful to late-medieval theatergoers, who were constantly enlarging their own geographical universes and, hence, were interested in hearing an explicit description of the netherworld by someone who had been resurrected miraculously. Lazarus's story brought to life the tortures and angst of the damned, a foreshadowing of what Christ himself would soon undergo.

These travails, albeit narrated ones, make Jesus' death and the redemption of the damned souls urgent; to avoid the punishments meted out for a life of sin, a sincere Christian was thus guided to choose good over evil. The same graphic information about a subterranean region (purgatory, "invented" in the twelfth century according to Jacques LeGoff, was designed to frighten the sinner) can be found in several passion plays.[8] This account appears in the *Passion Sainte Geneviève* and in that of Semur, as well as in Gréban's and Michel's *Mystères*, in the passions of Troyes, Châteaudun, and Valenciennes. As shown on our figure 1, there is a city seen in the distance, probably the Heavenly Jerusalem, suggesting that Lazarus must die again and may go to Paradise.[9] Many passion plays include the sickness, death, and burial of this emblematic figure; and Jean Michel's *Mystère de la Passion* (1486) even features Lazarus's and Mary Magdalene's previous (sinful) lives.[10]

Generally, in late-medieval Europe, the Raising of Lazarus, like other sight-provoking incidents played out in drama and art during Holy Week, seems to defy logic: faith — borne out in gesture — in fact triumphs over reason. Believing Lazarus staggered forth from his motley tomb requires suspending logic (made clear by skeptical remarks coming from bystanders — in the biblical narrative), and faith becomes the dominant human response to an otherwise incorporeal concept conveyed by the miracle.

Figure 2, from the same manuscript, depicts Christ's Entry into Jerusalem. As shown on the back panel of Duccio de Buoninsegna's *Maestà* (early fourteenth century) in Siena, people can be seen spreading a garment on the ground in front of Christ, who sits on the donkey, lifting his right hand in a blessing.[11] The Roman towers of Jerusalem (in Duccio: Siena) are reminiscent of the structures depicted in the upper right of the *Isabeau* Lazarus miniature. Here, as in the Duccio painting and in the *Biblia Pauperum* (28), Jesus comes from the left, whereas the two men spreading the garment can be noticed on the right; as in the Italian painting, the figures wave palm branches behind the frontal scene (one person, perhaps Zacchaeus, leans down from a tower, to look and cut a branch). The disciples on the left behind Christ gesture with their right hands which are not open-palmed; instead, they point in demonstration; a Pharisee, recognizable by his headdress, appears at the left border of the miniature.

This Entry into Jerusalem (a scene soon to become symbolic for sudden reversals of opinion) was dramatized many times in the fifteenth century. It is the kind of procession of which medieval people were fond and in which the audience even participated, fitting, as the scene does, right into pre-Easter festivities. The conventional iconography varied little; in the *Biblia Pauperum* (28) the scene depicted is similar to the Duccio painting and shows Zacchaeus in a tree, cutting his palm branch. The procession resembles the entrance festivities staged for princes' visiting one of their cities; in turn, these arrivals are often modeled after Christ's entry into Jerusalem.

The scene of welcome is followed in the manuscript by figure 3, a Munich miniature with a French text and conversational gestures enacted by the personages (Biblioteca Regia Munacensis, gall. 22). Indoors at Bethany, Jesus talks to his mother who makes the four requests, which he refuses: that he save humankind without having to die; that he die without having to suffer; that she might die before him, in order not to see his death; or that she see her son die without sustaining profound spiritual pain. In all late-medieval passion plays, the role of the Virgin Mary extends beyond the scope of the biblical narrative due to several concomitant influences: late-medieval devotion to the Holy Mother; a Christianization of courtly love (influenced by mysticism); and the Franciscan tendency to humanize holy figures. The dialogue between mother and son, a debate about her requests, one by one, can occur in a room adjoining the other scenes on the simultaneous stage.

Figure 3 is divided into three parts: on the left, Christ speaks to his mother, while his left hand takes hers; she places her right hand on her heart in emphasis of, and anticipatory pain over, his suffering and death. Her face shows expectation and fear, while the son's countenance remains strict and stern; he is barefoot, whereas Mary wears shoes in the fashion of the late Middle Ages. This conversation is not mentioned in the *MVC* or in other apocryphal sources, nor is it depicted in passion iconography preceding the fifteenth century.

In the middle section of the illumination the disciples and the women huddle, standing on a tiled floor. St. Peter gestures in blame (of Judas) with his left hand, while his right hand holds a Bible, no doubt for pointing out prefigurations of Christ's death established in the Old Testament. Next to him seems to be St. John, who conveys blame, when he sees Judas leaving with the infamous money pouch, as shown in the third section of the illustration. The idea of blame evidenced within John's gesture is intriguing, because both Peter and John are evidently capable of stopping Judas; the gestures seem to preclude the disciples' active involvement at this point (in order to fulfill Scripture). Indeed, the traitor's face shows decision. All disciples appear as barefoot, and the two women look grieved at the news of Christ's impending death; the background of the miniature is blue with gold or silver stars. In Gréban's and Michel's presentations of the scene on a simultaneous stage, the three divisions could have been easily reproduced. On the second day of Gréban's work, the only rubric specifies: "Icy se tire Jhesus et Nostre Dame a part" [here, Jesus and Our Lady step aside], before verse 16,423; at the end of Michel's scene there is a very effective stichomythic dialogue between the two holy persons (234 in Jodogne's edition).[12]

Our next section of the passion story (figure 4) shows Judas's Betrayal and the Arrest of Christ, again taken from the Munich codex, a scene framed at the lower part of the illustration by an enclosure (similar to the *St. Apollonia* scene by Jean Fouquet, 1452).[13] The master/disciple pair of Christ/Judas is in the middle, where Judas can be evidenced bestowing the ironical kiss of betrayal onto his Lord, as he holds Christ's right arm with his own right hand.[14] Judas's left hand grips Jesus' left shoulder firmly, and Christ suffers the embrace having knowledge of prefigured fulfillment. The youth in the left foreground (did he fall to the ground when Jesus spoke, as in some passion plays?)[15] is wearing shoes, as are the arresting knights in helmets. St. Peter, on the left, takes a sword out of its sheath, and the other persons (one other disciple, Pharisees, soldiers, and citizens with fifteenth-c. headdresses) mill around. The evening sky is dark blue with gold or silver stars (shown on the original manuscript), and a woman holds a lantern: according to Michel, she is Hedroit, the smith's wife, who later forges blunt nails for the crucifixion (278). Judas's right hand with its soft, delicate touch contrasts with the forceful mercenary's left hand used in the arrest; this man seems to sport an air of satisfaction, as he grips Christ firmly (noticeable in the contracting folds of the Savior's garment), while banners of joy are raised by the soldiers, signifying exhilaration that the "hypocrite" is finally arrested.[16] In the Betrayal shown in the *Hours of Étienne Chevalier* (Fouquet), Judas kisses Christ from the beholder's right, and Peter unsheathes his sword also on the right, where a woman stands with a lamp (Mâle, 59).

In several plays the Arrest is conflated with Judas's Betrayal, just as in the *Pl*, the *Biblia Pauperum* (35), and the Fouquet miniature. The Agony in Gethsemane is depicted by Duccio below the panel for the Betrayal and Arrest; in the latter, the configuration Judas/Christ/arresting mercenary is the same as in our figure 4; in the panel Christ stands on a vertical axis, just as in the illustration, and, in both instances, Jesus wears a dark-colored mantle, in contrast to the other persons' garments. Perhaps the *Maestà* has really influenced northern iconography (but there could be other sources as well), and it is of course possible that some versions of the *MVC* or the *Gospel of Nicodemus* had similar miniatures.[17]

Figure 5 illustrates the Flagellation, from MS 978 of the BNF. Christ is tied tightly to a column or pillar, so that he and the post form a reinforced pillar, as it were; two mercenaries or torturers whip him all night (in some plays and in Duccio, there are four scourgers who, in Gréban and Michel, take turns). Here, the two men raise their whips far above their heads to achieve better impact. On the (negative) left, some persons are watching, including Judas with his purse, all of these onlookers pointing at the scene with their right hands; this basement has Romanesque arches.

Since the second half of the thirteenth century, the scene of the Flagellation inspired late-medieval groups of flagellants who performed passion plays in the churches of their patrons, hoping to expiate their sins by so doing. Called *disciplinati* in Italy, these groups alternated the singing of *laude* (praises of the holy persons) with the administering of self-flagellation.[18] In England, Margery Kempe imagined sixteen men wielding scourges, each of which was fixed with eight spurlike lead pellets; in the N-Town mocking, Christ is made to sit "on a stol" and has the crown of thorns forced on him, while in the German *Donaueschingen* passion play (1485), this stool is removed from under him at the very moment when he sits down.[19] Davidson mentions an alabaster (Hildburgh) displaying four tormentors engaged in the act of whipping (98). Duccio had an elaborate flagellation on one of two elegant pillars, with two tormentors and rope scourges; there Christ, in a loin-cloth and placed just off center, faces the viewer directly, as Pilate looks on, gesturing open-palmed toward Christ (*adlocutio*[20]). As Mulvaney has remarked, the Duccio Christ is isolated by being depicted in a visibly hostile environment.[21]

Figure 6, from Peniarth 482 (a Welsh testimony), shows the *iacente cruce* nailing in a lovely miniature of the so-called international style, resembling the scene in the *Grandes Heures du Duc de Berry* (Mâle, 22) and in Gérard David's *Nailing* (1480). Thus, Christ is hammered to the cross lying on the ground and erected later. The *iacente cruce* position in most fifteenth-c. painted passions followed theatrical practice that may have influenced the iconography: it would be impossible to nail (or tie) someone to an upright cross. Both traditions, the *erecto cruce* and the *iacente cruce* nailing, were traceable in early Christian iconography, that is, in Byzantine illustrations of psalters from the ninth through the twelfth centuries; but the *iacente cruce* form did not appear in northern paintings until the late Middle Ages.[22] In the *MVC*, however, Christ climbed a ladder onto the standing cross.

Figure 6 is characterized by diagonals which enliven the nailing and emphasize the forceful pulling of Christ by the "chevaliers" (as Christ's tormentors are called in the *PI* text). One of the men exerts so much force that he stems his entire body against the cross and the transverse beam with Christ's left hand (the holes for the nails are placed too far from the middle axis). The depicted scene swarms with black tools, later called "holy instruments" of torture (symbols of the passion[23]), which stand in stark contrast to Christ's white body. There are also two baskets with tools, just in case; a man in the foreground seems to be forging more nails; on the right, another pounds in the feet (with *one* nail). In the distance at left is Jerusalem with late-Romanesque architecture and a lovely pond, a boat, and a swan — a truly superb landscape, contrasting with the violence in the foreground. In the far distance on the right a château can be seen on a hill, which forms a parallel, as it were, with another hilly landscape more in the foreground, behind which people and mercenaries are moving forward to see the crucifixion. This (out)line, in turn, parallels the man pulling very hard to stretch Christ's left arm, as described above. Miniatures 6 and 8 are of superior quality; this manuscript was obviously illustrated (in full color) by an outstanding artist of the late fifteenth century. In Gréban the nailing becomes a grim and ironic *rondeau grinçant*.[24]

Figure 7 (from French MS 978) shows the Crucifixion, with Christ in the center, his enemies on the right, evincing gestures of demonstration (the high priests, with soldiers behind them), and three women on the left, mourning and praying, and the same positioning is noticeable in the *Biblia Pauperum* (39); in some reports, Mary had fainted; the background is dark, as for a storm. In a French alabaster of 1430, now in Warsaw, the collapsing Mary is supported by two women, an artistic solution comparable to that of an altarpiece (in the Poor Clare convent) created by Luis Borrasscá (1414–15) and to another of 1427 by Thomas de Kolozsvár.[25]

The Descent from the Cross (figure 8, from Peniarth) allows for ample movement. Christ's body, bent backwards, is held by the left arm of a mercenary (or burial assistant) and by the right arm of another; both men stand on ladders and steady their own bodies by holding onto the cross with their free hands. A third person holds Christ's legs, while Mary Magdalene touches his right thigh, and the other women pray and gesticulate sorrowfully.[26] In a miniature from a Vienna Missal of 1409, Magdalene embraces the cross itself (Białostocki, 37). In figure 8 the wooden cross stands out black against a sunny and peaceful background showing the impressive Temple of Jerusalem, a symbol for the powers that executed Jesus. Neither at the Crucifixion nor at the Descent do we see the thieves. This miniature resembles the Descent in the *Grandes Heures du Duc de Berry* (Mâle, fig. 10); and in the magnificent *Deposition* by Rogier Van der Weyden (before 1443 — an altarpiece as well), the bodies of Christ and the fainting Mary form the same parallel inflection.[27] The Virgin's address at this point is by far the most expressive lamentation in Michel's passion (vv. 29,425–65).

Thus, what the eight miniatures reveal is a complete *gestural vocabulary*, depicting movements which speak a language, as in silent films. For the beholder, the gestures are logical: the astonishment and reflection responses of Lazarus; the joyful greetings by Jerusalem's citizens at Christ's arrival (to be contrasted by the merriness of his capturers later on);[28] gestures of supplication (the four requests by Mary) and demonstration/persuasion (Christ's answers to Mary); gestures of the disciples, blaming Judas; the awe of the mercenaries at seeing Christ in Gethsemane; a kiss of betrayal and the brutality of the arrest; infliction of pain (whipping, mocking, and nailing); prayer, grief, and sadness of the women at the cross; the careful lowering of Christ's body by the executioners in the Descent from the Cross.

To sum up and complete our findings, it is obvious that *Fatistes* and painters offered planned movements that must be understood by beholders to be effective, body language accompanying or replacing words, and interpreting moods and tonalities. What we know about gestures is slowly helping to decode both stage and iconography. Moreover, it should be kept in mind that the artist of a miniature or dramatic performance brings his/her age, social status, etc., into the creative mix.

Thus, we must interpret gestures portrayed in paintings which convey the passion story by making explicit reference to medieval dramatic performances, to scenes closely allied to conventional iconography, even Byzantine. Narrative passion tracts should likewise be exploited; the conversation between Jesus and Mary (figure 3), for example, is a logical depiction of the corresponding scene in the *PI* text. The controversy about the relationship between iconography and the stage has an astonishing longevity: Frederick Pickering, the German critic and historian, has established the iconic character of the stage and the theatricality of iconography;[29] and Patrick J. Collins has called our attention to the narrative pictorial cycles existing long before the fifteenth-c. mysteries in miniatures and murals, series which even seem to have determined the sequence of events selected for the passion stage.[30]

While formerly literary critics were attuned mostly to the *written* texts, we should read the miniatures of any passion story, whether expressed in narrative or in dialogue, as closely related to scenic visualization. According to Jean-Claude Schmitt,

> [l]e rapport très étroit de l'iconographie et du drame . . . se vérifie dans d'autres cas encore. L'image peut non seulement figurer les gestes des *acteurs*, mais rappeler, avec plus de force encore, les gestes réels de la Passion dont le drame . . . est la *sainte représentation*, la mémoire vivante. Les deux types de représentation ont leur propre logique, leurs propres significations, leurs propres fonctions.[31]

The crucifixion miniatures of the *PI* are undoubtedly more than illustrations of a written text; on a few occasions the words actually describe the pictures! Both the miniatures and the text, operating in conjunction with one another, lead to complete meditations on Christ's life.

The communicative gestures in the *Passion Isabeau* miniatures are such that the illustrations could be *read* even when separated from the known narrative conveyed within the text — except for the famous debate between Christ and his mother which cannot be transmitted entirely by gestures. Through inference and demonstration, meditation would thus be possible *in lieu of* the text, just as conventional religious iconography (risen in Byzantine times) — and the scenes of all passion dramas — lead to contemplation and spiritual participation.[32]

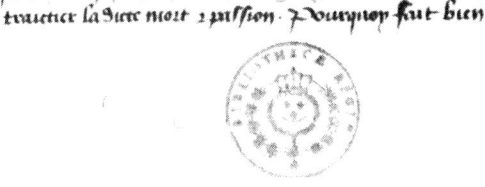

Fig. 1: Resurrection of Lazarus: B.N. fr. 978, fol. 1r.
With permission of the Bibliothèque Nationale de Paris.

Fig. 2: Entry into Jerusalem: B.N. fr. 978, fol. 5v.
With permission of the Bibliothèque Nationale de Paris.

Fig. 3: Jesus talks to his mother: Cod. Gall. 22, fol. 16v.
With permission of the Bayerische Staatsbibliothek.

Fig. 4: Betrayal and Arrest at Gethsemane: Cod. Gall 22, fol. 24v.
With permission of the Bayerische Staatsbibliothek.

Fig. 5: Flagellation: B.N. fr. 978, fol. 39r.
With permission of the Bibliothèque Nationale de Paris.

Fig. 6: *Iacente cruce nailing*: Peniarth 482, fol. 76r.
With permission of the National Library of Wales.

Fig. 7: Crucifixion: B.N. fr. 978, fol. 42v.
With permission of the Bibliothèque Nationale de Paris.

Fig. 8: Descent from the cross: Peniarth 482, fol. 103r.
With permission of the National Library of Wales.

Notes

[1] A la louenge de Dieu, de la Vierge souveraine, et tous sains et toutes saintes, et a la requeste de tres excellante et redoubtee dame et puissant princesse dame Ysabel de Baviere, par la grace de Dieu royne de France, j'ay translaté ceste Passion de Jhesus Nostre Sauveur de latin en françoiz sans y adjouster moralités, hystoires, exemples ou figures, l'an 1398, prenant mon commencement dès la suscitacion du ladre pource que celuy miracle avec les autres par avant fais furent occasion aux faulx felons Juifs de machiner la mort et passion de Jhesus.

While it is not clear to what extent the text's illuminations were indebted to conventional passion iconography, they do enliven certain passages and bring out the story's emotional tonality (conventional sources are: Émile Mâle, *L'Art religieux de la fin du moyen âge en France* [Paris: A. Colin, 1925], chs. ii–iv; James Marrow, *Passion Iconography in Northern European Art of the Late Middle Ages and Early Renaissance* [Kortrijk: Van Ghemmert, 1979]; Louis Réau, *Iconographie de l'art chrétien* [Paris: PUF, 1955–59]; Gertrud Schiller, *Iconography of Christian Art*, trans. Janet Seligman, 2 vols. [Greenwich: New York Graphic Society, 1971–72], vol. 2; Jan Białostocki, *L'Art du XVe siècle des Parler à Dürer*, trans. Pierre-Emmanuel Dauzat [Paris: Librairie Française, 1993]). When editing the *PI*, a text commissioned by Isabeau de Bavière, Queen of France, I examined some twenty-three manuscripts, most of which came from the Paris region (Île de France): DuBruck, ed. *La Passion Isabeau. Une édition du manuscrit fr. 966 de la Bibliothèque Nationale de Paris* (New York: Peter Lang, 1990). See also: "The Narrative Passion of Our Lord Jesus Christ Written in 1398 for Isabeau de Bavière, Queen of France: An Important Link in the Development of French Religious Drama," *Michigan Academician* 18 (1986): 95–107; "The *Passion Isabeau* (1398) and Its Relationship to Fifteenth-Century *Mystères de la Passion*," *Romania* 107 (1986): 77–91; and "Image — Text — Drama: The Iconography of the *Passion Isabeau*," 287–310 in *Studies in Honor of Hans-Erich Keller*, ed. Rupert T. Pickens (Kalamazoo: MIP, 1993). All of the manuscripts (depicting the events of Holy Week) were anonymous and untitled; I chose the title *Passion Isabeau* because nearly all the incipits of the manuscripts attested to the queen's commissioning. Émile Roy has proved that Arnoul Gréban's *Mystère de la Passion* (1453) was influenced by the *PI*, mostly because of an important conversation (which appears in the *PI*) between Christ and the Virgin, a passage containing her four requests (or reasons for Jesus to avoid his own suffering and death), evident nowhere else before Gréban (see Émile Roy, *Le Mystère de la Passion en France du XIVe au XVIe siècle. Étude sur les sources et le classement des mystères de la passion* [Dijon: Damidot, 1903–1904]: 249; also, Jean-Pierre Bordier, "Les quatre requêtes de Notre-Dame," in Bordier, ed. *L'Économie du dialogue dans l'ancien théâtre européen* [Paris: Champion, 1999], 187–210).

Passion narratives in the vernacular were created in a considerable number of manuscripts throughout late-medieval Europe, texts which 'translated' or adapted the passion sequence of the thirteenth-c. prose work *Meditationes Vitae Christi* (hereafter: *MVC*). See: Isa Ragusa and R. B. Green, tr. *Meditations on the Life of Christ* (Princeton: Princeton University Press, 1961). Modern scholars agree that the author of the *Meditationes* must have been a Franciscan monk living in Tuscany during the second half of the thirteenth century. The work is called "a life of Christ, a biography of the Blessed Virgin, the fifth gospel, the last of the apocrypha, one of the masterpieces of Franciscan literature, a summary of medieval spirituality, a religious handbook of contemplation, a manual of Christian iconography" (*Smaointe Beatha Chríost*, ed. Cainneach Ó'Maonaigh [Dublin: Baile Átha Cliath, 1944], 325). The *MVC* spread over all of Europe in many copies, inspiring similar works in the vernacular; the influence of St. Bernard (who is quoted in the text) is obvious. Émile Mâle was the first to emphasize the great influence of the *MVC* on fifteenth-c. religious art and drama: *L'Art religieux de la fin du moyen âge en France* (see above), chs. ii to iv. English fourteenth-c. equivalents are Nicholas Love's *Mirror of the Blessed Life of Jesus Christ*, the *Cursor Mundi*, the *Northern Passion*, and a German witness is the *Erlösung*. The *Mirror of the Blessed Life of Jesus Christ* by Nicholas Love (fl. 1410), first printed in Douai by C. Boscard, c.1606, was edited by Michael G. Sargent (New York: Garland, 1992). On the *Cursor Mundi*, see John J. Thompson, *The Cursor Mundi: Poem, Texts and Contexts* (Oxford: Oxbow Books, 1998); *The Northern Passion* was published by Frances Foster, EETS, 2 vols. (1913–16; repr. New York: Kraus, 1971). Following the *MVC*, the authors of these vernacular texts incorporated many apocryphal elements which also appeared in passion plays.

What was the purpose of creating narrative passion texts? Not only did literate Christians in châteaux and crowded late-medieval cities need vernacular versions of the holy stories, but monks whose Latin had deteriorated were now able to read indigenous texts; in addition, cloistered women assembled to hear the stories read to them. Isabeau de Bavière probably wanted the passion report for her library; the multiplicity of manuscripts in the region near Paris attests to the popularity of this text, even in country congregations.

[2]I owe these last remarks to Barbara I. Gusick. On gestures, many works have been helpful: Moshe Barasch, *Gestures of Despair in Medieval and Early Renaissance Art* (New York: New York University Press, 1976); Robert Boenig, ed. *The Mystical Gesture: Essays on Medieval and Early Modern Spiritual Culture in Honor of Mary E. Giles* (Aldershot: Ashgate, 2000); Jan N. Bremmer and Herman Roodenburg, ed. *A Cultural History of Gesture: From Antiquity to the Present Day* (Cambridge: Polity Press, 1991); Clifford Davidson, "Gesture in Medieval Drama With Special Reference to the Doomsday Plays in the Middle English Cycles," *EDAM Newsletter* 6 (1983): 8–17, and "Gesture in Medieval British Drama," 66–127 in Davidson, ed. *Gesture in Medieval Drama and Art* (Kalamazoo: MIP, 2001); Francis Edeline, J. M. Klinkenberg, and P. Minguet, *Traité du signe visuel (Pour une rhétorique de l'image)* (Paris: Seuil, 1991); Jody Enders, *Rhetoric and the Origins of Medieval Drama* (Ithaca: Cornell University Press, 1992), and "Of Miming and Signing: The Dramatic Rhetoric of Gesture," 1–25 in Davidson, ed. *Gesture* (above); François Garnier, *Le Langage de l'image au moyen âge*, 2 vols. (Paris: Le Léopard d'Or, 1982); Ernst Gombrich, "Ritualized Gesture and Expression in Art," *Philosophical Transactions of the Royal Society of London*, B series # 772, vol. 251 (1966): 393–401; Peter Meredith and John Tailby, ed. *The Staging of Religious Drama in Europe in the Later Middle Ages: Texts and Documents in English Translation*, trans. Raffaella Ferrari, P. Meredith, R. Muir, M. Sleeman, and J. E. Tailby (Kalamazoo: MIP, 1983): 177–83; Beth A. Mulvaney, "Gesture and Audience: the Passion and Duccio's *Maestà*," 178–220 in Davidson, ed. *Gesture*; Dunbar H. Ogden, *The Staging of Drama in the Medieval Church* (Cranbury, N.J.: Associated University Presses, 2002): 164–72; Barbara D. Palmer, "Annunciations, Sacred and Secular," 128–57 in Davidson, ed. *Gesture*; Silke Philipowski, "Geste und Inszenierung," *Beiträge zur Geschichte der deutschen Sprache und Literatur* 122 (2000): 455–77; Anke Roeder, *Die Gebärde im Drama des Mittelalters: Osterfeiern, Osterspiele* (Munich: Beck, 1974); Jean-Claude Schmitt, *La Raison des gestes dans l'occident médiéval* (Paris: Gallimard,

1990), and Schmitt, ed. *Gestures* (London: Harwood Academic Publishers, 1984); Pamela Sheingorn, "The Visual Language of Drama: Principles of Composition," 173–91 in *Contexts for Early English Drama*, ed. Marianne G. Briscoe and J. C. Coldewey (Bloomington: Indiana University Press, 1989). On "Wechselbeziehungen zwischen bildender Kunst und Theater," see Roeder (above), 18–24.

[3] See Dunbar Ogden, "Gesture and Characterization in the Liturgical Drama," 26–47 in Davidson, ed. *Gesture* (above, note 2); also: Roeder (ibid.), 24–29; Jean-Claude Schmitt and Jody Enders (ibid.); Schmitt, ch. vii. On the difference between gestures and gesticulation, see Schmitt, 30 and 131: Christian and monastic gestures are prescribed to be moderate, reflecting the inner person, whereas *gesticulationes* are exterior movements with histrionic content, without rational control. A good example of gesticulations can be seen in a miniature of Christ's Buffeting displayed in the *Petites Heures de Jean de Berry*: Jan Białostocki, *L'Art du XVe siècle des Parler à Dürer* (above, note 1): 97.

[4] See above, note 2.

[5] Not all *PI* texts have miniatures. Our images come from costly manuscripts in the Bibliothèque Nationale de France, the Bayerische Staatsbibliothek, and the National Library of Wales.

[6] On Lazarus, see Davidson, "The Visual Arts and Drama, with Special Emphasis on the Lazarus Plays," 45–59 in *Le Théâtre au Moyen Âge*, ed. Gari Muller (Montréal: Aurore, 1981); Kathleen M. Ashley, "The Resurrection of Lazarus in the Late Medieval English and French Cycle Drama," *Papers on Language and Literature* 22 (1986): 227–44; Barbara I. Gusick, "Death and Resurrection in the Towneley *Lazarus*," 331–54 in *Death and Dying in the Middle Ages*, ed. Edelgard E. DuBruck and B. I. Gusick (New York: Peter Lang, 1999); Walter Puchner, *Studien zum Kulturkontext der liturgischen Szene: Lazarus und Judas als religiöse Volksfiguren in Bild und Brauch, Lied und Legende Südosteuropas*, 2 vols. (Vienna: Österreichische Akademie der Wissenschaften, 1991); Mark C. Pilkinton, "The Raising of Lazarus: A Prefiguring Agent to the Harrowing of Hell" (on English drama), *Medium Aevum* 44 (1975): 51–53; on Lazarus in N-Town, see Davidson, "Gesture" (above, note 2), 95–96.

[7] Avril Henry, ed. *Biblia Pauperum* (Ithaca: Cornell University Press, 1987), 68. Also: Albert C. Labriola and J. W. Smeltz, ed. and trans., *The Bible of the Poor* (Pittsburgh: Duquesne University Press, 1990): 25. Here, however, the coffer tomb is on the left side.

[8] LeGoff, *La Naissance du purgatoire* (Paris: Gallimard, 1981). On Lazarus's report from hell, see E. DuBruck, "Lazarus's Vision of Hell: A Significant Passage in Late-Medieval Passion Plays," 53–63 in DuBruck and Yael Even, ed. *Violence in Fifteenth-Century Text and Image* (vol. 27 of *Fifteenth-Century Studies*, 2002); Edward Gallagher, "The *Visio Lazari*, the Cult and the Old French Life of Saint Lazarus: An Overview," *Neuphilologische Mitteilungen* 3–4 (1989): 331–39; Clifford Davidson and Thomas H. Seiler, ed. *The Iconography of Hell* (Kalamazoo: MIP, 1992).

[9] See Barbara I. Gusick, "Time and Unredemption: Perceptions of Christ's Work in the Towneley *Lazarus*," *Fifteenth-Century Studies* 22 (1995): 19–41.

[10] See also: Lynette R. Muir, *The Biblical Drama of Medieval Europe* (Cambridge: Cambridge University Press, 1995): 116–21.

[11] See Beth A. Mulvaney (above, note 2), 186–89. On blessings, see Schmitt, 108–109. The influence of Italian on northern art has been highlighted by Mâle (ch. i); Italian

iconography, in turn, was still based on Byzantine patterns; these connections were not probed in Mulvaney's article.

[12] All translations of passages in French are my own. Jean Michel, *Le Mystère de la Passion (Angers 1486)*, ed. Omer Jodogne (Gembloux: Duculot, 1959). Also: Muir, 245–46, note 9; Gertrud Schiller (above, note 1), 2: 129.

[13] On page 35 of the *Biblia Pauperum*, Judas kisses Christ from the beholder's right, and the mercenary grabs Jesus from the left. St. Peter unsheathes his sword on the left.

[14] See Davidson, "Gesture," 74–75 and 78–79. On the kiss, furthermore, Schmitt, 298, and Roeder (note 2, above), 60.

[15] Compare this scene to Białostocki's Arrest miniature (22) by the Limburg Brothers of 1416, where all the soldiers fall to the ground before arresting Christ: they are awed by the luminous appearance of Jesus in the dark night.

[16] Judas's suicide is not mentioned in the *PI*, nor in the *MVC*, while it is included in Gréban and Michel; the latter gives an elaborate treatment of Judas's oedipal adolescence, thereby furnishing psychological reasons for the man's deed. On his repentance and death, see DuBruck and Gusick, *Death and Dying* (above, note 6), 355–75 (361) in DuBruck's "The Death of Christ on the Late-Medieval Stage: A Theater of Salvation."

[17] According to Zbigniew Izydorczyk, the apocryphal *Gospel of Nicodemus* (hereafter *GN*) in Greek, was perhaps the most popular passion/resurrection narrative of late-medieval Europe, nourishing, as it were, the stage in many ways; the Latin translation dates from the fifth century A.D. This gospel enlarged the canonical accounts and provided much detail, illustrating the history of salvation. According to Vincent de Beauvais, this text contained pure truth, an opinion then held generally: Nicodemus was considered an eyewitness to Christ's death (*Speculum naturale*, Prologue, col. 8). See Izydorczyk, ed. *The Medieval 'Gospel of Nicodemus': Texts, Intertexts, and Contexts in Western Europe* (Tempe: Medieval and Renaissance Texts and Studies, 1997), ix–xiii.

[18] See DuBruck, "Image — Text — Drama," 293–94. Muir, 21.

[19] Davidson, "Gesture," 97; see DuBruck, "The Death of Christ on the Late-Medieval Stage," 355–75 (363) in *Death and Dying* (above, note 6).

[20] See Schmitt, 52–53, 109, 137.

[21] Mulvaney (above, note 2), 205, and fig. 40 in Davidson, ed. *Gesture*.

[22] See DuBruck, "The Passion Plays in Continental Europe: Adapting Biblical Stories to the Stage," 75–94 in *New Approaches to European Theater of the Middle Ages: An Ontology*, ed. Barbara I. Gusick and E. E. DuBruck (New York: Peter Lang, 2004). Also: Schiller, 2: 86 and fig. 316.

[23] Schiller, 2: 691.

[24] *grinçant* = squeaking. Arnoul Gréban, *Le Mystère de la Passion*, ed. Omer Jodogne, 2 vols. (Brussels: Palais des Académies, 1965–83): vv. 24,738–53. Also: Jody Enders, "The Music of the Medieval Body in Pain," 93–112, and Robert Mills, "'For They Know Not What They Do': Violence in Medieval Passion Iconography," 200–216 in *Violence in Fifteenth-Century Text and Image* (above, note 8).

[25] Białostocki, 69–70.

[26] In the late Middle Ages, *gesticulatio* was losing its negative connotation.

[27] Białostocki, 135.

[28] See Barbara D. Palmer, "Gestures of Greeting: Annunciations, Sacred and Secular," 128–57 in Davidson, ed. *Gesture*. Of all gestures, greetings are closely related to everyday life, and Palmer pointed out (ibid., 144–45) that gestures showing the converse of greetings communicate the gesticulating person's rejection, rudeness, disrespect, and even scatology (as in profane theater, on miniatures, and in drawings at the margins of manuscripts). Especially in carnival plays a whole repertory of *reversed* gestures is imaginable by the medievalist.

[29] *Literatur und darstellende Kunst im Mittelalter* (Berlin: Schmidt, 1966): 106 and ch. iv.

[30] "Narrative Bible Cycles in Medieval Art and Drama," *Comparative Drama* 9 (1975): 125–46.

[31] Schmitt, *La Raison des gestes*, 277–78:

> [(T)he close relationship of iconography and drama . . . can be noticed in yet other cases. An image may not only show the actors' gestures but recall, with yet more emphasis, the real gestures of the Passion of which the drama . . . is the sacred representation, its living memory. The two types of shows have their own logic, their proper significance, their own functions. My translation].

[32] A valuable list of gestures (drawings) was provided by John Bulwer in *Chirologia, or the Naturall Language of the Hand . . . Whereunto is added Chironomia: or, the Art of Manuall Rhetoricke* (1644), ed. James W. Cleary (Carbondale and Edwardsville: Southern Illinois University Press, 1974): 155. Another listing is in Walter Lipphardt, *Lateinische Osterfeiern und Osterspiele*, 9 vols. (Berlin: Walter de Gruyter, 1975–90), here motions from rubrics, reprinted by Ogden Dunbar (above, note 3), 26–47 in Davidson, ed. *Gesture*. Furthermore, the following lines from Charles R. Dodwell (*Anglo-Saxon Gestures and the Roman Stage* [Cambridge: Cambridge University Press, 2000]: 101–54, passim), were quoted by Davidson ("Gesture," 107):

> [P]uzzlement, signaled by moving hand or finger toward the face or taking hold of the beard; grief or melancholy, by placing the hand to the side of the face; approval, or agreement, by curving the thumb and forefinger (or another finger) around until they touched each other; supplication, by outstretched, imploring arms; fear, by throwing up . . . arms from the elbows; and reflection or meditation, by resting the chin on the back of the hand.

Marygrove College

Some Renaissance Views about Madness and Genius: Reading Ficino and Paracelsus

Leonardas Vytautas Gerulaitis

During the late 1400s, an important shift in the spiritual and factual orientations of humankind began to take place, as Christian teleology became challenged by a worldly anthropology. Whereas before, God and religious concerns held sway in the world, now secular matters came to preoccupy the lives and fears of humankind and became the center of attention. As Georges Duby observes, "there can be no doubt that a subjective experience of the presence of evil did exist; but, as has often been observed, the most frightening demons are those within."[1] Duby's comment captures the temper of an individualistic era, one empowering humankind by validating its authority to achieve progress — while providing subject matter for moralists.

Culturally, this was a time of brilliant accomplishments in scholarship, literature, science, and the arts, and the beginning of a revolution in commerce. The Renaissance first appeared in Italy, where relative political stability, economic expansion, wide contact with other cultures, and a flourishing urban civilization provided the background for a new view of the world. The humanist emphasis on the individual was typified in the ideal of the Renaissance man, the man of universal genius, best exemplified by Leonardo da Vinci. Soon, the northern states, above all France, benefited from and adopted the ideas, practices, and world view of the Italian Renaissance. Geographic exploration — as well as the first investigations into mental processes and the human behavioral microcosm — were now underway.

During the Middle Ages what was known about mental ailments derived from Greek and Arabic medicine. Guessing at a relationship between corporeal and mental symptoms, authors such as Gregory of Nyssa, Nemesius of Emesa, and Hugo of St. Victor believed that the theory of the four humors held by Hippocrates and Galen was still applicable. For Hildegard of Bingen, *dyscrasia* (an imbalance of humors) sometimes indicated the afflicted person's moral failure. While treatment might have been possible by diet, pharmacology, sport, and music, the mentally disabled (primarily the responsibility of their families) were often feared as outsiders, who were forced to live in prisons, leper hospitals, or forests, or they were loaded onto a boat floating down a stream. The insane frequently included demented oldsters; in fact, solitary wandering was believed to be a symptom of insanity. Madness (a term first used in the fourteenth century, as far as we know) might take many forms, with sufferers sometimes exhibiting the behavior of carnival fools or village idiots.[2]

Madness and genius are often related, such as depicted in the film *A Beautiful Mind*, where Nash, an ingenious mathematician, endures bouts of schizophrenia. In psychological terms, a genius is a person of extraordinary intellectual power, with an IQ of 140 or more, demonstrating potentiality, not necessarily manifested in attainment. The word *genius* is also used to designate creative ability of a high degree such as that as typified by Raffael, Leonardo da Vinci, Erasmus, and Martin Luther. Another theory underway today views genius as related dangerously close to neurosis and psychosis, and, in any case, a result of both hereditary and environmental factors.[3] In this study, we examine primarily the views of Marsilio Ficino (1433–99) and Theophrastus Bombastus von Hohenheim, called Paracelsus (1493–1541), in order to illustrate how the concepts of mental disease and ingenuity changed during the sixteenth century: attributed at first to divine or infernal forces, both qualities began to be considered functions of the brain.

During the Middle Ages and the Renaissance it was just as impossible to doubt the Lord's Word (unless one was an atheist) as it is today to distrust mathematical proofs. Diagnosing madness were two authorities: the supreme Church and the university, the latter operating outside the purview of the Church's jurisdiction. We should view Renaissance universities not as being in the vanguard of progress, but rather as establishing and endorsing authorities found in ancient texts covered by the curriculum. Between the twelfth and the nineteenth centuries, European medicine remained virtually unchanged in its basic paradigm as established by Hippocrates and Galen, then synthesized by the Arabs, and ultimately christianized by medieval scholastics. During the sixteenth century madness was considered a malady attributable to some magico-religious cause, or a psychosomatic condition explainable through ancient philosophy and medicine.[4]

Before discussing the positions of Ficino and Paracelsus, we examine the two views on madness just mentioned: the magico-religious perspective and the ancient realistic outlook. Renaissance medicine accepted in fact both positions and helped the patient in some way. What were the causes of a mental disease? A magical "explanation" was that somebody or something must have implanted the ailment, perhaps an evil spirit, according to the ancient Egyptians.[5] A similar idea prevailed in primitive cultures and was accepted by the Greeks before the emergence of pre-Socratic realistic thinking; the concept of such an agent is promoted throughout the Bible.[6] While in polytheistic societies various gods were believed to be responsible for this invasion of the body, in monotheistic religions the condition was held to be the work of demons or that of the devil himself. Jesus personally freed many persons from demonic possession, the best known example being the case of the Gadarene swine (Mark 5: 1–13). With the collapse of classical civilization the demonic view came to predominate once more in western Europe during the Middle Ages and reached its apogee during the sixteenth- and seventeenth-c. witch-craze.[7]

To ancient authorities the varying states of madness and genius were explainable through natural causes. Starting in Ionian Greece with Thales and Pythagoras, the concepts culminated in Plato and Aristotle, continued in a secondary role with Cicero and Lucretius, and became tinged by a religious outlook even before the fall of the Roman empire.[8] In medicine and psychiatry in particular, Hippocrates of Cos (460–370 B.C.) played a key role, rejected any supernatural causes for epilepsy in his *The Sacred Disease*, and attributed this condition, as all other diseases, to natural causes.[9] This rational approach did not prevail further because of its subsequent dilution with magical and religious views; yet during the Renaissance Hippocrates regained some popularity over Galen and Avicenna among humanist medieval doctors. Gradually, the influence of Neoplatonism and its various manifestations became noticeable in astrology, alchemy, magic, and finally demonology and religion. While medicine was practiced with some independence from religion during the Middle Ages, psychiatry (a nineteenth-c. term) was almost totally within the domain of the Church, because mental diseases were considered to be ailments of the soul — or possession by evil spirits.

What happened to the search for natural causes of madness and genius? Often, the Renaissance is hailed as the harbinger of modern times, and yet the Age constituted a rebirth, a revaluation of classical antiquity. Those who were most successful in the fields of literature and art — Renaissance thinkers, men of letters, and artists — did not totally reject the medieval period, but instead tried to combine a classical, primarily Neoplatonic, world view with Christian ideas; only when this combination failed as applied to certain phenomena, did science in the modern sense begin to develop.

Like the medieval art of healing, Renaissance medicine remained firmly embedded in the four-humor system of Hippocrates and Galen (from Empedocles's [c.450 B.C.] four elements: fire, water, earth, and air, equated with blood, yellow bile, black bile, and phlegm). Health consisted in the proper proportion of all four humors (*eucrasia*), while disease was the consequence of humoral disproportion; a surplus of black bile (*melancholia*) would produce mental disturbances in the form of extreme depression, hallucinations, and delusions, typical for manic-depressive psychosis.[10] Generally, the human mind was equated with the psyche and its Christian form, the soul; psychiatry as such was avoided by the medical profession and was left in the hands of the clergy. Probably the most famous form of mental disturbance, the belief in and practice of witchcraft, was identified and persecuted by the *Malleus maleficarum* (*Hammer of Witches*) by Heinrich Krämer (c.1450–1505) and Jacob Sprenger (1436 or 1438–95), two Dominican inquisitors mentioned in the bull *Summis desiderantes affectibus* issued by Pope Innocent VIII in 1484, a text which established the use of the Inquisition to hunt down supposed witches. Before publishing the *Malleus* in 1487 at Speier, the authors received an endorsement from the faculty of the University of Cologne and from Maximilian, King of Rome.[11]

While many symptoms for identifying a witch would be used today to pinpoint some mental disorder, the official intention of the *Malleus* and that of the papal bull was to combat the heresy of witchcraft:

> For the imagination of some men is so vivid that they think they see actual figures and appearances which are but reflections of their thoughts, and then those are believed to be the apparitions of evil spirits or even the spectres of witches. But this is contrary to the true faith, which teaches that certain angels fell from heaven and are now devils, and we are bound to acknowledge that by their very nature they can do many wonderful things which we cannot do. And those who try to induce others to perform such evil wonders are called witches. And because infidelity in a person who has been baptized is technically called heresy, therefore such persons are plainly heretics.[12]

One of the first books against witchcraft was the *Formicarius* written in 1435/37 by the Dominican reformer Johannes Nider (1380–1483);[13] the impact of the *Malleus* was great, and until 1501 six more editions were printed. The persecution of witches continued for some three hundred years, and the last witch was burned in Poland in 1793. One of the first attacks of the *Malleus* by a medical doctor was the *De praestigiis daemonum* by Johann Weyer, published in 1563.[14]

The only doctors who brought new ideas to the fields of medicine and psychiatry were Ficino and Paracelsus; actually, their ideas revived the tradition of Neoplatonism, specifically its hermetic branch.[15] Ficino was a medical doctor and priest, but he is best known as a philosopher and humanist.[16] A leading light of the Florentine Platonic Academy and translator of Plato, Plotinus, and other Greek philosophers, Ficino also translated the Greek *Corpus Hermeticum*, the main source for all scholars in pursuit of esoteric knowledge.[17] The *Corpus* was a collection of texts from late antiquity, writings which (during the Renaissance) were believed to be even older, since their author, Hermes Trismegistus, was thought to have been a contemporary of Moses. Hermeticism and magic in general, including alchemy and astrology, were for several centuries the leading paradigms until the emergence of modern science. Even Isaac Newton entertained many hermetic ideas.[18]

Ficino's concepts concerning mental processes followed Pseudo-Aristotle's *Problemata*, problem 30, # 1, which stated that melancholy was the source not only of madness but also of true creativity, a sign of genius.[19] The

Italian wrote two major medical texts: *Consiglio contra la pestilenza*, which appeared in 1481 and was not reprinted; and the more substantial and popular *De triplici vita*, first published in Florence by Antonio Miscomini in 1489, reprinted five times until 1501.[20] The *Triplici vita* is the first work devoted to the health of intellectuals, whose prevalent humor is believed to be melancholy. This book consists of three parts, "De vita sana," "De vita longa," and "De vita coelitus comparanda," and gives advice for a healthy, long, and heavenly life. Throughout the work Ficino pays more attention to *spiritus* than to body or soul. As he states,

> [O]nly the priests of the Muses, only the hunters after the highest good and truth, are so negligent (oh shame!) and so unfortunate, that they seem wholly to neglect that instrument with which they are able in a way to measure and grasp the whole world. This instrument is the spirit, which is defined by doctors as a vapor of blood — pure, subtle, hot, and clear.[21]

Ficino continues by saying that the spirit, not the soul, of scholars needs special care, because these humans consume spirit by constantly using it; since this vital principle (spirit) has to be replaced from blood, the fluid that remains becomes dense, dry, and black, and as a consequence such persons are always melancholy. Spirits arising from black bile (melancholy humor) are especially fine, hot, agile, and combustible; they are liable to ignite and produce a temporary state of mania in a person, followed by such symptoms as exhaustion and lethargy, as a consequence of the black smoke "left after the fire" [sic].[22] Since melancholy is under the influence of Saturn, it should be the physician's goal to attract for the patient the astral beneficent powers of the Sun, Jupiter, Mercury, and Venus, by botanical and other means, such as wine, odors, light, and music, especially the singing of Orphean hymns — all these remedies being a revival of Neoplatonic views.[23]

The third part of Ficino's *De triplici vita* is about pure astral magic, built not on mathematics (as astrology and modern astronomy were), but on astral power captured through an amulet or an engraved talisman — like Wilhelm Reich's orgone box;[24] modern scholars like Walker, Garin, Yates, and others are intrigued by such stipulations.[25] In general, Ficino's thought was traditional but daring to introduce new (old) notions in a very limited field, astral magic, a dangerous area, as he said.[26] His ideas on melancholy remained active within subsequent ages, for example in Albrecht Dürer's *Melencolia I* of 1514, and Robert Burton's *The Anatomy of Melancholy* (1621).[27]

Theophrastus Bombastus von Hohenheim, called Paracelsus, was the product of a university education, lost his professorship at Basle, and spent the remainder of his life wandering all across Europe, a stranger in a (then) strange land. Living from 1493 to 1541, he was caught in the webs of alchemy (a combination of metallurgy and Neoplatonic and Gnostic speculation), searching to understand the world from the viewpoint of this ancestor of modern chemistry.[28] Because Paracelsus was believed (by his fellow scholars) to have been crazy, he was liberated in a sense, thereby being able to think the unthinkable and tell about it,[29] as shown below.

Paracelsus dared in fact to venture beyond Empedocles's four elements, and, like Copernicus or Keppler, he stepped outside established limits to seek the truth. He was a genius, indeed; for him, his personal experience and knowledge were to be instrumental: counting madness among the so-called "invisible diseases," he learned his craft not from books alone, but also in the course of an empirical search. According to Sir Francis Bacon, Paracelsus was a natural philosopher, a Saturnian *Übermensch* (Nietzsche) who dared to reject Hippocratic-Galenic medicine and replace it with his own. Instead of being governed by four humors, humankind has three natures, Paracelsus said: animal, human, and divine; like Pico della Mirandola, Theophrastus did not prescribe a place for humans in the chain of being, because he viewed them as determining their own function in this world (and therefore not being subject to or governed by any systemic determinism).

Paracelsus never presented a unified view of mental illness;[30] instead he based all medicine on four pillars: natural philosophy (science), astronomy (astrology), alchemy, and virtue. Finding specific causes of diseases drove his intellectual search, and, because he refused to bequeathe a new system, he merely offered views and opinions which were sometimes conflicting; therefore, his contribution was appreciated only gradually by university faculties and soon sank into theosophic quagmire. His most systematic presentation on mental ailments was his *Von den Krankheiten, so die Vernunfft berauben*, which has been translated into English.[31] Even this work is not very succinct; the doctor divided mental diseases into five groups: epilepsy, or falling sickness; mania, a corruption of reason; St. Vitus dance, produced by "cursing, excessive frivolity, or a natural corruption of the imagination"; a "suffocation" of the intellect; loss of senses, further divided into the following categories of afflicted persons: lunatics; those insane from birth "because of the parents' sexual pleasure"; those poisoned by food or drink; the bewitched; those with the disease of melancholy.[32] His major contribution was to shun the humoral theory and to recognize diseases as results of observable physical causes; witchcraft, however, was still part of his *scientific* world.[33]

To conclude, let me quote Freeman J. Dyson on a different period, namely the present, to illustrate the way we consider the thinkers of the Renaissance:

> We are in the position of anthropologists observing the rituals and liturgy of an alien culture. As anthropologists, we try to understand the alien way of thinking and we try to enter into the alien culture

as far as we can. We make friends with individual members of the alien culture and listen to their stories. We respect them as human beings, struggling in their own way to deal with the mysteries of life and death, sharing with us our common weaknesses, fears, passions, and bewilderments. We respect their faith in the love of God, whether or not we share it. We observe them with a sympathetic eye, but from a distance. We do not for a moment imagine that their detailed vision of a world to come, with heaven and hell and eschatological verification, the vision that they find emotionally satisfying or intellectually compelling, is actually true.[34]

To look at Renaissance medicine and early psychology is to perceive many areas of doubt in the basic paradigms taught at the universities. Except for some empiricism, these fields were still unsatisfactory, but, with another rebel genius of his age, Ulrich von Hutten, Renaissance scholars would have proudly confessed "Ich hab's gewagt," or, as we would say in English, "I dared to think and do it." My excursion into psychic phenomena among Renaissance humans and the causes and significance of such conditions has brought us closer to an understanding of genius and madness, with the help of Ficino and Paracelsus. Ultimate explanations, based partially on DNA, may be expected in the future. Perhaps.

Notes

[1] Georges Duby, ed. *A History of Private Life. Revelations of the Medieval World*, tr. Arthur Goldhammer (Cambridge: Belknap Press of Harvard University Press, 1988): 629. Vol. 2 of *A History of Private Life*, 5 vols., ed. Philippe Ariès and Georges Duby.

[2] See Michel Foucault, *Histoire de la folie à l'âge classique* (Paris: Gallimard, 1972), 13–37; Peter Dinzelbacher, ed. *Sachwörterbuch der Mediävistik* (Stuttgart: Kröner, 1992), s.v. "Wahnsinn," 889–90. Also: Andrew McCall, *The Medieval Underworld* (London: Hamish Hamilton, 1979): ch. 5.

[3] *The New Encyclopaedia Britannica, 'Micropaedia,'* 12 vols. (Chicago: Encyclopaedia Britannica, Inc., 2002), 5: 180–81; Claude Kappler, *Monstres, démons et merveilles à la fin du moyen âge* (Paris: Payot, 1980); Robert Volmat (*L'Art psychopathologique* [Paris: Presses Universitaires de France, 1956]: 149), who speaks of "la double incidence du génie et de la folie" among artists; Heinrich Schipperges, "Die Assimilation der arabischen Medizin durch das lateinische Mittelalter," in *Sudhoffs Archiv für Geschichte der Medizin und der Naturwissenschaften*. Beiheft 3 (1964): 1–240.

[4] Richard Kieckhefer, *Magic in the Middle Ages* (Cambridge: Cambridge University Press, 1989), ch. 6.

[5] John F. Nunn, *Ancient Egyptian Medicine* (Norman: Oklahoma University Press, 1996): 96–112.

[6] Julius Preuss, *Biblical and Talmudic Medicine* (Northvale, N.J.: Jason Aronson, 1993): 139–40.

[7] Edelgard E. DuBruck, "Thomas Aquinas and Medieval Demonology," *Michigan Academician* 7 (1974): 167–83.

[8] See Giorgio de Santillana, *The Origins of Scientific Thought: From Anaximander to Proclus, 600 B.C.–300 A.D.* (New York: New American Library, 1961).

[9] Geoffrey E. R. Lloyd, ed. *Hippocratic Writings* (New York: Penguin Books, 1978): 237 ff.

[10] Schipperges, "Melancolie als ein mittelalterlicher Sammelbegriff für Wahnvorstellungen," in *Studium Generale* 20 (1967), passim; see also: Bernard Ribémont, tr. *Le Livre des propriétés des choses. Une encyclopédie au XIVe siècle* (Paris: Stock, 1999), on the four humors: 110–11.

[11] Gregory Zilboorg, M.D., in collaboration with George W. Henry, M.D. *A History of Medical Psychology* (New York: Norton and Company, 1967): 144–74.

[12] Heinrich Krämer and James Sprenger, *The Malleus Maleficarum*, tr. Montague Summers (New York: Dover Publications, 1971): 2–3.

[13] See Andreas Blauert, *Frühe Hexenverfolgung: Ketzer-, Zauberei- und Hexenprozesse des 15. Jahrhunderts* (Hamburg: Junius, 1989).

[14] See Ina Lommatzsch, "Der *Malleus Maleficarum* (1487) und die Hexenverfolgung in Deutschland," *Fifteenth-Century Studies* 27 (2002): 185–99; Émile Grillot de Givry, *A Pictorial Anthology of Witchcraft, Magic, and Alchemy*, tr. J. Courtenay Locke (New Hyde Park, N.Y.: University Books, 1958); Martha J. Crowe, ed. *Witchcraft: Catalogue of the Witchcraft Collection in Cornell University Library* (Millwood, N.Y.: KTO Press, 1977); Joseph Hansen, ed. *Quellen und Untersuchungen zur Geschichte des Hexenwahns und der Hexenverfolgung im Mittelalter* (Bonn, 1901; repr. Hildesheim: Olms, 1963); Richard Kieckhefer, *European Witch Trials: Their Foundations in Popular and Learned Culture, 1300–1500* (London: Routledge, 1976) and "The Rise of the Witch Trials," in *Magic in the Middle Ages* (above, note 4), 194–200; Alan C. Kors and Edward Peters, ed. *Witchcraft in Europe, 1100–1700: A Documentary History* (Philadelphia: University of Pennsylvania Press, 1972); Henry Charles Lea, *Materials Toward a History of Witchcraft*, 3 vols. (Philadelphia: University of Pennsylvania Press, 1939); Rossell Hope Robbins, *The Encyclopedia of Witchcraft and Demonology* (New York: Crown Publishers, 1959); Jeffrey Burton Russell, *Witchcraft in the Middle Ages* (Ithaca, N.Y.: Cornell University Press, 1972); Hugh R. Trevor-Roper, *The European Witch-Craze of the Sixteenth and Seventeenth Centuries* (New York: Harper, 1969); Joseph R. Strayer, *Dictionary of the Middle Ages*. 13 vols. (New York: Charles Scribner's Sons, 1982–89), 12: 658–65; George Mora et al., ed. *Johann Weyer, De praestigiis daemonum: Witches, Devils, and Doctors in the Renaissance* (Binghamton: Medieval and Renaissance Texts and Studies, 1991).

[15] See Walter Pagel, *Religion and Neoplatonism in Renaissance Medicine*, ed. Marianne Winder (London: Variorum Reprints, 1985).

[16] See Paul O. Kristeller, *Il pensiero filosofico di Marsilio Ficino* (Florence: Le Lettere, 1988).

[17] See Brian P. Copenhaver, *Hermetica: The Greek 'Corpus Hermeticum' and the Latin 'Asclepius' in a New English Translation* (Cambridge: Cambridge University Press, 1992): xlvii–1.

[18] Betty Jo Teeter Dobbs, *The Foundations of Newton's Alchemy, or, 'The Hunting of the Greene Lyon'* (Cambridge: Cambridge University Press, 1975).

[19] H. C. Erik Midelfort, *A History of Madness in Sixteenth-Century Germany* (Stanford: Stanford University Press, 1999), 23.

[20] *Gesamtkatalog der Wiegendrucke*, 9882–87. A good English translation exists: *Marsilio Ficino, Three Books on Life*, tr. and ed. Carol V. Kaske and John R. Clark (Tempe: Medieval and Renaissance Texts and Studies, 1989).

[21] *Three Books*, 111.

[22] See Daniel P. Walker, *Spiritual and Demonic Magic from Ficino to Campanella* (Notre Dame: University of Notre Dame Press, 1975), 4.

[23] Ibid., 22–23.

[24] Copenhaver, "Scholastic Philosophy and Renaissance Magic in the *De vita* of Marsilio Ficino," *Renaissance Quarterly* 37 (1984): 523–54. Orgone is a vital energy held to pervade nature and to be made available for use by the human body after one sits in a specially designed box. This energy was declared a fraud by the Food and Drug Administration. Reich's dates were 1897–1957.

[25] Eugenio Garin, *Astrology in the Renaissance. The Zodiac of Life*, tr. Carolyn Jackson and June Allen (London: Routledge, 1983); Frances A. Yates, *Giordano Bruno and the Hermetic Tradition* (London: Routledge; Chicago: Chicago University Press, 1964).

[26] "Apology," *Three Books*, 394–405.

[27] Raymond Klibansky, Erwin Panofsky, and Fritz Saxl, ed. *Saturn and Melancholy: Studies in the History of Natural Philosophy, Religion, and Art* (London: Nelson, 1964): 362; Michael O'Connell, *Robert Burton* (Boston: Twayne, 1986): 64.

[28] Alchemy is speculative as well as experimental, concerned primarily with discovering methods for transmuting baser metals into gold, with finding a universal solvent, and an elixir of life. Some alchemists strove to create an *homunculus*, an artificially made dwarf, supposedly produced in a test-tube, perhaps from sperm. See: Herwig Buntz, *Deutsche alchemistische Traktate des 15. Jahrhunderts*. Diss. Munich, 1968; Gerhard Eis, "Von der Rede und dem Schweigen der Alchemisten," *Deutsche Vierteljahresschrift für Literaturwissenschaft und Geistesgeschichte* 25 (1951): 415–35; Dinzelbacher (above, note 2), 14–16; Johannes Fabricius, *Alchemy: The Medieval Alchemists and Their Royal Art* (Copenhagen: Rosenkilde and Bagger, 1976); Jean Favier, *Dictionnaire de la France médiévale* (Paris: Fayard, 1993): 30–31; Karl Frick, "Einführung in die alchemiegeschichtliche Literatur," in *Sudhoffs Archiv* 45 (1961): 147–63; Wilhelm Ganzenmüller, *Die Alchemie im Mittelalter* (Paderborn: Bonifacius, 1938); Eric J. Holmyard, *Alchemy* (Harmondsworth: Penguin, 1957); Kieckhefer (above, note 4): 133–39; Edmund O. von Lippmann, *Entstehung und Ausbreitung der Alchemie*, 3 vols. (1919–54; repr. Weinheim: Verlag Chemie, 1954); William R. Newman, "An Introduction to Alchemical Apparatus in the Late Middle Ages," *Technologia* 6 (1983): 82–92; Barbara Obrist, *Les Débuts de l'imagerie alchimique (XIVe–XVe siècles)* (Paris: Le Sycomore, 1982).

[29] See Edelgard E. DuBruck, "Theophrastus Bombastus von Hohenheim, Called Paracelsus: Highways and Byways of a Wandering Physician (1493–1541)," *Fifteenth-Century Studies* 25 (2000): 1–10.

[30] Midelfort (above, note 19), 110 ff.

[31] "The Diseases That Deprive Man of His Reason, Such as St. Vitus Dance, Falling Sickness, Melancholy, and Insanity, and Their Correct Treatment," tr. Gregory Zilborg, in: Henri E. Sigerist, *Four Treatises of Theophrastus von Hohenheim, Called Paracelsus* (Baltimore: Johns Hopkins University Press, 1941): 127–212.

[32] On Paracelsus, see also: Karl Sudhoff et al., ed. *Sämtliche Werke*, 24 vols. (Munich: Barth, 1922–33); Jolande Jacobi, ed., and Norbert Guterman, tr. *Paracelsus. Selected Writings* (Princeton: University Press, 1979, second ed.); Franz Spunda, *Das Weltbild des Paracelsus* (Wien: Andermann, 1941); Alexandre Koyré, *Paracelse* (Paris: Allia, 1997; first ed. Gallimard, 1971); Lucien Braun, ed. and tr. *Évangile d'un médecin errant* (Paris: Arfuyen, 1991); Bernard Gorceix, *Paracelse. Oeuvres médicales* (Paris: Presses Universitaires de France, 1968).

[33] Midelfort, 116–18.

[34] Freeman J. Dyson, "Science and Religion: No Ends in Sight," *New York Review of Books* 49 (2002): 6.

Oakland University

Christ's Transformation of Zacchaeus in the York Cycle's 'Entry into Jerusalem'

Barbara I. Gusick

Christ's miracles as dramatized in the York cycle of Corpus Christi plays convey a representative selection of the Savior's works, attesting to his efficacy. His miracles of physical regeneration can be strikingly theatrical as borne out through contemporary production: the lame man hurls his crutches aside; and Lazarus staggers from his tomb resuscitated, still encumbered by his funeral garments. In addition to these works conducive to stage action, spiritual healings unaccompanied by physical metamorphosis are also enacted, though such transformations are less disposed toward external manifestation, making it necessary for spectators to *imagine* what the wondrous act, once effected, would entail; for example, the rehabilitated life of the Woman Taken in Adultery once the transgressor has reversed her sinning ways. One such miracle of spiritual renewal is the conversion of Zacchaeus, the publican sinner called down by Christ from a sycamore tree, into which the short-statured man had climbed to witness Jesus' entry into Jerusalem (cf. Luke 19, 1–10). In Play No. 25, this episode occurs after two miracles of physical healing have already taken place: the bestowing of sight upon the man born blind and the granting of bodily wholeness to the lame man. While Zacchaeus's transmutation from ostracized tax collector to believer in Christ is unremarkable vis-à-vis the stage action one would normally expect of a miraculous feat, it is his climbing of the sycamore tree, undertaken as the crowd sees him doing so, that emphasizes how instrumental the event of seeing (and *being seen*) is to this play in particular. In medieval art, miniatures and engravings portray one or two men scaling a tree to see Jesus riding through Jerusalem Gate; and the idea of an arboreal observer is likewise conveyed through the iconographic image of a man nestled in a tree (figs. 1–2), there to witness Christ moving forward through Jerusalem on his donkey.[1]

Yet the treetop perspective can also be used as a metaphor to express the importance of social visibility when we consider how a practitioner of a scorned profession, once reformed, would assimilate himself back into the community in which no new space has been created for him. The Zacchaeus episode, I intend to argue, yields various tensions heretofore unaddressed. Most of these tensions arise while considering scorned professions, reorientation options existing in late-medieval York, and notions of community (or lack thereof). Before examining the interplay of social factors within which context the Zacchaeus miracle expands considerably, I want to provide a brief overview of the scene and then establish several linkages between the biblical episode and late-medieval attitudes.

What we know about Zacchaeus from the dramatic text is that he emerges from the crowd of onlookers welcoming Christ into Jerusalem after Christ has healed the lame man of his infirmity, whereupon the healed man has just flung his crutches aside.[2] The tax collector marvels at the miracle he has just witnessed but claims not to know what the act signifies. Struggling to assess the miracle's import, he assesses Christ's strengths; for instance, his amassing of profits and acquisition of widespread fame. Yet Jesus has overturned existing law, which Zacchaeus operates in conjunction with, and in its place established his own law, which the people flock to uphold. As prince of publicans, Zacchaeus says he lacks knowledge of, or access to, Jesus (and within such a profession can never bridge that gap), equating this ineptitude with his short stature. The tax collector then mounts the sycamore tree, vowing to see Christ even if Jesus fails to see or acknowledge him in return. Praising the Creator for making such an awesome tree, the man pledges to remain high in heart and thought until he can catch a glimpse of Jesus — whatsoever befalls, as he puts it, revealing his uncertainty. At this juncture, Jesus has reached Zacchaeus and calls the publican down, whereupon the man hastily descends, and, convicted by his sins, immediately falls upon his knees. What Zacchaeus must now do, Christ says, is perform new service and make amends for his transgressions. Ashamed, Zacchaeus vows to give all his unspent money to the poor and make restitution to those he has defrauded; and Christ promises the converted man everlasting life and grants peace to the man's household provided its inhabitants live without offense.

What we know about taxation in England during the late-medieval period enables us to posit how spectators in York may have viewed Zacchaeus. Historian Peter Spufford establishes that direct taxation in England was initiated during the end of the twelfth century, and during the next century "subsidies exacted by Henry III and Edward I were based on a proportionate levy, frequently a fifteenth part, of the 'goods' of the peasantry" — that is, their produce harvested and ready for sale around Michaelmas at the end of September.[3] While direct taxing of production was the norm relative to rural areas, within urban settings, a more prevalent method of taxation became "indirect taxation of consumption, for example . . . gate-taxes on goods passing into the city."[4] In England, according to Gerald L. Harriss, the most critical role of Parliament as the king saw it was taxation. As reflected on a parliamentary record, Henry VI in 1453 appeared personally before the Commons to thank members for an especially bountiful grant of taxes, and Edward IV in 1467 likewise addressed the Commons in person, proclaiming his desire to ask for taxes only when urgent causes affecting the entire population made such recourse unavoidable.[5] During the late fifteenth century, royal taxes were at times referred to "benevolences," offerings that enabled subjects to demonstrate their "fondness" to the monarch. The chronicler Polydore Vergil writes that Henry VII continued the practice (initiated by Edward IV) of raising money by encouraging subjects to view their contributions as forms of "loving kindness" whereby the donor providing the most liberal offering was viewed by the crown as being most dutiful subject. Despite the gracious language through which such moneys were procured and acknowledged, this chronicler records that many subjects begrudged making their so-called contributions, describing these coerced funds as "malevolences" instead.[6] Relative to the city of York, we can substantiate that the English crown received a substantial portion of its income by taxing wool, a flourishing industry in Yorkshire during the late Middle Ages,[7] though George Sheeran, in his recent study of medieval Yorkshire towns, documents that a number of profitable industries existed in York besides the wool trade.[8]

Alongside these coin-of-the-realm factors, we must consider when we analyze the Zacchaeus episode the spiritual dimension of money as a medium of exchange. Saint John of Damascus had pointed out that, in the New Testament, Christ is called the "coin-impression" of God,[9] and an eighth-c. narrative describes Christ as a coin in his mother's womb. Fifteenth-c. art reveals Mary receiving God's golden semen conveyed by Gabriel's chrysographic characters.[10] During the sixteenth century, Titian's painting *The Tax Penny* (fig. 3) captures the essence of the controversy-generating question posed to Christ by the Scribes and Pharisees, who had asked Jesus what God's law said about paying taxes to the Roman Empire. Marc Shell, in his study *Art and Money*, offers several explanations for Christ's response that one should "Render . . . to Caesar the things that are Caesar's, and to God the things that are God's," among these, that the political sphere and the religious realm require entirely different tokens acknowledging their disparate authorities.[11]

In addition to considering the spiritual aspects of money, economic and social factors relevant to the late-medieval period enhance our understanding of the Zacchaeus miracle. While it is incontestable that the spiritual conversion Zacchaeus undergoes is the gift he receives — assurance of everlasting life, rendered even more bounteous by Christ's extending this plenitude to souls within the man's household — the emphatic use of gift-giving language used in the scene engenders other meanings. Before climbing the tree in order to view Christ as he passes through Jerusalem (and concomitantly, York), Zacchaeus had described Christ as the reaper of profits, this assessment couched in the tax collector's own materialistic language. After repenting of his sins and receiving salvation, Zacchaeus had vowed to divest himself of ill-gotten gains, promising that unspent goods be distributed to the poor as well as restitution be made toward taxpayers from whom he had extracted extra money.

How spectators reacted to the prospect of these newly distributable funds, had they overlaid late-medieval gift-giving principles upon the biblical context, can be postulated. Andrew Galloway, in his study of gift-giving in England, has demonstrated that during the late fourteenth century, social pressures obliged the recipient of a gift to do more than express gratitude to the gift-giver. Beginning with St. Thomas in the thirteenth century, Galloway asserts, sermons made it clear that gift recipients were expected to "recognize and remunerate any benefits" extended to them. For instance, Vincent of Beauvais considered those who refused to reciprocate a benefit as being ungrateful, and John Bromyard in his fourteenth-c. sermons presented numerous exempla of ingratitude, arguing that even animals expressed gratefulness.[12]

While no one would dispute the fact that Christ's transformation of Zacchaeus was a gift, there is another aspect of the exchange dynamics to consider (what Zacchaeus owes in return): restitution must take place. That is, the tax collector's funds must be redistributed; and this non-recurring windfall must be bequeathed upon the poor and those formerly swindled by the man in the city of York. Before focusing upon the reappropriation of Zacchaeus's funds, we must ask two snarly questions, which touch upon how the saved man challenges the social network: (1) how significant is Zacchaeus's Jewishness? Once converted by Christ, has Zacchaeus ceased being a Jew? The Jews were expelled from England in 1290 by edict of Edward I, more than a century before the staging of this miracle; and (2) what do we make of the man's forswearing of tax collecting, associated with usury? These monetary practices would not have been eradicated in York because one man relinquished them.

When confronting the issue of Zacchaeus's Jewish heritage, we must point out, of course, that *most* of the characters in this play are Jewish, including Jesus. As the Corpus Christi plays dramatize the entire spectrum of salvation history, audiences cannot miss seeing that Christianity subsumes Judaism.[13] Yet what stands out about the Zacchaeus miracle when examined alongside the other two miracles Christ enacts in this play — the healings of the man born blind and the lame man — is that Zacchaeus, after his spiritual transformation, has to destigmatize himself from the misappropriated funds in his possession, a reminder of the usury or other nefarious practices he admits having engaged in as a tax collector. The reality that Jews engaged in the sinful activity of usury was well known; and despite the fact that no Jews remained in England when the York plays were being performed, anti-Semitic feelings were kept alive through literary tracts and iconography, for instance.

Jews were portrayed as having not only stereotypical features (enormous hooked noses [see fig. 4], bulging lips, protruding jaws, elongated eyes) and offensive gestures (such as sardonic grins) but also repulsive bodies,[14] effeminate tendencies (in the case of males) and/or hypersexuality,[15] and swinelike characteristics.[16] Along with lepers, Jews were viewed as being walking pollutants, health threats traceable to Judas's effluvia;[17] and they were required to wear external signs—pointed hats, special badges, and distinctive clothing[18] — marking them as fundamentally different from other people. During the late Middle Ages the word *synagogue*, referring to the Jewish house of worship, came to be applied to any assemblage of witches or heretics.[19] Besides these social indicators suggesting Jews were inferior, there were theological texts (patristic writings) which unintentionally promoted anti-Semitism; Judaism was a disease in need of a cure.[20] Whether converting a Jew from Judaism to Christianity was socially expedient became disputable. In 1280 English law mandated that Jews attend weekly sermons (conversionist vehicles) preached by Dominicans,[21] and to encourage conversion, the king waived his right to claim converts' land for a period of seven years.[22] Although baptized Jews lived in safety in the House of Converts (*Domus Conversorum*), a royal foundation near London,[23] Jewish persons no longer inhabited cities like York after 1290, though their influence remained, albeit in a ghostly fashion. Late medieval texts — Mirk's *Festial* (a collection of sermons), Chaucer's *Canterbury Tales*, the *Holkham Bible Picture Book*, the Croxton *Play of the Sacrament*, and *The Siege of Jerusalem* (a poem)[24] — kept Jewishness alive. Having been removed corporally, Jews nonetheless became absent presences — "virtual Jew[s]" — as Sylvia Tomasch has referred to the displaced minority group.[25] Atrocities committed upon the Jews have even been silenced by historical societies such as the English Heritage foundation. Although Hebrews were massacred in the city of York in 1190, a 1943 English Heritage publication written to tell the history of Clifford's Tower, site of the mass homicide, *fails to mention* that Jews even died there.[26]

Jews, tax collectors, moneylenders, and short people[27] have all been marginalized — treated as Other — to one degree or another. That within the York play Zacchaeus sees himself as an outsider, separate and distinct from the physically disabled persons with whom he competes for Christ's attention, is undeniable. Further, the man confesses to Jesus that he has "beguiled" people in monetary matters (line 52), suggesting he has practiced usury, an activity condemned by Christian authorities. A usurer loaned money with the stipulation (and expectation) that he would "receive back more" than the amount he loaned,[28] although he knew that the Church denounced usurers for selling time, which could only belong to God.[29] Medieval economic theory held that usury was an unnatural act because money was sterile and should not be made to reproduce itself when detached from human labor.[30] Usurers because they were involved in shady dealings were despised, even though they provided a necessary service, becoming indispensable to some rulers and, in fact, receiving royal protection from others.[31] During the late Middle Ages, consumer lending survived the expulsion of

Jews from England,[32] and to impress upon ourselves that the image of the Jewish moneylender lived on, we need only envision Marlowe's Barabbas in *The Jew of Malta* or Shakespeare's Shylock in *The Merchant of Venice* as theatrical reminders.

Earlier I alluded to Zacchaeus's forswearing of illicit activities associated with his tax collecting duties and now move toward considering the social ramifications of his healing. What we know of charitable giving in York can facilitate understanding what the spiritually healed man's reappropriated funds, bequeathed upon the poor, would have meant to spectators. Cullum and Goldberg, in examining over 2,000 wills executed during the late-medieval period in York, have documented the impetus for and characteristics of charitable giving. Probate evidence reveals that saint cults, such as those venerating St. Martin or St. Anne, stressed the importance of providing for the poor as one of the Seven Corporal Works of Mercy and that this ongoing need was met within the city by providing for the needy with doles of food and drink, donations of cloth or items of apparel, and patronage of almshouses, hospitals (of which St. Leonard's was the oldest), and the city's five leper-houses. Moreover, bequests were made to prisoners, motivated by recalling saints who had suffered imprisonment; for instance, Saints Peter, Paul, Catherine, and John the Baptist.[33] Despite substantial testamentary evidence of charitable contributions in York, we would not consider these forms of largesse disinterested giving because charity "was one means of gaining remission from the pains of Purgatory and of assuring one's own salvation."[34]

What anthropologists have demonstrated about gift-giving from a social perspective is even more suited to our purposes here. Spectators would not have seen the post-miracle Zacchaeus as in need of procuring spiritual favors regarding the disposition of his soul. Yet the retribution that he must effect does become a monetary enterprise subject to social interpretation. We can substantiate that the *nature* of gift-giving had changed by the fourteenth and fifteenth centuries, attributable, as one scholar has said, to "the rise of monetary economy, . . . agrarian development, and . . . demographic growth" and that benefactors gifted others with "annuities, hereditary rent-charges, and leases, or amounts of cash out of their personal property." Unlike in the earlier medieval period, the concept of land grants as gifts underwent reconsideration; land at this time came to be viewed as a "means of production and of profit-making."[35]

The preceding factors enable us to gain a better sense of how spectators may have viewed Zacchaeus's normalized wealth, suddenly available for dispersal, but fail to address the issue of how he was understood as achieving assimilation. According to medical anthropologist John J. Pilch, all religious healing is symbolic healing in which the healer mediates culture. There are four distinct phases to the healing ritual whereby this cultural mediation is effected. Stage One is the establishment of a *symbolic bridge* (creation of a myth), wherein the healer and person in need of healing agree to "particularize a segment of the cultural mythic world" in effecting healing. Stage Two involves *communication*, whereby the sick person relates (in some way) to the mythic world. At this stage of the healing process, both the healer and the patient seeking a cure agree upon key meanings. Stage Three involves *transactional symbols*, meaning that both participants express mutual expectations and arrive at an agreement that configures and "name[s] the clinical reality." The last phase of the healing, Stage Four, requires *confirmation* which is expressed through efficacy. As Pilch makes clear, "healing is efficacious when the people who seek it say it is"; he emphasizes that for healing to have taken place, the individual cured must "leave the marginal situation of sickness and [be] reincorporated — in health or even death — back into the social body."[36]

Bringing this anthropological model to bear upon the Zacchaeus episode, we can attest to Phase One of the "healing" (the creation of a symbolic bridge) by reflecting upon Zacchaeus's climb into the sycamore tree with the resultant effect that Christ, despite being bodily restricted by a clamoring crowd, fortuitously sees and acknowledges the tree-nestled man. By the action of validating the sycamore and its inhabitant, Christ evokes (in our minds) a mythological framework — cosmic tree representing life everlasting — prelapsarian Eden,[37] Christ's own death upon the cross (fig. 5) imminent in dramatic time,[38] vegetation cults,[39] and the rich panoply of associative meanings connected with that emblem. Exploring a few of these tree-associated ideas will enable us to consider the man-in-tree image as the highly theatrical tableau that it must have been. In some ways, the man in a tree, looking down at others from amongst green (and perhaps dense) foliage, exemplifies the *quintessential* spectator, one who has competed for a superior vantage point and won. Certainly, townspeople would have experienced the tax collector in their lives as holding sway over others, even in ceremonial events, gaining the optimal view; one might even say that Zacchaeus as chief of publicans was superior to others within his sphere of daily operations. Although we must acknowledge what is obvious — the tax collector was too short to view Christ moving through the city unless he had a lofty perspective — there seems to be more to this arboreal happening than has been explored. A tree is known not only for its height but also as a metaphorical means by which family heritage may be illustrated. In late-medieval York, spectators knew the Tree of Jesse image from cathedral glass and sculpture (fig. 6); that family tree depicted how Jesus originated from Jesse through King David, Jesse's son, and also through Mary.[40] Besides knowing about the stage property and genealogical features of a tree, spectators would have discerned that God provided comfort through a tree. An Apocryphal Infancy Gospel from the Gospel of

Matthew states that during the Holy Family's journey to Egypt, the child Jesus responded to his weary mother's expressed desire for the fruit of a tree by commanding the tree to give forth its fruit, whereupon the tree bowed down from its utmost branches, bringing its bounty earthward, even laying the fruit at Mary's feet, obliging Jesus' request.[41] Even if spectators failed to see Zacchaeus's tree in one of the ways I have briefly outlined — stage prop, emblem for a family tree, or conduit for God's grace — there were trees everywhere within the natural environment,[42] attesting to the vegetative virtues of these organisms; for example, through the Green Man images peering down at townsfolk from cathedral settings.

Legendary and mythical connections aside, we can say with assurance that spectators in York would, through iconographic images abounding, have had familiarity with tree imagery, at which point we can now focus on the argument proper: how the tree facilitates healing from a medical anthropological perspective. If Stage One (as I mentioned earlier) involves Zacchaeus being validated through ascending the tree, we can correlate Christ's calling Zaccheaus *down* from the tree with Stage Two, whereupon core meanings of the mythic world are assented to. Biblical commentators have shown that Zacchaeus came down expeditiously, showing no hesitancy: what we see of his obeisance in kneeling before Christ is the man's unswerving willingness and commitment to join the world Christ represents. Stage Three of the miracle requires the expressing of *mutual expectations*. The "new service" which Christ states will rectify wrongdoings Zacchaeus has committed in the past (extracting excessive, unjustified funds from taxpayers) will be a converse operation countering (if not undoing) damages sustained by persons who had been swindled. Audiences hear Zacchaeus saying that *because* he renounces sin, he disowns proceeds obtained while willfully engaging in sin; therefore the "new service" paradigm instituted by Christ expunges the "old service" model exemplified by Zacchaeus and his now-foresworn practice of extracting unjustified monies from taxpayers. The agreement of both parties to authenticate the healing through socially validating its effectiveness, is signaled by Stage Four, in which *confirmation* takes place. In this regard, the York play affirms that Zacchaeus is to return to the social network because Christ instructs the converted man to go home. But when we scrutinize the text more thoroughly, we find it is at this point, Stage Four, where the dramatic text appears to turn back upon itself, by on the one hand proposing reintegration for Zacchaeus — positing a normalized existence for the man—and on the other hand, endorsing a post-healing assimilation into the social network, an aim which remains unachievable. Can a child return to its mother's womb? At this culminating stage of the healing process, Zacchaeus would be deemed *totally and irrefutably* healed if he were judged by the people of York as having been "reincorporated" as Pilch suggests, "in health or even death . . . back into the social body."

The importance of social wholeness to community has been examined by a growing number of scholars, most notably Mervyn James, who demonstrated that the concept of body was instrumental to Corpus Christi plays, becoming the means through which "social wholeness and social differentiation" were both affirmed and revealed as being in tension with each other.[43] Christ's body as a mediating factor is a *sine qua non* of medieval drama studies; suffice it to say here that, as Sarah Beckwith has shown in a study of the York plays, "symbolic utterances that circulate around the symbol of Christ's body are the very densest sites of signification."[44] Further, physical space expressed the social body through archaeology, for instance: hospitals placed at major gates of cities such as York not only framed communities but also displayed stigmatized bodies while exhibiting the town's charitable standing to the widest possible audience.[45]

The authentication of social space through the erection of buildings, hospitals, and other framing devices leads us to question whether spectators viewed Zacchaeus as *reentering* the mainstream of daily life in their city, an outcome established in the play by Christ's instructing Zacchaeus to return to his household. Whether he would have borne the stigma of his former detestable profession within the community can be extrapolated. In the biblical account from which he derives (Luke 19: 1–10), Zacchaeus is identified as a Jew. Although the Jews were expelled from England toward the end of the thirteenth century, gross caricatures of Jews remained, particularly in the *Holkham Bible Picture Book*; and anti-Semitism manifested itself in means other than art; for instance, through allegations "of ritual murder, blood libel, profanation of the Host, and well poisoning."[46] Prior to the expulsion of the Hebrews from England, a government document depicted the wealthy Jew Isaac fil Jurnet of Norwich, a moneylender, as being not only three-faced (seen at the top of fig. 4) but also surrounded by usurers, devils, and a coin clipper holding the scales at far left.[47] In order to be conceived of as effecting reinstatement within York, Zacchaeus would have to shed his identification with tax collecting in the same way perhaps that the disciple Matthew left gathering taxes to follow Christ. However, records substantiate that as late as the seventeenth century, and conceivably thereafter, tax collectors were considered dishonest outcasts (together with barbers, for instance). Groups revolting against tax collectors cited the Bible, and a song of 1623 expresses loathing for Jews, tax collectors, and princes who devalue coins.[48] Indeed, records suggest that the taxpayers of York might have reacted to money gatherers — even reformed ones — as being contemptible. Late in the fourteenth century, groundswell movements arose to protest unfair tax advantages given to the wealthy, and taxes became burdensome in England until British defeat in the wars with France during the middle of the fifteenth century. A number of economic factors — the scarcity of coins because of the bullion famine, diminishing personal wealth, and a declining cloth industry in the city of York — may have further contributed to a public sense of dissatisfaction with what tax collectors represented.[49]

Despite any resentment spectators may have harbored against tax collectors, one point is indisputable: Zacchaeus — like his counterparts in the play (the man born blind and the lame man) — has been transformed by Christ. Witnessing the exuberant feat of a man jumping down from his leafy abode to join Christ and his followers on earth must have been a delight to behold, and many citizens of York undoubtedly viewed this miracle. As Peter Womack has suggested, a substantial portion of the 8,000–10,000 people living in York during the late Middle Ages would have been immersed (in some way) in the "single spectacle" of the plays dominating their lives as much as their city.[50] Because of this play's emphasis upon communal involvement (procession, humanitarianism, crowd control), the transformational space — that sanctified area within which the Zacchaeus miracle takes place — is socially validated. The community participates in what the healed person as microcosm undergoes; or, as Don Handelman has stated: "healing does the repair and synthesis of the world."[51] Since Zacchaeus is no longer spiritually bankrupt, he can now enter a realm of eternal reward, and his vacated tree makes that point clear. Christ will die on a tree, leaving it behind — while this stage-foliage sycamore (unoccupied) evokes God's superabundance, ever ready to all. Like the mustard seed which grew into a huge bush, this (short, Jewish, tax-collecting) man is extremely valuable to the kingdom.

Within a social context, however, assurances are far less forthcoming. Spectators are *shown* that Zacchaeus has been reconstituted, and images from the natural environment support such an optimistic view. When the metamorphosed man stands before viewers — not in the guise of who he once was but representing (perhaps in some physical way) who he will be — he appears entirely liberated. Using an ecological analogy which would have been familiar to audiences, I suggest that Zacchaeus has (in a sense) been "born" of a tree since the tree serves as God's conduit for the man's renewal. He has therefore become a human embodiment of God and Nature, recalling the arboreal images mentioned earlier.[52] In York as throughout Europe, foliate heads referred to as Green Men looked down upon (or, in their grotesque versions, appeared to threaten) people from the heights of churches and other buildings; these quasi-human heads or torsos announced the inevitability of biological renewal, an earthly concept which is socially meaningful through humankind's dependence upon natural resources. One particular Green Man sculpture gracing a portal in Southwell seems to capture the joint physical/spiritual transformation which I believe the Zacchaeus figure is meant to exemplify. In this version of the Green Man archetype, a youthful figure is seen emerging from his vegetative refuge (fig. 7), appearing liberated in some newfound way. As William Anderson has proposed, the man whom we see may be "point[ing] to new wonders in life,"[53] and it seems to me that Zacchaeus, the dramatic character, may be interpreted as "springing forth" (being born of a tree) in much the same way. Audiences in York would have known of the man-in-tree image from any number of contexts — Christ crucified on the tree of life, Tree of Jesse, tree as conduit for God's grace — and may have viewed Zacchaeus as *wholly* rejuvenated (not just spiritually remade) as this Green Man image suggests. After having been destigmatized by Christ, Zacchaeus would be fit to be absorbed into the social body of the city.

However, the text resists such an encouraging conclusion and appears to question itself by, for example, depicting Zacchaeus as autonomous (since he relies upon no one but himself) and, by implication, assimilation-aversive within the community — unlike the other recipients of Christ's miracles in this play, who provide fellowship to one another. The uncomfortable fit between the celebratory tone conveyed within the play and social inequities remaining in (and extending beyond) the non-theatrical space of York — like the haunting loss of Jews from their city[54] — provokes us to assess the implications of Christ's works more pointedly.[55] While Zacchaeus himself, having gone up a tree and out on a limb[56] to meet Jesus, has been memoralized through iconography, this tax-collector's role in medieval drama warrants much more attention.

Fig. 1: Zacchaeus in the Tree. Gospels from Gross St. Martin, Cologne. Manuscript illumination, first quarter of the thirteenth-c. Cologne School. MS 9222, fol. 168r. By permission of the Bibliothèque Royale de Belgique.

Fig. 2: Zacchaeus and a Child in the Tree / Entry into Jerusalem. Nicolas of Verdun (c.1150–1205), from the Verdun Altar. Sammlungen des Stiftes Klosterneuburg. By permission of Erich Lessing / Art Resource, New York.

Fig. 3: *The Tribute Money*. Titian (Tiziano Vecellio, c.1488–1576.
Gemäldegalerie, Staatliche Kunstsammlungen.
By permission of Foto Marburg / Art Resource, New York.

Fig. 4: Anti-Semitic cartoon on a Jewish receipt roll, thirteenth century. Public Record Office, London, Great Britain. By permission of HIP / Scala / Art Resource, New York

Fig. 5: *Tree of the Cross* (fourteenth century). Pacino da Bonaguida Accademia, Florence. By permission of Alinari / Art Resource, New York.

Fig. 6: *Tree of Jesse* (twelfth century). The British Library. London, MS Lansdowne 383, fol. 15r. By permission of The British Library.

Fig. 7: Green Man (c.1290). Southwell. The man appears out of the vine leaves at the apex of the external face of the Chapter House portal of Southwell Minster. Photo and permission courtesy of Clive Hicks.

Notes

[1] Theresa Coletti and Kathleen M. Ashley, "The N-Town Passion at Toronto and Late Medieval Passion Iconography," *Research Opportunities in Renaissance Drama* 24 (1982): 181-92. On visual analogues to the episode (as seen in York Minster glass and the *Holkham Bible Picture Book*), see also Clifford Davidson, *From Creation to Doom: The York Cycle of Mystery Plays* (New York: AMS Press, Inc., 1984): 89, and notes 30, 31 (209). For a complete analysis and illustrations of the Entry into Jerusalem and Zacchaeus episodes, see the following art-historical source: Gertrud Schiller, *Iconography of Christian Art*, trans. Janet Seligman, 2 vols. (London: Lund Humphries / New York Graphic Society, 1971-72). Vol. 1: 119, 151, 156, 171, 181, figs. 49, 53, 57-58, 425, 441; vol. 2: 18-23, 29, 33, 125, 206, figs. 11-13, 15, 21, 25, 31-34, 36-40, 41, 42, 44-47, 49-50, 379. Also see: Earl Baldwin Smith, *Early Christian Iconography and a School of Ivory Carvers in Provence* (London: Oxford University Press, 1918): 121-28, especially fig. 114 (125), depicting a panel from the sixth-c. chair of Bishop Maximianus (Alexandria); and Walter L. Hildburgh, "Notes on Some English Alabaster Carvings," *The Antiquaries Journal* 4 (1924): 378-99. Hildburgh describes the image just mentioned as "a small bearded figure, with widespread arms, standing in a tree" (378, n. 3). Also see Alexander Coburn Soper's "The Italo-Gallic School of Early Christian Art," *The Art Bulletin* 20 (1938): 145-92. Soper discusses a fifth-c. Trivulzio ivory (Milan), which depicts Zacchaeus; the image appears on door panels of the Holy Sepulcher: 154, 168 (and n. 70); also fig. 16. Further documentation of Zacchaeus representations can be found in Hildburgh's "English Alabaster Carvings as Records of the Medieval Religious Drama," *Archaeologia, or, Miscellaneous Tracts Relating to Antiquity* XCIII (1949): 51-101 (especially 73-77 and Plate IXA). Hildburgh cites convincing evidence suggesting that real stage foliage might have been used in certain dramatic episodes (75). On staging possibilities, see Martin W. Walsh, "High Places and Travelling Scenes: Some Observations on the Staging of the York Cycle," in *Early Theatre* 3 [Special Volume: *The York Cycle Then and Now*] (2000): 137-54. Walsh believes that the tree into which Zacchaeus climbs may have been "braced against the wagon itself" in some way and that the actor might have stepped "off the wagon-top into his 'tree' where he would then have sufficient height to play his scene with Jesus riding below" (143).

[2] The edition used is *York Plays*, ed. Richard Beadle (London: E. Arnold, 1982). The episode spans lines 392-474.

[3] Peter Spufford, *Money and Its Use in Medieval Europe* (Cambridge: Cambridge University Press, 1988): 382-83.

[4] Ibid., 383-84.

[5] Gerald L. Harriss, "The King and His Subjects," in *Fifteenth-Century Attitudes: Perceptions of Society in Late Medieval England*, ed. Rosemary Horrox (New York: Cambridge University Press, 1994): 13-28, especially 22.

[6] Andrew Galloway, "The Making of a Social Ethic in Late-Medieval England: From *Gratitudo* to 'Kyndenesse,'" *Journal of the History of Ideas* 55 (July 1994): 365-83, especially 383, n. 48.

[7] Peter Speed, ed., *Those Who Worked: An Anthology of Medieval Sources* (New York: Italica Press, 1997): 133-34.

[8] George Sheeran, *Medieval Yorkshire Towns: People, Buildings and Spaces* (Edinburgh, U.K.: Edinburgh University Press, 1998): 10.

[9] Marc Shell, *Art and Money* (Chicago: University of Chicago Press, 1995): 12.

[10] The image is that of Sandro Botticelli's *The Annunciation* (1481), fig. 13 in Marc Shell's *Art and Money* (see n. 9).

[11] Ibid., 44–46.

[12] See n. 6, above, 372.

[13] Sometimes this point of Christianity's subsuming Judaism is quite manifest; for instance, the N-Town *Marian* plays depict Jewish clergymen singing Christian hymns. See Lawrence M. Clopper's "English Drama: From Ungodly *Ludi* to Sacred Play," in *The Cambridge History of Medieval English Literature*, ed. David Wallace (Cambridge, U.K.: Cambridge University Press, 1999): 739–66, especially 762.

[14] Particularly useful to this study has been Ruth Mellinkoff's work on anti-Semitic representation in medieval art, especially *Outcasts: Signs of Otherness in Northern European Art of the Late Middle Ages*, 2 vols. (Berkeley: University of California Press, 1993); also "Cain and the Jews," *Journal of Jewish Art* 6 (1979): 16–38. For a brief description of the salient features caricatured, see Mellinkoff's *Outcasts*, vol. 1, 127–30 and 229–30.

[15] Michael Uebel states that Jewish men have been rendered effeminate in Western discourse. See his "On Becoming Male," in *Becoming Male in the Middle Ages*, ed. Jeffrey Jerome Cohen and Bonnie Wheeler (New York: Garland Publishing, Inc., 2000): 367–84, especially 377. See also: Christine M. Rose, "The Jewish Mother-in-Law: Synagoga and the *Man of Law's Tale*," in *Chaucer and the Jews*, ed. Sheila Delany (New York: Routledge, 2002): 3–23 (22, n. 15). There is a hypersexuality associated with being Jewish as well, because of the relationship between Jews and capital (through usury), according to Sander Gilman. He argues that "Jews, in taking money, treated money as if it were alive, as if it were a sexualized object." This attitude/practice makes the Jew akin to the prostitute. See Gilman's *The Jew's Body* (New York: Routledge, 1991): 124.

[16] On the connection between pigs and Jews, see Peter Stallybrass and Allon White, *The Politics and Poetics of Transgression* (Ithaca: Cornell University Press, 1986): 44–58. Dietary restrictions prohibited Jews' ingesting pork, linking the pig to what is forbidden to Jews. Attitudes toward pigs were ambivalent; despite the animals' repugnant habits, pigs served utilitarian purposes. During fair and carnival periods throughout Europe, pigs (analogous to scapegoated people) were stoned in public forums; these stonings enabled townspeople to display hatred ("displaced abjection") against marginal groups like Jews (53). In Germany (Nuremberg) animosity toward the Jews was manifestly shown: a fifteenth-c. image of "The Jewish Sow" depicts a huge pig encircled by Jews (54).

[17] On Jews as health threats, see Paul Freedman's "The Medieval Other: The Middle Ages as Other," in *Marvels, Monsters, and Miracles: Studies in the Medieval and Early Modern Imaginations*, ed. Timothy S. Jones and David A. Sprunger (Kalamazoo: Medieval Institute Publications, 2002): 1–24, especially 9.

[18] About Jews' headgear, badges, and clothing, see the sources provided in n. 14 (Melinkoff, *Outcasts*). On the obligatory wearing of badges, see Frédérique Lachaud, "Dress and Social Status in England," in *Heraldry, Pageantry and Social Display in Medieval England*, ed. Peter Coss and Maurice Keen (Woodbridge, Suffolk, U.K.: Boydell Press, 2002): 105–23. The badges were "two white tablets, of linen or of parchment" which, after the Fourth Lateran Council of 1215, Jews were required to wear "on the upper

vestment of the chest" so that Jewish persons could be differentiated from Christians (110). This badge, stitched onto and exhibited on a garment, represented the tablets of the Mosaic Law. See David A. Hinton, "Medieval Anglo-Jewry: the Archeological Evidence," in *The Jews in Medieval Britain: Historical, Literary and Archeological Perspectives*, ed. Patricia Skinner (Woodbridge, Suffolk, U.K.: Boydell Press, 2003): 97–111, especially 109. In 1275, law required all Jews who were seven years old and above to wear felt badges (Lachaud, 111, n. 37).

[19] Howard M. Solomon, "Stigma and Western Culture: A Historical Approach," in *The Dilemma of Difference: A Multidisciplinary View of Stigma*, ed. Stephen C. Ainlay, Gaylene Becker, and Lerita M. Coleman (New York: Plenum Press, 1986): 59–76 (71).

[20] Among the patristic writings reflecting anti-Semitic references are the works of St. John Chrysostom, according to John Boswell: see Boswell's "Jews, Bicycle Riders, and Gay People: The Determination of Social Consensus and Its Impact on Minorities," *Yale Journal of Law & the Humanities* 1 (1989): 205–28 (208–209). Anti-Semitic in tone are Jesus' own words as registered in an apocryphal infancy manuscript (expanded Anglo-Norman Bodleian MS Selden Supra 38) discussed by Mary Casey in "Conversion As Depicted on the Fourteenth-Century Tring Tiles," in *Christianizing Peoples and Converting Individuals*, ed. Guyda Armstrong and Ian N. Wood (Turnhout, Belgium, U.K.: Brepols Publishers, 2000): 339–46, especially 344. Casey explains that "infancy stories [which] were excluded from the canonical Bible . . . enjoyed renewed popularity in the thirteenth and fourteenth centuries" (339). The only known portrayal of these stories (known outside manuscripts) were the Tring Tiles (red clay tiles in existence before the second century — 339–40). For general background on anti-Semitism, see Robert Chazan's "The Deteriorating Image of the Jews — Twelfth and Thirteenth Centuries," in *Christendom and Its Discontents: Exclusion, Persecution, and Rebellion, 1000–1500*, ed. Scott L. Waugh and Peter D. Diehl (Cambridge, U.K.: Cambridge University Press, 1996): 220–33.

[21] On conversionist sermons designed to Christianize Jews, see Haidee Lorrey, "Religious Authority, Community Boundaries and the Conversion of Jews in Medieval England," in *Authority and Community in the Middle Ages*, ed. Donald Mowbray, Rhiannon Purdie, and Ian P. Wei (U.K.: Sutton Publishing Limited, 1999): 85–99 (88).

[22] This land incentive was offered by Edward I. See Reva Berman Brown and Sean McCartney's "Living in Limbo: The Experience of Jewish Converts in Medieval England," in *Christianizing Peoples* (ed. Armstrong and Wood: n. 20, above): 169–91 (177).

[23] On the House of Converts (*Domus Conversorum*), see Brown and McCartney (n. 22, above): 179–91. The following studies are also extremely useful: Colin Richmond, "Englishness and Medieval Anglo-Jewry," in *Chaucer and the Jews* (n. 15, above): 213–27 (224–25); John Edwards, "The Church and the Jews in Medieval England," in *The Jews in Medieval Britain* (n. 18, above): 85–95, especially 92–93.

[24] A number of late-medieval texts kept Jewish issues alive after the expulsion of the Jews; see *Chaucer and the Jews* (n. 15, above), particularly Elisa Narin van Court's "*The Siege of Jerusalem* and Augustinian Historians: Writing about Jews in Fourteenth-Century England," 165–84 (169).

[25] On the concept of the "virtual Jew," see Sylvia Tomasch, "Postcolonial Chaucer and the Virtual Jew," in *Chaucer and the Jews* (n. 15, above): 69–85. Tomasch asserts that "while the English may have eliminated the Jews, they never eradicated 'the Jew'" (77).

This absent presence phenomenon is also discussed by Elisa Narin van Court in the same collection, who suggests that even though the Jews were physically missing from England, "their presence in narratives becomes a kind of pedagogical category into which other sources of anxiety are displaced" (166). A related point — that critics have demonstrated a sort of "selective blindness," whereby Jews are written out of rigorous studies — is adeptly argued by Sheila Delany in her "Chaucer's Prioress, the Jews, and the Muslims" (note 15, above): 43–57 (52).

[26] The silencing of the York massacre in Clifford's Tower is carefully explored in the following study: Barrie Dobson, "The Medieval York Jewry Reconsidered," in *Jews in Medieval Britain* (ed. Skinner, n. 18, above): 144–56. The guide book *Clifford's Tower* (English Heritage, 1987) says:

> In 1190 a murderous riot took place at York. The Jewish community in England had loyally appeared at the coronation of Richard the Lionheart in the previous year, only to be attacked by a mob. This event sparked off similar outrages elsewhere; the harassed Jews of York were permitted to shelter in the tower on the motte, but when they refused to readmit the sheriff, they were besieged. Offers of ransom money were refused, and the heads of several leading Jewish families thereupon killed themselves and their kinfolk. The whole castle was burnt down in an over-hasty attempt to cremate the bodies (17).

Clifford was a Lancastrian leader hanged at that tower in 1322. The suicidal slaughter of the Jews had a complicated background and was silenced; "the Archbishop of York did not condemn the atrocities" of that massacre (Colin Richmond, "Englishness and Medieval Anglo-Jewry," in *Chaucer and the Jews*, ed. Delany, 220). On the erasing of Jews throughout the history of the West, see also Steven F. Kruger, "The Spectral Jew," *New Medieval Literatures* 2 (1998): 9–35, especially 19–21.

[27] Regarding short-statured persons, see Melinkoff, *Outcasts*, vol. 1 (n. 14, above). Melinkoff explains that having too much or too little of a physical feature was considered ugly during the medieval period. Anything that was a "minority feature" was detestable; for instance, "ugliness associated with excess or deficiency, with anything thought to be too large or too small . . . *too tall or too short*" (emphasis mine, 115).

[28] The following studies on medieval usury have been most helpful to this essay: Diana Wood, *Medieval Economic Thought* (Cambridge, U.K.: Cambridge University Press, 2002); Diana Wood, "'Lesyng of Tyme': Perceptions of Idleness and Usury in Late Medieval England," in *The Use and Abuse of Time in Christian History*, ed. Robert N. Swanson (Woodbridge, Suffolk, U.K.: Boydell Press, 2002); Jacques Le Goff, *Your Money or Your Life: Economy and Religion in the Middle Ages*, trans. Patricia Ranum (New York: Zone Books, 1990); Joel Kaye, *Economy and Nature in the Fourteenth Century: Money, Market Exchange, and the Emergence of Scientific Thought* (Cambridge, U.K.: Cambridge University Press, 1998); and D. Vance Smith, "Body Doubles: Producing the Masculine *Corpus*," in *Becoming Male* (n. 15, above). The late-medieval English poet John Gower developed his own colloquially rendered definition of usury, as cited by Wood (*Medieval Economic Thought*): usury was "lending a small pea and receiving back a bean" (160).

[29] On stealing time, which belonged to God: Le Goff (39); Kaye (80 ff.); Wood (161), see n. 28, above. About the economic implications of time having a price, see Alfred W. Crosby, *The Measure of Reality: Quantification and Western Society, 1250–1600* (Cambridge,

U.K.: Cambridge University Press, 1997). Crosby poses the question: "If time had a price, if time were a thing that could have a numerical value, then what about other unsegmented imponderables, like heat or velocity or love?" (71).

[30] Kaye (n. 28, above) demonstrates that after the thirteenth century, Aristotelian theory on usury (*Politics*) was increasingly influential (86–87). Evoking the myth of Midas, Aristotle maintained that money in itself fails to satisfy any *natural* human need, and human desire for money is unlimited. Usury is not only detestable but perverse, because in a usurious transaction, money is made to give (unnatural) birth to itself; further, usurers bypass human labor. Le Goff cites Thomas of Chobham on the usurer's circumventing God's plan (as established in Gen. 3:19, i.e., that man's needs be met through his labor): "The usurer wants to make a profit without doing any work, even while he is sleeping, which goes against the precepts of the Lord" (42; see n. 28, above). Other valuable studies which touch upon usury are the following: Jochen Hörisch, *Heads or Tails: The Poetics of Money*, trans. Amy Horning Marschall (Detroit: Wayne State University Press, 2000): 103–105; Barry Gordon, *Economic Analysis Before Adam Smith: Hesiod to Lessius* (Great Britain: Macmillan Press, Ltd., 1975): chapter 7, "Scholastic Monetary Thought: 1300–1600," 187–217; Andrew Cowell, *At Play in the Tavern: Signs, Coins, and Bodies in the Middle Ages* (Ann Arbor: University of Michigan Press, 1999): 58–67, 77–78; and Odd Langholm, *Economics in the Medieval Schools: Wealth, Exchange, Value, Money and Usury According to the Paris Theological Tradition 1200–1350* (Leiden: E. J. Brill, 1992): chapter 22, especially 586–89.

[31] Diana Wood, in *Medieval Economic Thought* (n. 28, above), demonstrates that after the twelfth century, kings increasingly protected usurers. English kings, for example, offered refuge to usurers in exchange for "claim[ing] the goods of dead usurers, Jew and Christian, layman, and even cleric" (167). Protesting such forms of royal protection were Thomas of Chobham and Robert Grosseteste, among others (167–68). An excellent chapter, "Credit in the Marketplace" (ch. 11), is particularly relevant to this study. See Jean Favier's *Gold and Spices: The Rise of Commerce in the Middle Ages*, trans. Caroline Higgitt (New York: Holmes & Meier, 1998): 193–214.

[32] On collusion between borrowers and lenders whereby usury was believed to be avoided, see Edwin S. Hunt and James M. Murray, *A History of Business in Medieval Europe, 1200–1550* (Cambridge, U.K.: Cambridge University Press, 1999): 70–74. About sources of capital, consumer credit, and how effectively capital met the changing needs of business during the late-medieval period, see 215–25. During the later Middle Ages, another group of moneylenders became readily identifiable with the practice: the Lombards of Italy (215–16). The following study concentrates upon France and the Crown of Aragon (rather than England) but is exceedingly helpful vis-à-vis minorities and moneylending in Europe: David Nirenberg, *Communities of Violence: Persecution of Minorities in the Middle Ages* (Princeton: Princeton University Press, 1996). Nirenberg discusses how the Jews procured funds from the general population and passed these moneys onto the king without the monarch's having to obtain approval or pay costs associated with tax collecting; in effect, this is how the Jews unofficially became tax collectors for the Crown (174 and n. 32). Ordinarily, the crown would justify a demand for a tax — the Commons discussed (and sometimes rejected [but rarely]) the crown's appeal for taxes.

[33] Patricia H. Cullum and J. P. Goldberg, "Charitable Provision in Late Medieval York: 'To the Praise of God and the Use of the Poor,'" *Northern History* 29 (1993): 24–39. Also

see Jenny Kermode, *Medieval Merchants: York, Beverley and Hull in the Later Middle Ages* (Cambridge, U.K.: Cambridge University Press, 1998): 143–50. On general prosperity in York that undoubtedly enhanced charitable giving, see Jeremy Goldberg, "Craft Guilds, the Corpus Christi Play and Civic Government," in *The Government of Medieval York: Essays in Commemoration of the 1396 Royal Charter*, ed. Sarah Rees Jones (York, U.K.: University of York, 1997): 141–63, esp. 149–52.

[34] Malcolm G. A. Vale, *Piety, Charity and Literacy Among the Yorkshire Gentry, 1370–1480* (York, U.K.: University of York, 1976): 7.

[35] See Arnoud-Jan Bijsterveld, "The Medieval Gift as Agent of Social Bonding and Political Power: A Comparative Approach," in *Medieval Transformations: Texts, Power, and Gifts in Context*, ed. Esther Cohen and Mayke B. DeJong (Leiden: Brill, 2001): 123–56, especially 148–49. On money and commerce during the late-medieval period, also see Alexandra Reid-Schwartz, "Economies of Salvation: Commerce and the Eucharist in *The Profanation of the Host* and the Croxton *Play of the Sacrament*," *Comitatus* 25 (1994): 1–20.

[36] John J. Pilch, *Healing in the New Testament: Insights from Medical and Mediterranean Anthropology* (Minneapolis: Fortress Press, 2000): 34.

[37] A comprehensive study of tree symbolism which discusses the Tree of Life (in prelapsarian Eden) is the following essay: Gerhardt B. Ladner, "Medieval and Modern Understanding of Symbolism: A Comparison," *Speculum* 54 (April 1979): 223–56, especially 235–38; and 236, fig. 3.

[38] Christ's crucifixion as depicted on a green cross, or tree, is discussed by Ladner (n. 37, above): 236–38. Illustrations linking the Tree of Life with the Cross are plentiful, including in Ladner: figs. 5 and 6. Also see Thomas N. Hall, "The Cross as Green Tree in the *Vindicta Salvatoris* and the Green Rod of Moses in *Exodus*," *English Studies: A Journal of English Language and Literature* 72 (1991): 297–307, especially 302–304. As depicted in late fifteenth-c. painted glass (Swabia in Germany), Christ appears as the Man of Sorrows in the midst of vegetation; see the work of the Lautenbach Master (one of Peter Hemmel's closest collaborators) as shown in illustration 230 of *Mirror of the Medieval World*, ed. William D. Wixom (New York: Metropolitan Museum of Art, 1999): 190–91.

[39] The vegetation cults to which I refer involve the *Green Man* archetype. The Green Man appears as an image in an architectural context, for instance, in a number of locations throughout Europe. While the image varies, the general impression the beholder has is as follows: a man-like face emerges from amidst foliage (often a tree), perhaps suggesting that the man/tree fusion which has already taken place is quite natural (though not always peaceful). The following study on the Green Man theme is enlightening: Kathleen Basford, *The Green Man* (New York: D. S. Brewer, 1998). Basford explains that the foliate head image sometimes graces Christian tombs as well as memorials and, in this context, may be conveying the concept of resurrection (21). Basford began conducting research into the Green Man image after seeing a striking portrayal of a human head spewing vegetation from its mouth while she was visiting Fountains Abbey in Yorkshire (7–8). Also see Fran and Geoff Doel's informative *The Green Man in Britain* (Charleston: Arcadia Publishing, Inc., 2001), where the authors focus upon England but link the image to Germany (*der grüne Mensch*) and France (*l'homme vert*) as well (17); they propose that "the power of the recurring symbol of the Green Man" during the late Middle Ages (thirteenth through fifteenth centuries) may partly relate to the subconscious and partly to figures from the shadowy region of folklore and legend" (18). Doel and Doel believe that the reason the green figure always seems to be male is because its function is to protect

others (22); on some occasions, the Green Man motif is grotesque, however (39). Regarding the city of York, these authors list the following two sites as places bearing Green Man images: All Saints Church (North Street) and York Minster Cathedral: chapter house and vestibule carvings; also "corbels and bosses in choir, crossing and aisles" (154). Most useful to my essay's line of investigation has been William Anderson's *Green Man: The Archetype of Our Oneness with the Earth / Photography by Clive Hicks* (London: Harper Collins, 1990). Of all the Green Man depictions I have perused, I find a possible analogue to the Zacchaeus-in-tree episode of the York play in fig. 81 of Anderson's text, where a man is shown emerging from vine leaves on a frieze at the apex of a chapter house entrance portal at Southwell. Anderson notes the man's peaceful expression as well as his demeanor, suggesting he has been freed; the vine surrounding the man symbolizes Christ. Besides the Green Man motif evoking Creation (as one of many themes), the emblem conveys "cosmic energies," a concept Hildegard of Bingen would equate with *viriditas* (greenness −163).

[40] Studies exploring Tree of Jesse images are numerous. Among those which have proven instrumental to this essay are the following: Gerhardt Ladner (see n. 37, above), especially 250–51 (and fig. 18); and Peter Coss, "Knighthood, Heraldry, and Social Exclusion in Edwardian England" (see Coss and Keen, ed., note 18, above): 39–68. Coss asserts that the Tree of Jesse image was quite popular in fourteenth-c. England (particularly among the gentry because of their focus upon heraldry and family lineage), demonstrating that "[f]aith and social status were strongly intertwined" (53). See also O. Elfrida Saunders, *A History of English Art in the Middle Ages* (Freeport: Books for Libraries Press, 1932), particularly chapter four. Saunders alludes to an example of this image in York (53) and believes (following Émile Mâle) that the picture may be linked to the drama (53–54). In Saunders, see fig. 18 for a twelfth-c. image from the Lambeth Bible and her later discussion of the York picture, though she provides no illustration for the latter. In that example, "a king [is] seated in the branches of a conventional tree, to which he holds on with either hand" (112). Fifteenth-c. motifs are mentioned in brief (201). For an interesting discussion of the Jesse Tree image in York, see Elisabeth Reddish, "The Fourteenth Century Tree of Jesse in the Nave of York Minster," *York Medieval Yearbook* 2 (2003): 1–15; the essay can be found through: http://www.historyjournals.de/journals/hjg-y00024.html.

[41] See the Gospel of Pseudo-Matthew in *Apocryphal Gospels, Acts, and Revelations*, 24 vols., ed. Alexander Roberts and James Donaldson, trans. Alexander Walker (Edinburgh: T. & T. Clark, 1873): 16, 16–52 (especially 37). The depiction of a tree bending downward to provide divine assistance is shown also in the *Holkham Bible Picture Book* (fol. 15), where a bowing tree assists Mary during the Flight into Egypt. God sustains Noah through this means as well: as Noah begins the overwhelming task of constructing the ark, a tree bows down to assist him (fol. 7): William O. Hassall, ed. (London: Dropmore, 1954). On God's giving the fruit of a tree to benefit humankind, the apple was known to signify Christ; see Pauline Larson, "The Medieval Use of the Apple as a Symbol for Christ," *The Covenant Quarterly* 43 (1985): 35–51.

[42] On the English woodland, see Mark Bailey, "Population and Economic Resources," in *An Illustrated History of Late Medieval England*, ed. Chris Given-Wilson (Manchester, U.K.: Manchester University Press, 1996): 41–57, especially 53–54.

[43] Mervyn James, "Ritual, Drama, and the Social Body in the Late Medieval English Town," *Past and Present* 98 (1983): 3–29 (4). On competing notions of social body (fra-

ternal versus familial) see Miri Rubin, "Small Groups: Identity and Solidarity in the Late Middle Ages," in *Enterprise and Individuals in Fifteenth-Century England*, ed. Jennifer Kermode (Great Britain: Alan Sutton Publishing, Ltd., 1991): 132–50. In 1303, the guild of burgesses in the city of York vowed to commit themselves one to another, this fraternal bond coming first over any family commitments individual members might have (140). As Michael Camille has demonstrated, there were competing notions of the body during the Middle Ages: not only was a body politic marginalized and framed as a picture, but shown as opened, divided into regions, conflicted with the soul (among many other images, including those portraying Christ). See Camille's "The Image and the Self: Unwriting Late Medieval Bodies," in *Framing Medieval Bodies*, ed. Sarah Kay and Miri Rubin (Manchester: Manchester University Press, 1994): 62–99.

[44] Sarah Beckwith, "Ritual, Theater, and Social Space in the York Corpus Christi Cycle," in *Bodies and Disciplines: Intersections of Literature and History in Fifteenth-Century England*, ed. Barbara A. Hanawalt and David Wallace (Minneapolis: University of Minnesota Press, 1996): 63–86 (77).

[45] See Roberta Gilchrist, "Medieval Bodies in the Material World: Gender, Stigma and the Body," in *Framing Medieval Bodies* (n. 43, above): 43–61, especially 47–48.

[46] Melinkoff, *Outcasts*, vol. 1 (n. 14, above): lviii.

[47] Lucienne Germain has demonstrated how negative artistic depictions of Jews sanctioned anti-Semitism. See her "From Usury to High Finance: The Metamorphosis of an Anti-Jewish Myth Viewed Through English Caricatures," *La Revue LISA* 1 (2003) [http://www.unicaen.fr/mrsh/anglais/lisa]: 75–84.

[48] See Werner Danckert, *Unehrliche Leute [Dishonest People]: Die verfemten Berufe* (Bern: Francke, 1979): 266.

[49] See Christopher Dyer, *Making a Living in the Middle Ages: The People of Britain 850–1520* (New Haven: Yale University Press, 2002): 265–329. On taxpayer grievances, see also the following: Irene M. W. Harvey, "Was There Popular Politics in Fifteenth-Century England?" (155–74, especially 166) and A. J. Gross, "K. B. McFarlane and the Determinists: The Fallibilities of the English Kings, c.1399–1520" (55–74), both in *The McFarlane Legacy: Studies in Late Medieval Politics and Society*, ed. Richard H. Britnell (New York: Stroud, 1995).

[50] Peter Womack, "Imagining Communities: Theatres and the English Nation in the Sixteenth Century," in *Culture and History 1350–1600: Essays on English Communities, Identities and Writing*, ed. David Aers (Detroit: Wayne State University Press, 1992): 91–145 (99).

[51] On healing, see Don Handelman's "Postlude: The Interior Sociality of Self-Transformation," in *Self and Self-Transformation in the History of Religions*, ed. David Shulman and Guy G. Stroumsa (Oxford: Oxford University Press, 2002): 236–53 (247). An extremely relevant article on the implications of social space in York is the following: Sarah Beckwith, "Ritual, Theater, and Social Space in the York Corpus Christi Cycle" (n. 44, above): 63–86, especially 70–78.

[52] The "man born of an elm-tree" image is depicted in fig 7 of the following source: Marie-Christine Pouchelle, *The Body and Surgery in the Middle Ages*, trans. Rosemary Morris (New Brunswick: Rutgers University Press, 1990). The illustration shows "a man emerging from a tree-trunk [holding] in the hollow of his hand a tiny tree exactly

like the first one." Pouchelle describes the portrayal as a "vegetable image for procreation" (165).

[53] William Anderson, *Green Man* (above, n. 39), 95 and fig. 81. I am indebted to Clive Hicks for his critical insights into the Green Man motif within Europe. Regarding the illustration (fig. 7) chosen for this *Fifteenth-Century Studies* essay, Hicks explains that the image of the youth appears to be the fruit of the tree.

[54] In a particular rendition of the Tree of Jesse, Jon Whitman explains that Jews appear "to survive for a time on a limb." See his "The Body and the Struggle for the Soul of Romance: *La Queste del Saint Graal*," in *The Body and the Soul in Medieval Literature*, ed. Piero Boitani and Anna Torti (Woodbridge, Suffolk: D. S. Brewer, 1999): 31–61 (53, and fig. 8). Jews were frequently likened to the fig tree which bore no fruit (53, n. 67).

[55] The Green Man images seen in York may have had social implications, according to Anderson (see notes 39 and 53, above). Referring to the Green Men portrayed in the York chapter house, Anderson considers whether such images depicted "the intelligence underlying Natural Law" which then became "a reminder to those who regulated communities or administered justice to the common man and woman of the principles by which they should be guided" (93). Two illustrations of Green Men as they appear in the York Minster chapter house can be seen in John Michell's book *The Traveler's Key to Sacred England* (New York: Alfred A. Knopf, 1988): 260. For a facile introduction to the Green Man theme, see Clive Hicks, *The Green Man — A Field Guide* (Fakenham, Norfolk: Compass Books, 2000).

[56] Although this expression is commonplace, I owe its application here to Ann Hagman, *Climbing the Sycamore Tree: A Study on Choice and Simplicity* (Nashville: Upper Room Books, 2001): 10.

Troy State University Dothan

Bibliographie des Miracles et Mystères français

Graham A. Runnalls et Jesse Hurlbut

Le lecteur trouvera ci-dessous une version publiée de la *Bibliographie des Miracles et Mystères Français*, créée par Graham A. Runnalls et disponible depuis quatre ans au site internet de Jesse Hurlbut, intitulé le *French Medieval Drama Database Project*, dont l'adresse internet est: www.byu.edu/~hurlbut/fmddp/bmmf.html

L'avantage d'une bibliographie en ligne est incontestablement le fait qu'elle peut être régulièrement augmentée, corrigée et mise à jour. Effectivement, cette version publiée de notre bibliographie, datée du 1 juin 2003, a déjà subi de nombreuses modifications depuis sa création en ligne en 2000. La publication de notre bibliographie dans *Fifteenth-Century Studies* ne signifie absolument pas que la version en ligne cessera d'exister. C'est notre intention de continuer à l'augmenter et à la mettre à jour; et sans doute, la version en ligne actuelle sera-t-elle plus complète encore que celle publiée ici dans le volume 30 de *Fifteenth-Century Studies*. Mais celle-ci permettra au lecteur du périodique d'en consulter un texte plus "concret," pour ainsi dire, un "cliché" qui reflète l'état de la bibliographie en ligne en mai 2003.

Notre bibliographie consiste en une liste d'éditions critiques et d'études portant sur le théâtre religieux en langue française des XIVe, XVe et XVIe siècles. Sont donc exclus: le théâtre en langue occitane; le théâtre liturgique; tout le théâtre (comique et religieux) des XIIe et XIIIe siècles; les farces, les sotties et les moralités; le théâtre humaniste et pré-classique; ainsi que les genres "para-dramatiques" (entrées princières, etc.).

Il s'agit d'une bibliographie personnelle, cumulative et non-classée. C'est-à-dire que c'est une oeuvre que Graham Runnalls a accumulée lui-même au cours des vingt-cinq dernières années, et qu'il a complétée récemment par des recherches plus explicitement bibliographiques. Elle est non-classée, dans la mesure où nous n'avons pas cherché à la diviser en une série de sous-catégories (par exemple: mise en scène, représentations, style, théologie), parce que nous nous sommes rendu compte de la nature inévitablement subjective de tout classement de ce genre. Ou bien nous aurions dû faire des décisions souvent arbitraires; ou bien nous aurions dû citer le même ouvrage plusieurs fois. D'ailleurs, tout lecteur qui consulte la bibliographie en ligne dispose nécessairement d'un ordinateur qui lui permet de rechercher un mot-clé sujet, auteur, titre, etc. — ce qui rend toute classification presque superflue.

Aucune bibliographie ne peut prétendre être originale. Par définition, une telle liste bibliographique est le résultat de dépouillements successifs de catalogues de bibliothèques et d'autres bibliographies. Nous sommes donc inévitablement redevables à tous nos nombreux prédécesseurs, auxquels nous tenons à exprimer notre reconnaissance.

La bibliographie est divisée en deux parties: les éditions critiques (surtout des XIXe et XXe siècles) et les études. Pour une liste des documents originaux qui conservent les miracles et mystères en question (manuscrits, éditions gothiques, etc.), nous renvoyons le lecteur à notre *Corpus du théâtre religieux français du moyen âge*, que l'on peut consulter au même site web de Jesse Hurlbut.

Les éditions critiques (environ 120) sont présentées dans l'ordre alphabétique du titre traditionnel du texte en question, sans tenir compte du nom d'auteur, même lorsque celui est connu. Les articles (le, la les) sont omis. Il faut se méfier du mot d'un titre qui renvoie au genre théâtral d'un texte. Il arrive souvent que, dans les documents originaux comme dans les éditions critiques, *Miracle* remplace *Mystère* ou *vice versa*, que certains *Mystères* sont parfois appelés *Vie*, que les titres des *Passions* ne sont pas précédés du mot *Mystère*, et ainsi de suite. En vérité, les titres traditionnels sont parfois trompeurs ou variables. Il existe un petit nombre d'anthologies modernes de miracles et de mystères, qui sont classés sous le nom de l'éditeur.

Les études (monographies, articles, essais, etc. environ 750 titres) sont présentées dans l'ordre alphabétique des noms des auteurs ou des titres des anonymes, suivant l'un des nombreux modèles typographiques recommandés par les périodiques et les maisons d'éditions, à cette exception près que le prénom de l'auteur suit son nom de famille (ce qui a facilité le triage alphabétique automatique par l'ordinateur).

Il va de soi que les lecteurs relèveront des erreurs et omissions. Comme nous l'avons déjà expliqué, c'est notre intention de corriger et d'augmenter, à des intervalles réguliers, la version en ligne de cette bibliographie. Nous serions donc reconnaissants à tous ceux qui trouveront des erreurs ou des omissions de nous les faire remarquer, en écrivant directement à l'adresse électronique de Jesse Hurlbut. Car, au fur et à mesure que cette bibliographie en ligne sera améliorée grâce aux suggestions de ses lecteurs, elle ne sera plus *la nôtre*, mais plutôt une liste bibliographique qui appartiendra à tout le monde, à toute la communauté de chercheurs dans ce domaine.

The entries do not follow the requirements of the *Chicago Manual of Style*, 14th edition, entirely, especially for nineteenth-c. items (note by the editors).

Editions

Collection de Poésies, Romans, Chroniques, une série publiée d'après d'anciens manuscrits et d'après des éditions des XVe et XVIe siècles. Paris: Silvestre, 1839–41. [*Miracles de Nostre Dame par personnages* 8 et 11; *la Nativité de Nostre Seigneur Jhesuchrist par personnages avec la Digne Accouchée; le Mystère de la Vie et Hystoire de Monseigneur Sainct Martin.*]

Cycle de Mystères des Premiers Martyrs, ed. Graham A. Runnalls. Geneva: Droz, 1976.

Du Méril, Édélestand. *Les Origines latines du théâtre moderne*. Leipzig-Paris: H. Welter, 1897 [*Miracles de Nostre Dame par personnages* 5 et 13].

L'Estoire de Griselidis, ed. Mario Roques. Geneva: Droz, 1957; éd. Barbara Craig. Lawrence, Kansas: University of Kansas Publications, 1954.

"Farce du Meunier" (du *Mystère de Saint Martin*), éd. André Tissier. *Farces du Moyen Age*. Paris: Garnier-Flammarion, 1984. Vol. 4, # 22 in *Recueil de farces (1450–1550)*. Geneva: Droz, 1989.

Fournier, Edouard. *Le Théâtre français avant la Renaissance, 1450–1550*. Paris: Laplace, 1873 [Le *Martire Saint Estiene*, la *Conversion Saint Pol* et la *Vie de Monseigneur Saint Fiacre* des *Mystères inédits du XVe siècle*; le *Mystère du Chevalier qui donna sa femme au diable*].

Le Geu Saint Denis, ed. Bernard Seubert. Geneva: Droz, 1974.

Jeu de l'Etoile, éd. Claude Thiry. Bruxelles: Palais des Académies, 1980.

Jeu des Trois Jeux des Rois de Neuchâtel, ed. Yves Giraud, N. King et S. de Reyff. Fribourg/Suisse, 1985; ed. André de Mandach. Geneva: Droz, 1982.

Jour du Jugement, éd. Émile Roy. Paris: E. Bouillon, 1902; Slatkine Repr. 1976; éd. et trad. en français moderne par Jean-Pierre Perrot et J.-J. Nonot. Besançon: Éditions Comp'Act, 2000.

Miracle de Saint Nicolas (prologues), ed. Charles Samaran. *Romania* 51 (1925).

Miracle de Saint Nicolas et d'un Juif, ed. Omer Jodogne. Geneva: Droz, 1982.

Miracle de Saint Nicolas, ed. Paul Aebischer dans *Neuf Études sur le théâtre médiéval*. Geneva: Droz, 1972.

Miracle des Trois Pèlerins, ed. G. Ouy. *Pluteus* 2 (1984).

Miracles de Madame Sainte Geneviève, ed. Clotilde Sennewaldt. Frankfurt am Main, 1937.

Miracles de Mont-Saint-Michel, ed. Robillard de Beaurepaire. Avranches, 1842.

Miracles de Nostre Dame par personnages, éd. Gaston Paris et Ulysse Robert, 7 vols. Paris: SATF, 1876–93: voici les titres abrégés des quarante miracles, avec la référence à cette édition, suivis de références aux autres éditions isolées de chaque miracle:

L'Enfant donné au diable (I, 3–59); éd. Adalbert von Keller. Tübingen: Tübinger Universitätsschriften, 1865.

L'Abbeesse grosse (I, 60–102).

L'Evesque que l'arcediacre murtrit (I, 103–48).

La Femme du roy de Portugal (I, 149–204).

La Nativité Nostre Seigneur Jhesuscrist (I, 205–50); ed. Édélestand Du Méril, *Les Origines latines du théâtre moderne*. Leipzig-Paris: H. Welter, 1897 (354–89).

Saint Jehan Chrisosthomes (I, 251–312); ed. W. Wahlund. Stockholm, 1875.

La Nonne qui laissa son abbaie (I, 313–54); éd. Nigel Wilkins, *Two Miracles*. Edinburgh: Scottish Academic Press, 1972.

Un pape qui vendi le basme (I, 355–400).

Saint Guillaume du désert (II, 3–56).

L'Evesque à qui Nostre Dame s'apparut (II, 57–90).

Un Marchant et un larron (II, 91–130).

La Marquise de la Gaudine (II, 131–73); dans *Collection de Poésies, Romans, Chroniques, etc., publiées d'après d'anciens manuscrits et d'après des éditions des XVe et XVIe siècles*. Paris: Silvestre, 1841.

L'Empereur Julien (II, 174–228); ed. Du Méril, *Les Origines latines du théâtre moderne*. Leipzig-Paris: H. Welter, 1897 (305–53).

Un Prevost que Nostre Dame delivra (II, 229–82).

Un Enfant que Nostre Dame resuscita (II, 283–347); éd. Graham A. Runnalls. Geneva: Droz, 1972.

La Mere du pape (II, 348–407).

Un Paroissien excomenié (III, 2–68).

Theodore (III, 69–135).

Un chanoine qui se maria (III, 136–88).

Saint Sevestre (III, 189–243).

Barlaam et Josaphat (III, 244–306); ed. Hermann Zotenberg et P. Meyer. Stuttgart: Litterarischer Verein 75, 1864 (368–417).

Saint Panthaleon (III, 307–70).

Amis et Amile (IV 5–70), ed. Louis Monmerqué et F. Michel, *Théâtre Français au moyen âge publié d'après les manuscrits de la Bibliothèque du Roi.* Paris: F. Didot, 1842 (216–64).

Saint Ignace (IV, 71–121); ed. L. Monmerqué et F. Michel, ibid. (265–93).

Saint Valentin (IV, 122–77); ed. L. Monmerqué et F. Michel, ibid. (294–326); ed. Nigel Wilkins, *Two Miracles.* Edinburgh: Scottish Academic Press, 1972.

Une Femme que Nostre Dame garda d'estre arse (IV, 178–238); ed. Louis Monmerqué et F. Michel, ibid. (327–64).

L'Empereris de Romme (IV, 239–316); ed. L. Monmerqué et F. Michel, ibid. (365–416).

Oton roy d'Espaigne (IV, 317–87); ed. L. Monmerqué et F. Michel, ibid. (417–80).

La Fille du roy de Hongrie (V, 2–90); ed. L. Monmerqué et F. Michel, ibid. (481–542).

Saint Jehan le Paulu hermite (V, 91–154).

Berthe femme du roy Pepin (V, 155–261); dans *Collection de Poésies, Romans, Chroniques*, etc. Paris: Silvestre, 1839.

Roy Thierry (V, 93–338); ed. L. Monmerqué et F. Michel, ibid. (551–608).

Robert le dyable (VI, 3–80); ed. Édouard Frère et Leroux de Lincy. Rouen, 1836; ed. Édouard Fournier. Paris, 1879.

Sainte Bauteuch (VI, 81–173); ed. Achille Jubinal et Leroux de Lincy: *Eustache-Hyacinthe Langlois. Essai sur les Énervés de Jumièges et sur quelques décorations singulières des églises de cette abbaye, suivi du Miracle de sainte Bauteuch.* Rouen: Édouard Frère, 1838.

Un Marchant et un Juif (VI, 174–226).

Pierre le changeur (VI, 227–99).

La fille d'un roy (VII, 3–121).

Saint Lorens (VII, 122–94).

Clovis (VII, 195–280); éd. L. Monmerqué et F. Michel, ibid. (609–68).

Saint Alexis (VII, 282–368).

Monmerqué, Louis, et F. Michel. *Théâtre Français au moyen âge publié d'après les manuscrits de la Bibliothèque du Roi.* Paris: F. Didot, 1842. [*Miracles de Nostre Dame par personnages* 23–29, 32, 39.]

Le Mistère d'une Jeune Fille laquelle se voulut habandonner à peché, edited by Lenita et M. Locey. Geneva: Droz, 1976.

Mystère de Judith et Holofernés (de Jean Molinet?, tiré du *Mystère du Viel Testament*), ed. Graham A. Runnalls. Geneva: Droz, 1995.

Mystère de l'Advocacie Nostre Dame, ed. Graham A. Runnalls. *Zeitschrift für romanische Philologie* 100 (1983): 41–77.

Mystère de l'Ascension de la Vierge, ed. Bernard Lunet. *Mémoires de la Société des Lettres, Sciences et Arts de l'Aveyron*, 4 (1842–43): 300–73.

Mystère de l'Incarnation et Nativité de Notre Sauveur et Rédempteur Jésus-Christ: représenté à Rouen en 1474, d'après un imprimé du XVe siècle: Éd. facsimilé, 3 vols. Pierre Le Verdier. Rouen: Imprimerie de Espérance Cagniard, 1884–86.

Mistère de l'Institucion de l'ordre des Frères Prêcheurs: texte de l'Édition de Jehan Trepperel (1504–12?), ed. Simone de Reyff, G. Bedouelle et M. Gérard-Zai. Geneva: Droz, 1997.

Mystère de la Nativité Nostre Seigneur Jesus Christ par personnages, avec la Digne Accouchée, dans Collection de Poésies, Romans, Chroniques. Publiées d'après d'anciens manuscrits et d'après des éditions des XVe et XVIe siècles. Ed. Auguste Veinant. Paris: Silvestre, 1839–41.

Mystère de la Nativité (fragments), ed. Albert Thomas. *Romania* 38 (1909): 193–?

Mystère de la Pacience de Job, mystère anonyme du XVe siècle (MS fr. 1774), ed. Albert Meiller. Paris: Klincksieck, 1971.

Les Mystères de la Procession de Lille, éd. Alan Knight. 5 vols. Tome I, *Le Pentateuque* [12 mystères]. Geneva: Droz, 2001; Tome II, *De Josué à David* [16 mystères]. Geneva: Droz, 2003.

Mystère de la Résurrection Angers (1456), ed. Pierre Servet, 2 vols. Geneva: Droz, 1993.

Mystère de la Vengeance (d'Eustache Mercadé). Des microfiches de l'édition critique des première et troisième journées par Andrée Kail (1955) et de celle de la deuxième journée par Adèle Cornay (1957) sont jointes à: Stephen K. Wright, *The Vengeance of our Lord: Medieval Dramatizations of the Destruction of Jerusalem.* Toronto: Pontifical Institute, 1989.

Mystère de Notre-Dame-du-Puy, ed. A. Chassaing, 2 vols., dans *Le Livre de Podio.* Le Puy-en-Velay: M.P. Marchessou, 1874.

Mystère de Saincte Susanne par personnaiges, ed. R. Giménez. Inedita et Rara 14. Montréal: Ceres, 1999 [= partie du *Mystère du Viel Testament*].

Mystère de Saint Adrien, ed. Émile Picot. Mâcon, 1895.

Mystère de Saint Bernard de Menthon, ed. Albert Lecoy de la Marche. Paris: Firmin Didot, 1988.

Mystère de Saint Christofle, ed. Graham A. Runnalls. Exeter: Exeter University, 1973.

Mystère de Saint Clément, ed. Carl F. Abel. Metz, 1861.

Mystère de Saint Crespin et de Saint Crespinien, ed. Léon Dessalles et F. Chabaille. Paris: Silvestre, 1836; ed. Élisabeth Lalou, thèse inédite, École des Chartes, 1980.

Mystère de Saint Didier, ed. J. Carnandet. Paris, 1855; ed. Alain-J. Surdel. Thèse inédite, Strasbourg, 1997.

Mystère de Saint Genis, ed. J. Mostert et E. Stengel. Marburg, 1895.

Mystère de Saint Laurent, ed. W. Söderhjelm et A. Wallensköld. Helsingfors, 1891.

Mystère de Saint Louis, éd. Francisque Michel. Westminster: Roxburghe Club, 1871; éd. Darwin Smith. Thèse inédite, Paris III, 1986.

Mystère de Saint Martin, dans *Collection de Poésies, Romans, Chroniques*. Ed. Karl Knudsen. Thèse inédite, University of Massachusetts, 1976.

Mystère de Saint Martin (Savoie), éd. F. Truchet. Travaux de la Société d'Histoire et d'Archéologie de Maurienne I, V (1881).

Mystère de Saint Martin (1496) d'André de La Vigne, ed. André Duplat. Geneva: Droz, 1979.

Mystère de Saint Quentin, ed. Henri Châtelain. Saint-Quentin: Imprimerie générale, 1909.

Mystère de Saint Rémy, éd. Jelle Koopmans. Geneva: Droz, 1997.

Mystère de Saint Sébastien, éd. Louis R. Mills. Geneva: Droz, 1965.

Mystère de Sainte Agathe, éd. Graham A. Runnalls. Montréal: Ceres, 1994 (*Le Moyen Français*: Inedita et Rara 9).

Mystère de Sainte Barbe (en deux journées), éd. P. Seefeld. Greifswald, 1908; éd. Mario Longtin. *Le Mystère de Sainte Barbe en deux journées*. Mémoire de maîtrise (inédit). Montréal: Université McGill, 1998.

Mystère de Sainte Barbe (rôle), ed. Jacques Chocheyras, dans *Le Théâtre religieux en Savoie au 16e siècle*. Geneva: Droz, 1971.

Mystère de Sainte Venise, éd. Graham A. Runnalls. Exeter: Exeter University, 1980. [http://www.uhb.fr/alc/medieval]

Mystère des Trois Doms représenté à Romans en 1509 et publié avec le compte, ed. Ulysse Chevalier et P. Giraud. Lyon, 1887.

Mystère des Trois Rois (fragments de la *Passion d'Arras*), ed. Paul Aebischer. *Romania* 51 (1925): 521–27; et Graham A. Runnalls, *Pluteus* 4–5 (1986–87): 47–54.

Mystère des Trois Rois (Manosque), ed. M. Isnard. *Bulletin Historique du Comité des Travaux Historiques,* 1896.

Mystère du Chevalier qui donna sa femme au dyable, ed. Eugène Viollet-le-Duc. *Ancien Théâtre François.* Paris: Jannet, 1854. 425–79. Edouard Fournier dans *Le Théâtre Français avant la Renaissance,* 1450–1550. Paris: Laplace, Sanchez et Cie, 1873.

Mystère du Jeune Enfant que sa mère donna au diable, éd. Jean Babelon dans *La Bibliothèque française de Fernand Colomb.* Paris: Champion, 1913.

Mystère du Roy Advenir, ed. Albert Meiller. Geneva: Droz, 1970.

Mystère du Sacrifice d'Abraham, tiré du *Mystère du Viel Testament,* éd. de trois versions du texte par Barbara Craig dans *The Evolution of a Mystery Play.* Orlando: French Literature Publications, 1983.

Mystère du Siège d'Orléans, ed. François Guessard et E. de Certain. Paris, 1862. Éd. Vicki Hamblin. Geneva: Droz, 2002; éd. Gérard Gros (avec traduction en regard). Paris: Livres de Poche, 2002.

Mystère du Viel Testament, ed. James A. Rothschild et E. Picot. 6 vols. Paris: Firmin Didot, 1878–91. Éditions critiques partielles: *La Creacion, la Transgression and l'Expulsion of the Mistere du Viel Testament,* éd. Barbara Craig. Lawrence: University of Kansas Press, 1969; voir aussi le *Mystère du Sacrifice d'Abraham,* le *Mystère de Judith et Holofernés* et le *Mystère de Saincte Susanne.*

Mystères et Moralités Liégeois, éd. Gustave Cohen. Paris: Champion, 1920.

Mystères inédits du XVe siècle, 2 vols., ed. Achille Jubinal. Paris: Téchener, 1837. [= Le recueil de mystères du manuscrit 1131 de la Bibliothèque Sainte-Geneviève de Paris: la *Résurrection,* la *Passion Nostre Seigneur,* la *Vie de Saint Fiacre,* la *Nativité,* le *Geu des Trois Roys,* le *Cycle de Mystères des Premiers Martyrs,* le *Geu Saint Denis,* les *Miracles de Madame Sainte-Geneviève.*] [http://www.uhb.fr/alc/medieval]

Nativité et le Geu des Trois Roys, ed. Ruth Whittredge. Bryn Mawr: Bryn Mawr College, 1944.

Passion d'Amboise, ed. Émile Picot, *Romania* 19 (1890): 260–82. Éd. Graham A. Runnalls. *Le Moyen Français* 26 (1991): 7–86.

Passion d'Arnoul Gréban (MS A), ed. Gaston Paris et G. Raynaud. Paris: Vieweg, 1878.

Passion d'Arnoul Gréban (MS B), ed. Omer Jodogne. Bruxelles: Palais des Académies, 1965, 1983.

Passion d'Arras, ed. Jules M. Richard. Arras, 1891.

Passion d'Autun, ed. Grace Frank. Paris: SATF, 1934.

Passion d'Auvergne, ed. Graham A. Runnalls. Geneva: Droz, 1982; et *The Baptism and Temptation of Christ*, éd. John R. Elliott et Graham A. Runnalls. New Haven: Yale University Press, 1978.

Passion de Jean Michel, ed. Omer Jodogne. Gembloux: Duculot, 1959.

Passion de Leyde, ed. Graham A. Runnalls. *Romania* 105 (1984): 88–110.

Passion de Mons, ed. Gustave Cohen. *Le Livre de Conduite du Régisseur et le Compte des Dépenses pour le Mystère de la Passion, joué à Mons en 1501.* Paris: Champion, 1925; et *Le Mystère de la Passion joué à Mons en juillet 1501. Livre des Prologues. Matinée IIIe.* Gembloux: Duculot, 1957.

Passion de Semur, éd. Émile Roy dans *Le Mystère de la Passion en France*. Dijon, 1903; ed. Peter Durbin et L. Muir. Leeds: University of Leeds, 1981.

Passion de Troyes, ed. Jean-Claude Bibolet. Geneva: Droz, 1987.

Passion du ms n.a.f. 10660 de la Bibliothèque Nationale de Paris (fragment), ed. Graham A. Runnalls. "Un Mystère de la Passion inconnu? Les Fragments du ms B.N. n.a.f. 10660." *Romania* 111 (1990): 514–41.

Passion du Palatinus, ed. Karl Christ. *Zeitschrift für romanische Philologie* 40 (1920): 405–89; ed. Grace Frank. Paris: Champion, 1922; republiée avec traduction par Jacques Ribard. Paris: Champion, 1992.

Passion en rimes franchoises: mystère du début du XVIe siècle, édition des trois premières journées procurée par Cécile Guérin. Tours: Mémoires, 1994.

Passion Nostre Seigneur (du manuscrit 1131 de la Bibliothèque Sainte-Geneviève, ed. Graham A. Runnalls. Geneva: Droz, 1974; ed. Edward J. Gallagher. Chapel Hill: University of North Carolina Press, 1976.

Passion Catalane-Occitane, édition, traduction et notes par Aileen A. MacDonald. Geneva: Droz, 1999 (édition de la soi-disant *Passion Didot* avec d'autres textes apparentés).

Passion Savoyarde (I) (en deux journées); manuscrit dans la possession d'Yves Michelland (Grenoble: Meylan); éd. Runnalls, dans *Les Mystères dans les provinces françaises (en Savoie et en Poitou, à Reims et à Amiens)*. Paris: Champion, 2003.

Passion Savoyarde (II) (troisième de quatre journées); manuscrit dans la possession d'Yves Michelland; éd. Runnalls (see above).

Vie de Marie-Madeleine par personnages: Bibliothèque Nationale, Réserve Yf 2914, ed. Jacques Chocheyras et Graham A. Runnalls. Geneva: Droz, 1986.

Vie de Monseigneur Saint Fiacre, éd. Edouard Fournier dans *Le Théâtre en France avant la Renaissance*. Paris, 1873; ed. J. Burks, B. Craig et H. Porter. Lawrence: University of Kansas Press, 1960.

Vie de Saint Louis de Pierre Gringore, dans *Oeuvres complètes*, ed. Anatole de Montaiglon et J. de Rothschild. 2 vols. Paris, 1877.

Viollet-le-Duc, Eugène. *Ancien théâtre français, ou: collection des ouvrages dramatiques les plus remarquables depuis les mystères jusqu'à Corneille*, 10 vols. Paris: Jannet, 1854–57.

Studies

Abrahams, P. "The Mercator Scenes in Medieval French Passion Plays." *Medium Aevum* 3 (1934): 112–23.

Accarie, Maurice. "Jean Michel homme de théâtre: la suppression du prologue dans la *Passion* de Jean Michel." Dans *Mélanges de langue et de littérature médiévales offerts à Pierre Le Gentil*. Paris: SEDES, 1973. 1–121.

——. "Théâtre religieux et théâtre profane au Moyen Âge: essai de classification." *Cahiers de Varsovie* 19 (1992): 15–22.

——. *Le Théâtre sacré de la fin du Moyen Âge: Étude sur le sens moral de la Passion de Jean Michel*. Geneva: Droz, 1979.

Actes du Ier Colloque de la SITM (Leeds 1974). Leeds: University of Leeds Press, 1975.

Actes du IIe Colloque de la SITM (Alençon 1977): Gari Muller éd. Le Théâtre au Moyen Âge. Montréal: L'Aurore, 1981.

Actes du IVe Colloque de la SITM (Viterbo, 1983): Maria Chiabò, F. Doglio, M. Maymone, éd. Atti del IV Colloquio della Società Internationale pour l'Étude du Théâtre Médiéval. Viterbo, 1983.

Actes du Ve Colloque de la SITM (Perpignan, 1986): Jean-Claude Aubailly, éd. Le Théâtre et la Cité. *Fifteenth-Century Studies* 13 (1988).

Actes du VIe Colloque de la SITM (Lancaster 1989): ed. Meg Twycross, Festive Drama. Cambridge: Brewer, 1996.

Actes du VIIe Colloque de la SITM (Gérone, 1992): ed. Francesc Massip. Formes Teatrals de la Tradició Medieval. Barcelona: Institut del Teatre, 1995.

Aebischer, Paul. "Fragments de moralités, farces et mystères retrouvés à Fribourg." *Romania* 51 (1925): 511–27; voir aussi: *Archivum Romanicum* 4 (1920): 342–61; 7 (1923): 288–336; 15 (1931): 512–40.

—. "Jasme Oliou, versificateur et auteur dramatique avignonais du XVe siècle." Dans Aebischer, *Neuf Études sur le Théâtre Médiéval*. Geneva: Droz, 1972. 37–65.

—. "L'auteur probable des farces en franco-provençal jouées à Vevey vers 1520." Ibid.: 144–54.

—. "Le lieu d'origine et la date des fragments de farces en franco-provençal." Ibid.: 117–43.

—. "Le théâtre dans le Pays de Vaud à la fin du moyen âge." Ibid.: 155–74.

—. "Un *Miracle de saint Nicolas* représenté à Avignon vers 1470." *Annales d'Avignon et du Comtat Venaissin* 18 (1932): 5–40.

—. "Un rôle d'une farce franco-provençale." Dans *Neuf Études sur le Théâtre Médiéval*. Geneva: Droz, 1972. 83–93.

—. "Une oeuvre littéraire valdôtaine? Le *Mystère de Saint Bernard de Menton*." *Augusta Praetoria* 7 (1925): 49–61.

—. *Neuf Études sur le Théâtre Médiéval*. Geneva: Droz, 1972.

Aimont, C. *Le Théâtre à Verdun à la fin du moyen âge*. Paris: 1910 (extrait des *Mémoires de la Societé des Lettres, Sciences et Arts de Bar-le-Duc*, quatrième série, 7).

Allegri, Luigi. *Teatro e spettacolo nel Medioevo*. Roma-Bari: LaTerza, 1988.

Andresen, Helga. "Bruchstück eines altfranzösischen Mystère." *Zeitschrift für romanische Philologie* 26 (1902): 76–100.

Andrus, Toni W. *The Devil on the Medieval Stage in France*. PhD thèse inédite, Syracuse University 1979; résumé dans *Treteaux* 3 (1981): 47–81.

Angeli, G. "Un esempio de bilinguismo nel teatro francese del Quattrocento." Dans *Testi e Interpretazioni*. Milan: Ricciardi, 1978. 3–35.

Anis, A-F. *Une page d'histoire locale. Les mystères représentés à Laval de 1493 à 1538*. Laval: Chaillaud, 1887.

Ashley, Kathleen M. "The Bourgeois Piety of Martha in the *Passion* of Jean Michel." *Modern Language Quarterly* 45 (1984): 227–40.

Aubailly, Jean-Claude. "L'Image du prince dans le théâtre de Gringore (*Vie de S. Louis*)" dans *Le Pouvoir Monarchique et ses supports idéologiques aux XIVe–XVIIe siècles*. Études réunies par Jean Dufournet, A. Fiorato et A. Redondo. Paris: Publications de l'Université de Paris IV–Sorbonne nouvelle, 1990. 175–83.

—. "Préface" de la réimpression (par Slatkine Reprints) de l'édition de la *Vie de Monseigneur saint Louis par personnages* de Pierre Gringore (éd. Francisque Michel; London, 1871), 1976. 1–49.

—. "Théâtre médiéval et fêtes calendaires." *Réforme Humanisme Renaissance* 11 (1980): 5–11.

—. "Variations dramatiques sur la parabole du fils prodigue à la fin du Moyen Âge." Dans *"Et c'est la fin pour quoy sommes ensemble": Hommage à Jean Dufournet. Littérature, histoire et langue du Moyen Âge*, edited by Jean-Claude Aubailly. 3 vols. Paris: Champion, 1993. 109–24.

Audisio, Gabriel, et I. Bonnot-Rambaud, *Lire le français d'hier: manuel de paléographie moderne, XVe–XVIIIe siècle*. Paris: Armand Colin, 1991 (vol. 1).

Axelsen, Angelina. *Supernatural Beings in the French Medieval Drama, with Special Reference to the Miracles of the Virgin*. Copenhagen: Munksgaard, 1923.

Axton, Richard. *European Drama of the Early Middle Ages*. London: Hutchinson, 1974.

Bapst, Germain. *Essai sur l'histoire du théâtre. La mise en scène, le décor, le costume, l'architecture, l'éclairage, l'hygiène.* Paris: Hachette, 1893.

—. *Étude sur les Mystères au Moyen Âge.* Paris: Leroux, 1892.

Bar, F. "Un cas de style 'humanistique': *Le Mystère de saint Didier.*" *Actes du Xe Congrès international de linguistique et de philologie romane* (Strasbourg, 1962). 2 vols. Paris: Klincksieck, 1965. II, 589–604.

Baugh, Albert C. "The Chester Plays and French Influence." Dans *Schelling Anniversary Studies.* New York: Russell and Russell, 1969. 35–63.

Baur, August. *Beitrag zu Untersuchungen über mittelalterliche Moral auf Grund der Miracles de Nostre Dame par Personnages.* Zürich, 1910.

Beauchamps, Pierre-François. *Recherches sur les théâtres en France.* 3 vols. Paris: Prault, 1735.

Beck, Jonathan. "Sainte-Apolline: l'image d'un spectacle, le spectacle d'une image." Dans André Lascombes ed. *Spectacle and Image in Renaissance Europe.* Leiden: Brill, 1993. 232–44.

Becker, Carl. *Die Mysterien "Le Siège d'Orléans" und "La Destruction de Troye la grant," eine sprachliche Untersuchung.* Marburg: R. Friedrich, 1886.

Bernard, P. "Le drame liturgique pour la *Présentation de la Sainte Vierge au Temple* de Philippe de Mézères (1372): entre hapax théâtral et chanson liturgique." Dans *Théâtre et spectacles hier et aujourd'hui.* 3 vols. Paris: Éditions du CTHS, 1991. I, 93–113.

Berriat Saint-Prix, J. *Remarques sur les anciens jeux de mystères faits à l'occasion de deux délibérations inédites prises par le conseil de ville de Grenoble en 1535 relativement à l'un de ces jeux.* Paris: Smith, 1823.

Beuve, O. *Le Théâtre à Troyes aux XVe et XVIe siècles.* Paris: Champion, 1913.

Biais, E. "Le théâtre à Angoulême: XVe siècle–1904." *Réunion des Sociétés des Beaux-Arts des Départements.* Paris: Plon, 1904.

Bibolet, Jean-Claude. "Les Descendants d'Adam et Ève dans trois mystères du XVe siècle." Dans *Les Relations de parenté dans le monde médiéval. Senefiance* 26 (1989): 425–36.

—. "Les Manifestations de la vieillesse dans le *Mystère de la Passion* d'Arnoul Gréban et dans le *Mystère de la Passion* de Troyes." Dans *Vieillesse et vieillissement au Moyen Âge. Senefiance* 19 (1987): 9–19.

Billington, Sandra. "Social Disorder, Festive Celebration, and Jean Michel's *Mistere de la Passion Jesus Crist.*" *Comparative Drama* 29 (1995): 216–47.

—. "King and Queen Games in English Mystery and French Passion Plays." In *Custom, Culture and Community in the Later Middle Ages*, ed. . Tom Pettitt et L. Sondergaard. Odense: Odense University Press, 1994. 85–104.

—. *Midsummer: A Cultural Sub-Text from Chrétien de Troyes to Jean Michel.* Turnhout: Brepols, 2000.

Billon, J. "Histoire du théâtre de Laon et de Soissons." *Mémoires de la Fédération des Sociétés Savantes de l'Aisne* 3 (1956): 64–73.

Blum, Claude. "La folie et la mort dans l'imaginaire collectif du Moyen Âge et au début de la Renaissance (XIIe–XVIe siècles): position du problème." In Herman Braet et al., ed. *Death in the Middle Ages.* Louvain: Leuven University Press, 1983. 258–85.

—. "Le fou, personnage populaire dans les mystères et les miracles." Dans *Aspects du théâtre populaire en Europe au XVIe siècle.* Éd. Madeleine Lazard. Paris: SEDES, 1989. 43–50.

Bodenheimer, Marie-Odile. "La représentation théâtrale de la violence dans quelques *Miracles de Nostre Dame par personnages.*" Dans *La Violence dans le monde médiéval. Senefiance* 36 (1994): 55–67.

—. "Le rôle de la mère dans les *Miracles de Nostre Dame par personnages.*" *Bien Dire et Bien Aprandre: Revue de médiévistique* # 6, *La Mère au Moyen Age.* Lille: Centre d'Études médiévales et dialectales de l'Université de Lille III, 1998. 490–98.

Borderie, A. "Représentations dramatiques en Bretagne aux XVe et XVIe siècles." *Bulletin de la Société des Bibliophiles Bretons* 1 (1878).

Bordier, Jean-Pierre. "Art du faux, miroir du vrai: les Mystères de la Passion (XVe siècle)." In André Lascombes, ed. *Spectacle and Image in Renaissance Europe.* Leyden: Brill, 1993. 60–79.

—. éd. *L'Économie du Dialogue dans l'ancien théâtre européen: Actes de la première rencontre sur l'ancien théâtre européen*, réunis par Jean-Pierre Bordier. Paris: Champion, 1999.

—. "Eustache Mercadé auteur de la *Passion d'Arras* et de la *Vengeance Nostre Seigneur*." Dans Marie-Madeleine Castellani et J.-P. Martin, ed. *Arras au Moyen Âge. Histoire et Littérature*. Arras: Artois Presses Université, 1994. 197–218.

—. *Le Jeu de la Passion: le message chrétien et le théâtre français (XIIIe– XVIe siècle)*. Paris: Champion, 1998.

—. éd. *Le Jeu Théâtral, ses marges, ses frontières: Actes de la deuxième rencontre sur l'Ancien Théâtre Européen*. Paris: Champion, 1999.

—. éd. *Langues, Codes et Conventions de l'ancien théâtre: Actes de la troisième rencontre sur l'ancien théâtre européen*. Paris: Champion, 1999.

—. "Lectures du *Palatinus*." *Le Moyen Âge* 80 (1974): 429–82.

—. "Magis mouent exempla quam uerba: une définition du jeu théâtral dans la *Moralité du jour saint Antoine* (1427)." Dans Bordier, éd. *Le Jeu Théâtral, ses marges, ses frontières*. Paris: Champion, 1999. 91–104.

—. "*Le Mystère d'Orléans*: de la politique à la religion." *Perspectives Médiévales* 18 (1992): 54–66.

—. "La *Passion* de Jean Michel et le nominalisme." Dans Michel Zink éd., *L'Hostellerie de Pensée. Études sur l'Art littéraire au Moyen Âge offertes à Daniel Poirion par ses anciens élèves*. Paris: Presses de l'Université de Paris-Sorbonne, 1995. 85–89.

—. "Les Quatre Requêtes de Notre-Dame." Dans Bordier, éd. *Économie du Dialogue dans l'Ancien Théâtre Européen: Actes de la Première Rencontre sur l'ancien théâtre européen*. Paris: Champion, 1999. 187–210.

—. "Rome contre Jérusalem: la légende de la *Vengeance Jhesucrist*." Dans *Jérusalem, Rome, Constantinople: l'Image et le mythe de la ville*, ed. Daniel Poirion. Paris: Presses de l'Université de Paris IV–Sorbonne, 1986. 93–123.

—. "Théophanie négative, amour des images: deux théâtres religieux au moyen âge." Dans J.-M. Houpert et P. Petitier, éd. *De l'irreprésentable en littérature*. Paris: l'Harmattan, 2001. 37–64.

Borgnet, J. "Recherches sur les anciennes fêtes namuroises." *Mémoires couronnés de l'Académie royale de Belgique* 27 (1885).

Bossuat, André. "Fragments d'un *Mystère de Sainte Agathe.*" *Bibliothèque d'Humanisme et Renaissance* 8 (1946): 182–97.

—. "Le théâtre à Clermont-Ferrand au XVIe et XVIIe siècles." *Bibliothèque d'Humanisme et Renaissance* 23 (1961): 105–71.

—. "Note sur les représentations théâtrales en Basse-Auvergne au XVe siècle." Dans *Mélanges Cohen*. Paris: Nizet, 1950. 177–83.

—. "Une représentation d'un Mystère de la Passion à Montferrand en 1477," *Bibliothèque d'Humanisme et Renaissance* 5 (1944): 327–45.

Bossuat, Robert. *Manuel Bibliographique de la Littérature Française du Moyen Âge.* Paris: Éditions du Centre National de la Recherche Scientifique, 1951; suppléments: I, 1955; II, 1961; III, 1986.

—. "Nicole Oresme et le théâtre à Paris au XIVe siècle," *Bulletin de la Société des Historiens du Théâtre* 1 (1933): 17–22.

Bouhaïk-Gironès, Marie. "Les clercs et les écoliers, auteurs de théâtre profane à Paris à la fin du XVe siècle et au début du XVIe siècle." *Le Théâtre français des années 1450–1550. État actuel des recherches.* Textes réunis par Olga Anna Duhl. Dijon: Centre de Recherches Le Texte et l'Édition, Université de Dijon, 2002. 29–36.

—. "Le Théâtre médiéval et l'espace parisien à la fin du Moyen Âge." *European Medieval Drama* 6 (2002): 49–64.

Bourgeois, Théodore. "Le personnage de la Sybille et la légende de l'*Ara Coeli* dans une Nativité wallonne." *Revue Belge de Philologie et d'Histoire* 18 (1939): 883–912.

Boutillier, Abbé. "Mystères et moralités du Moyen Âge joués par personnages ou simplement figurés aux entrées des princes dans la ville de Nevers." *Bulletin de la Société nivernaise des Sciences, des Lettres et des Arts* 8 (1880): 146–60.

Boutiot, T. "Recherches sur le théâtre à Troyes au XVe siècle." *Mémoires de la Société d'Agriculture, des Sciences, Arts et Belles-Lettres du Département de l'Aube* 18, 2ème série, 5 (1854): 419–54.

Braet, Herman, J. Nowé, et G. Tournoy, ed. *The Theatre in the Middle Ages.* Louvain: Leuven University Press, 1985.

Brandenburg, M. *Die festen Strophengebilde und einige metrische Künsteleien des Mystère de Sainte Barbe, ihr weiteres Vorkommen und ihre verwandten Formen in anderen Mysterien.* Greifswald: Reineke, 1907.

Brooks, Neil C. "Notes on Performances of French Mystery Plays." *Modern Language Notes* 39 (1924): 276–81.

Brouchoud, C. *Les Origines du Théâtre de Lyon: mystères, farces et tragédies. Troupes ambulantes.* Lyon: Scheuring, 1865.

Brouwers, D. "Fêtes publiques à Dinant du XVe au XVIIIe siècle." *Annales de la Société Archéologique de Namur* 28 (1990): 59–?

Brown, Cynthia J. "Du nouveau sur le *mistere* des *Douze Dames de Rhétorique*: le rôle de Georges Chastellain." *Bulletin de la Commission Royale d'Histoire* 153 (1987): 181–221.

Bulard, M. "Un manuscrit du *Mystère de la Passion* découvert en Savoie." *Mélanges de la Société Toulousaine d'Études Classiques* 1 (1947): 260–65.

Bürger, P. *Über typische Durchbrechungen der dramatischen Einheit im französischen Theater in seiner Entwicklung bis an den Ausgang der klassischen Zeit: Das mittelalterliche Theater.* Breslau: Markus, 1901.

Burgoyne, Lynda. "La rime mnémonique et la structuration du texte dramatique médiéval." *Le Moyen Français* 29 (1991): 7–20.

Busch, Robert L. *Über die Beteuerungs- und Beschwörungsformeln in den Miracles de Nostre Dame par personnages.* Marburg, 1886.

Butterworth, Philip. "Jean Fouquet's 'The Martyrdom of St. Apollonia' and 'The Rape of the Sabine Women' as Iconographical Evidence of Medieval Theatre Practice." *Leeds Studies in English* 29 (1998): 55–68.

———. *Theatre of Fire: Special Effects in Early English and Scottish Theatre.* London: Society for Theatre Research, 1998.

Caieu, P. de. "Le Théâtre à Abbeville." *Mémoires de la Société d'Émulation d'Abbeville*, IVe série, 20 (1889).

Callahan, Leslie A. "The Torture of Saint Apollonia: Deconstructing Fouquet's Martyrdom Stage." *Studies in Iconography* 16 (1994): 119–38.

Calonne, le Baron A. de. "Une représentation à Amiens en 1500." *Mémoires de la Société des Antiquaires de la Picardie* 17 (1881).

Campbell, Thomas P. "Cathedral Chapter and Town Council: Cooperative Ceremony and Drama in Medieval Rouen." *Comparative Drama* 27 (1993): 100–13.

Cariani, Gianni. "Autorité et théâtre à la fin du Moyen Age." *Revue d'Histoire du Théâtre* 4 (1993): 35–44.

Carlier, E. *Le Mystère de Valenciennes en 1547.* Valenciennes: Girard, 1878.

Carlson, Marla. "Spectator Responses to an Image of Violence: Seeing Apollonia." *Fifteenth-Century Studies* 27 (2002): 7–20.

—. "Painful Processions in Late Medieval Paris." *European Medieval Drama* 6 (2002): 65–82.

Carnahan, David. *The Prologue in the Old French and Provençal Mystery Play.* New Haven: The Tuttle, Morehouse & Taylor Company, 1905.

Carpenter Sarah, et G. A. Runnalls. "The Entertainments at the Marriage of Mary Queen of Scots and the French Dauphin François, 1558: Paris and Edinburgh." *Medieval English Theatre* 22 (2000 [2002]): 145–61.

Cartier, M. "Représentations dramatiques à Amboise aux XVe et XVIe siècles." *Mémoires de la Société des Antiquaires de l'Ouest* 8 (1841): 241–58.

Cazal, Yvonne. "L'épaisseur d'un signe: le recours à la langue vulgaire dans le drame latin des XIIe et XIIIe siècles." Dans Jean-Pierre Bordier, éd. *Langues, Codes et Conventions de l'ancien théâtre*. Paris: Champion, 2002. 7–20.

Cazelles, Brigitte. "Bodies on Stage and the Production of Meaning." *Yale French Studies* 86 (1994): 56–74.

Chabaneau, C. "Le rôle de Moréna, du *Mystère* provençal *des Innocents.*" *Revue des Langues Romanes* 7 (1882): 414–18.

Chambers, E. K. *The Mediaeval Stage.* 2 vols. Oxford: Oxford University Press, 1903.

Champion, Pierre. *Histoire Poétique du XVe siècle.* 2 vols. Paris: Champion, 1923.

Charpentier, Hélène. "Figures de la mère dans le *Mystère du Vieux Testament.*" *Bien Dire et Bien Aprendre: Revue de médiévistique,* # 6: *La Mère au Moyen Âge.* Lille: Centre d'Études médiévales et dialectales de l'Université de Lille III, 1998. 59–70.

—. "Le rire et le comique dans le *Mistere du Viel Testament*." Dans *Le Rire au Moyen Âge*, ed. Thérèse Bouché et H. Charpentier. Talence: Presses Universitaires de Bordeaux, 1990. 107–35.

Charvet, E. *Recherches sur les anciens théâtres de Beauvais*. Beauvais: Père, 1881.

Chatelain, Henri L. *Recherches sur le vers français au XVe siècle: rimes, mètres et strophes*. Paris: Champion, 1908 (Genève: Slatkine Reprints, 1974).

Chauvin, M. *The Role of Mary Magdalene in Medieval Drama*. Washington: Catholic University of America Press, 1951.

Chiabò, Maria et F. Doglio. Ed. *Esperienze dello spettacolo religioso nell'Europa del Quattrocento*. Viterbo: Centro Studi del Teatro Medioevale et Rinascimentale, 1993.

Chocheyras, Jacques. "La *Conversion de la Madeleine* représentée à Auriol en 1543." *Recherches et Travaux, Université de Grenoble, Lettres, Bulletin* 26 (1984): 25–42.

—. "La Place du *Mystère de Saint Bernard de Menthon* dans le théâtre de son époque." Dans *Histoire Linguistique de la Vallée d'Aoste du Moyen Âge au XVIIIe siècle*. Vallée d'Aoste, 1985. 185–89.

—. "La *Vie de sainte Marie Madeleine par personnages*: illustrations." Dans *Aspects du théâtre populaire en Europe au XVIe siècle*, éd. Madeleine Lazard. Paris: SEDES, 1989. 173–79.

—. "Les Éditions de la *Passion* de Jean Michel au XVIe siècle." *Romania* 87 (1966): 175–93.

—. "Où sont les manuscrits du théâtre religieux de Savoie du XVIe siècle?" Dans *Actes du Congrès des Sociétés Savantes des Départements* 90 (1965). Paris: Bibliothèque Nationale, 1966. 685–90.

—. *Le Théâtre Religieux en Dauphiné du Moyen Âge au XVIIIe siècle*. Geneva: Droz, 1975.

—. *Le Théâtre Religieux en Savoie*. Geneva: Droz, 1971.

Choux, J. "Un mystère joué à Dombasle en 1537." *Annales de l'Est* 20 (1968): 119–21.

Christ, Marinus. "Die Aufführung von Mysterien in Issoudun und Bourges (1536) nach dem Bericht der Zimmerischen Chronik." *Zeitschrift für französische Sprache und Literatur* 46 (1922): 315–20.

Clark, Robert L. "Charity and Drama: the Response of the Confraternity to the Problem of Urban Poverty in Fourteenth-Century France." Dans *Actes du Ve Colloque de la SITM (Perpignan, 1986)*: ed. Jean-Claude Aubailly, *Le Théâtre et la Cité dans l'Europe médiévale*, dans *Fifteenth-Century Studies* 13 (1988): 359–69.

—. "Community Versus Subject in Late Medieval French Confraternity Drama and Ritual." Dans Alan Hindley, ed. *Drama and Community: People and Plays in Medieval Europe*. Turnhout: Brepols, 1999. 34–56.

—. "Othered Bodies: Racial Cross-Dressing in the *Mistère de la Sainte Hostie* and the Croxton *Play of the Sacrament*." *Journal of Medieval and Early Modern Studies* 29 (1999): 61–87.

—. et Sheingorn, Pamela. "Performative Reading: the Illustrated Manuscripts of Gréban's *Mystère de la Passion*." *European Medieval Drama* 6 (2002): 129–54.

Clouzot, Henri. "Le Théâtre populaire de Doué en Anjou." *Revue d'Art Dramatique* (1902): pages ?

—. "Un ordonnateur de mystères, Jean Bouchet," *Revue des Provinces de l'Ouest* 5 (1901): 151–54.

—. *L'Ancien Théâtre en Poitou*. Niort: L. Clouzot, 1901.

Cohen, Gustave. "Fragment Inédit d'un Mystère de la Passion." Dans *Festschrift Édouard Wechssler. Berliner Beiträge zur romanischen Philologie* 1 (1929): 208–16.

—. "La mise en scène au XVIe siècle: la présentation de Marie au Temple." *Revue d'Histoire du Théâtre* 3 (1958): 155–67.

—. "Le costume dans le théâtre religieux du moyen âge." *Revue de Belgique* 38 (1903): 29–53.

—. "Le livre de scène du *Mystère de la Passion* joué à Mons." Dans *Mélanges Gustave Lanson*. Paris: Champion, 1922. 63–76.

—. "Le personnage de Marie-Madeleine dans le drame religieux français du Moyen Âge." *Convivium* 24 (1956): 141–63.

—. "Le personnage de saint Joseph dans le *Grand Mystère de la Passion* d'Arnoul Gréban." *Cahiers de Josephologie* (Montréal) 4 (1956): 181–200.

—. "Le plus ancien document du théâtre liégeois: Mystères et moralités du ms. 217 de Chantilly." Dans *Études de dialectologie romane: dédiées à la mémoire de Charles Grandgagnage*. Paris: Droz, 1932. 79–95.

—. "Le Théâtre à Paris et aux environs au quatorzième siècle." *Romania* 37 (1909): 587–95.

—. "Le thème de l'aveugle et du paralytique dans la littérature française." Dans *Mélanges M. Wilmotte*. Paris: Champion, 1910. 393–494.

—. "Le vocabulaire de la scénologie médiévale: lieu ou mansion." *Zeitschrift für französische Sprache und Literatur* 66 (1956): 15–21.

—. "Le Vrai Mystère de Saint Sébastien." *Grande Revue* (25-6-1911): 673–87.

—. "Mystères religieux et profanes en Avignon à la fin du XIVe siècle." *Neophilologus* 24 (1938): 310–13.

—. "Notes sur le *Mystère de S. Quentin*." *Romania* 39 (1910): 92–93.

—. "Notre-Dame, d'après A. Gréban et J. Michel." *Revue des Deux Mondes* 23 (1923): 402–23.

—. "Un terme de la scénologie médiévale." Dans *Mélanges Huguet*. Paris: Droz, 1940. 52–58.

—. "Une grande représentation théâtrale en juillet 1501." Dans Cohen, *Études d'Histoire du théâtre en France au Moyen Âge et à la Renaissance*. Paris: Gallimard, 1956. 231–44.

—. *Études d'Histoire du Théâtre en France au Moyen Âge et à la Renaissance*. Paris: Gallimard, 1956.

—. *Histoire de la Mise en scène dans le théâtre religieux français du Moyen Âge*. Paris: Champion, 1926.

—. *Le Livre de Conduite du Régisseur et le Compte des Dépenses pour le Mystère de la Passion joué à Mons en 1501*. Paris: Champion, 1925.

—. *Le Mystère de la Passion joué à Mons en juillet 1501. Livre des Prologues. Matinée IIIe*. Gembloux: Duculot. (Société Belge des Bibliophiles séant à Mons, tiré à 216 exemplaires): 1957.

—. *Le Théâtre à Huy au XVe siècle*. Huy, 1922.

—. *Le Théâtre en France au Moyen Âge*. Paris: Presses Universitaires de France, 1948.

—. *Le Théâtre Français en Belgique au Moyen Âge*. Bruxelles: Renaissance du Livre, 1953.

Coleman, Joyce. *Public Reading and the Reading Public in Late Medieval England and France*. Cambridge: Cambridge University Press, 1996.

Collingwood, Sharon. *Market Pledge and Gender Bargain: Commercial Relations in French Farce, 1450–1550*. New York: Peter Lang, 1996.

Combarieu du Grès, Micheline de, et J. Subrenat. Arnoul Gréban, *Le Mystère de la Passion de Notre Sauveur Jésus-Christ: traduction (en français moderne) et présentation*. Paris: Gallimard, 1987.

—. "Ceux d'Orléans: les Orléanais dans le *Mystère du Siège d'Orléans*." *Perspectives Médiévales* 18 (1992): 44–53.

—. "Dieu le Père, Dieu le Fils dans le mystère de la Passion d'Arnoul Gréban." Dans *Les Relations de parenté dans le monde médiéval*. *Senefiance* 26 (1989): 437–68.

Coornaert, E. *Les Corporations en France avant 1789*. Paris: Gallimard, 1941.

Cornagliotti, Anna. "Apocryphes et mystères." Dans Gari Muller, éd.: *Le Théâtre au Moyen Âge*. Montréal: L'Aurore, 1981. 67–78.

Couffon, O. "L'amphithéâtre de Douces." *Bulletin de Mayenne-Sciences*. Laval: Université de Laval, 1912–13.

Couturier, Mary, et G. A. Runnalls. *Compte du Mystère de la Passion à Châteaudun 1510*. Chartres: Société Archéologique d'Eure-et-Loir, 1991.

Craig, Barbara. "Didactic Elements in Medieval French Serious Drama." *Esprit Créateur* 2 (1962): 142–48.

—. "Prefiguration and Literary Creativity in the *Sacrifice d'Abraham* of the *Mistere du Viel Testament*." Dans Raymond Cormier et E. Sellin, ed. *Voices of Conscience*. Philadelphia: Temple University Press, 1974. 183–98.

—. *The Evolution of a Mystery Play*. Orlando: French Literature Publications, 1983.

—. "The Staging and Dating of the *Mystère du Siège d'Orléans*." *Res Publica Litterarum* 5 (1982): 70–83.

Crist, Larry S. "La Chute de l'Homme sur la scène dans la France du XIIe et du XVe siècle." *Romania* 99 (1978): 207–19.

Crohn-Schmidt, Natalie. "Was There a Medieval Theatre in the Round?" Dans Jerome Taylor and A. Nelson, ed. *Medieval English Drama: Essays Critical and Contextual.* Chicago: University of Chicago Press, 1972.

Cuisard, C. "Mystères joués à Fleury et à Orléans." *Lectures et Mémoires de l'Académie de Sainte-Croix d'Orléans* 4 (1880): 284–313.

Dabrowka, Andrzrej, "Trial Scenes in Medieval Drama." Dans Sydney Higgins et F. Paino, ed. *European Medieval Drama, 1998.* Camerino: Università degli Studi di Camerino, 1999. 77–98.

Dahan, G. "Les Juifs dans le théâtre religieux en France du XIIe au XIXe siècle." *Archives Juives* 13 (1977): 1–10.

David, C. *Die drei Mysterien des Heiligen Martin von Tours. Ihr Verhältnis und ihre Quelle.* Frankfurt am Main, 1899.

Davidson, Clifford, ed. *The Saint Play in Medieval Europe.* Kalamazoo: Medieval Institute Publications, 1986.

—. et al., ed. *The Drama of the Middle Ages. Comparative and Critical Esssays.* New York: AMS Press, 1982.

—, ed. *Gesture in Medieval Drama and Art.* Kalamazoo: MIP, 2000.

—, ed. *Material Culture and Medieval Drama.* Kalamazoo: MIP, 1999.

Decugis, Nicole et S. Reymond. *Le Décor de Théâtre en France du Moyen Âge à 1925.* Paris: Compagnie française des arts graphiques, 1953.

Deierkauf-Holsboer, Sophie. "Représentations à Athis-sur-Gorge en 1542." Dans *Mélanges Cohen.* Paris: Nizet, 1950. 199–203.

Delbouille, Maurice. "De l'intérêt des Nativités hutoises de Chantilly et de Liège." Dans *Mélanges Cohen.* Paris: Nizet, 1950. 75–84.

—. "Essai sur la genèse des Nativités wallonnes de Chantilly et sur leur adaptation au XVIIe siècle." Dans *Mélanges Jean Haust.* Liège, 1939. 97–125.

Delisle, L. "Documents parisiens de la Bibliothèque de Berne." *Mémoires de la Société de l'Histoire de Paris et d'Île-de-France* 23 (1896): 225–98.

Demartres, A. *Histoire et Organisation de la Confrérie Parisienne de la Passion (1402-1677)*. Thèse (inédite) de l'École des Chartes, 1939 [exemplaire photocopié déposé aux Archives Nationales de France, Paris; coté en sous-série AB XXVIII {thèses et diplômes}]. Résumé dans: *Position des Thèses*: Écoles des Chartes, 1939. 43–52.

—. "La Confrérie de la Passion." *Bulletin de la Société des Historiens* 7 (1939): 20–29.

—. "La Confrérie de la Passion: recrutement et fonctionnement." *Bulletin de la Société d'Histoire du Théâtre* 8 (1939): 20–29.

Despierre, Gabriel. *Le Théâtre et les Comédiens d'Alençon au XVe siècle*. Paris: Plon, 1892.

Destranges, Étienne. *Le Théâtre à Nantes depuis ses origines jusqu'à nos jours (1430-1901)*. Paris: Fishenbacher, 1902.

Detcheverry, A. *Histoire des théâtres de Bordeaux depuis leur origine jusqu'à nos jours*. Bordeaux, 1860.

Devaux, Jean. *Deux représentations de mystères à Pithiviers en 1528*. Paris, 1892.

—. "Edification et Grande Rhétorique: Jean Molinet et le *Mystère de Saint Quentin*." *Revue d'Histoire Religieuse du Comté et de la Province d' Hainaut* 17 (1996): 16–26.

Devilliers, L. "Anciens Usages, fêtes et solennités à Mons." *Annales du Cercle archéologique de Mons* 9 (1869): 321 et seq.

Di Stefano, Giuseppe. "A propos de la rime mnémonique." Dans Bruno Roy et P. Zumthor, ed. *Jeux de mémoire. Aspects de la mnémotechnique médiévale*. Montréal-Paris: Vrin, 1985. 35–42.

—. "Structure métrique et structure dramatique dans le théâtre médiéval." Dans Herman Braet et al. ed. *The Theatre in the Middle Ages*. Leuven: Leuven University Press, 1985. 194–206.

—. et R. Bidler, ed. *La Langue, le Texte, le Jeu: Perspectives sur le théâtre médiéval. Le Moyen Français* 19 (1986).

Dictionnaire des Lettres Françaises. Le Moyen Âge, ed. Geneviève Hasenohr et M. Zink. Paris: Fayard, 1992.

Dictionnaire des Lettres Françaises: Le XVIe siècle, éd. Michel Simonin. Paris: Fayard, 2001.

Dominguez, Véronique. "Une expérience de Dieu: Mystique et théâtre dans la quatrième journée du *Mystère de la Passion* d'Arnoul Gréban." *European Medieval Drama* 5 (2002): 1–16.

—. "Voir l'invisible au théâtre: les mystères de la foi dans quelques mystères de la Passion." Dans Michèle Gally et M. Jourde, ed. *Par la vue et par l'ouïe. Littérature du Moyen Âge et de la Renaissance*. Fontenay-aux-Roses: Éditions ENS, 1999: 111–34.

Douhet, Jules de. *Dictionnaire des Mystères* (dans Jacques Paul Migne, *Nouvelle Encyclopédie Théologique*, vol. 43). Paris: Migne, 1854.

Doutrepont, Georges. *La Littérature Française à la Cour des Ducs de Bourgogne*. Paris: Champion, 1909.

Drzewicka, Anna. "De la narration au jeu: les *Miracles de Notre-Dame*." *Cahiers de Varsovie* 19 (1992): 33–45.

Dubois, A. *Mystères joués à Amiens dans les XVe et XVIe siècles*. Amiens: Mémorial, 1878.

DuBruck, Edelgard E. "Changes of Taste and Audience Expectation in Fifteenth-Century Religious Drama," *Fifteenth-Century Studies* 6 (1983), 59–91 (Gréban vs. Michel).

—. "The Current State of Research on Late-Medieval Drama, 1992–93: Reviews, Notes, and Bibliography." *Fifteenth-Century Studies* 21 (1994), 17–53; 1993–94: vol. 22 (1996), 163–91; 1994–95: vol. 23 (1997), 236–57; 1995–96: vol. 24 (1998), 1–16; 1996–97: vol. 25 (2000), 365–85.

—. "The Current State of Research on Late-Medieval Drama, 1997–98. Survey, Bibliography and Reviews." *Fifteenth-Century Studies* 26 (2001): 1–20.

—. "The Current State of Research on Late-Medieval Drama: 1998–2000. Survey, Bibliography, and Reviews." *Fifteenth-Century Studies* 28 (2003): 1–36.

—. "The Death of Christ in French Passion Plays of the late Middle Ages: Its Aspects and Sociological Implications." Dans Jane H. M. Taylor, ed. *Dies Illa: Death in the Middle Ages*. Liverpool: Cairns, 1984. 81–92.

—. "The Death of Christ on the Late-Medieval Stage: A Theater of Salvation." 355–75 in *Death and Dying in the Middle Ages*, ed. E. DuBruck and Barbara I. Gusick. New York: Peter Lang, 1999.

—. "The Devil and Hell in Medieval French Drama." *Romania* 100 (1979): 165–79.

—. "Image — Text — Drama: the Iconography of the *Passion Isabeau (1398)*." 287–307 in *Studies in Honor of Hans-Erich Keller*, ed. Rupert Pickens. Kalamazoo: MIP, 1993.

—. "Lazarus's Vision of Hell: a Significant Passage in Late-Medieval Passion Plays." *Fifteenth-Century Studies* 27 (2002): 44–55.

—. "The Narrative *Passion of Our Lord Jesus Christ* Written in 1398 for Isabeau de Bavière, Queen of France: An Important Link in the Development of French Religious Drama." *Michigan Academician* 18 (1986), 95–106.

—. "The *Passion Isabeau* (1398) and Its Relationship to Fifteenth-Century *Mystères de la Passion*." *Romania* 107 (1986): 77–91.

—. "The Perception of Evil in Jean Michel's *Mystère de la Passion (1486)*." *Michigan Academician* 15 (1983): 253–63.

—. "The Theme of Self-Accusation in Early French Literature: Adam and Théophile." *Romania* 94 (1973), 410–18.

Dubuis, Roger. "Jeu narratif et jeu dramatique dans la littérature française du moyen âge." Dans Guy Mermier, ed. *Contemporary Readings of Medieval Literature*. Ann Arbor: Romance Languages, University of Michigan, 1989. 203–26.

Dufournet, Jean. "Les Jeux de l'intertextualité dans *Courtois d'Arras*: de la parabole évangélique à la farce." Dans Dufournet, éd. '*Si a parlé par moult ruiste vertu*': *Mélanges de Littérature Médiévale offerts à Jean Subrenat*. Paris: Champion, 2000. 197–208.

Duhl, Olga A., éd. *Le Théâtre français des années 1450–1550. État actuel des recherches*. Dijon: Centre de Recherches Le Texte et l'Édition, Université de Dijon, 2002.

Dull, Olga A. "À la recherche du jeu médiéval comique: texte, théorie et spectacle virtuel." Dans Giuseppe Di Stefano et R. Bidler, ed. *La Recherche: bilan et perspective*. Vol. I: *Moyen Français* 44–45; vol. II: *Moyen Français* 46–47. Montréal: Editions CERES, 1999. 209–21.

Dumont, Pascale. "Monologues, dialogues et mimes dans la gestion spatiotemporelle du *Jeu d'Adam* et du *Prologue* du *Mystère de la Passion* d'Arnoul Gréban." Dans Jean-Pierre Bordier, éd. *L'Économie du Dialogue dans l'Ancien Théâtre Européen*. Paris: Champion, 1999. 175–86.

———. "Du texte narratif au drame: codes et conventions d'ordre spatiotemporel dans quelques *Miracles de Nostre Dame par personnages*." Dans Bordier, éd. *Langues, Codes et Conventions de l'ancien théâtre*. Paris: Champion, 2002. 101–20.

Dupire, Noël. "Le *Mystère de la Passion* de Valenciennes." *Romania* 48 (1922): 571–84.

———. Jean Molinet: *La Vie, les oeuvres*. Paris: Droz, 1932.

———. "La *Passion de Molinet* (MS 560 de Valenciennes)." Dans Jean Molinet: *La Vie, les oeuvres*, 170–201.

Duplat, André. "Comparaison des quatre mystères de saint Martin récités ou présentés aux XVe et XVIe siècles, en français ou en provençal." Dans *Actes du IVe Colloque de la SITM (Viterbo, 1983)*, ed. Maria Chiabò, F. Doglio, et M. Maymone. Viterbo: Centro studi sul teatro medioevale e rinascimentale, 1984. 235–50.

Durrieu, A. "Le théâtre à Cambrai avant et après 1789." *Mémoires de la Société d'Émulation de Cambrai* 39 (1883): 5–241.

Dusevel, H. "Notes sur le théâtre à Amiens au XVIe siècle." *Revue des Sociétés Savantes*, 2e Série, 2 (1859): 107–10.

———. "Documents relatifs à la représentation du *Mystère de la Passion* dans la ville d'Amiens à la fin du quinzième siècle." Dans *Revue des Sociétés Savantes des Départements*, 3e série, 4 (1864): 388–89.

———. *Documents relatifs aux mystères et jeux de personnages représentés à Amiens pendant le XVe siècle*. Amiens: Caron-Vitet, 1842.

Dust, A. *Die Magdalenenszene in den französischen und provenzalischen geistlichen Spielen des Mittelalters*. Münster, 1939.

Emmerson, Richard K., et D. Hult. *Antichrist and Judgment Day: The Middle French 'Jour du Jugement'* (translated into English) with an Introduction. University of North Carolina at Asheville: Pegasus Press, 1998.

Enders, Jody. *Death by Drama and Other Medieval Urban Legends.* Chicago: University of Chicago Press, 2002.

––. "Medieval Snuff Drama." *Exemplaria* 10 (1998): 171–206.

––. *The Medieval Theater of Cruelty: Rhetoric, Memory, Violence.* Ithaca: Cornell University Press, 1999.

––. "The Music of the Medieval Body in Pain." *Fifteenth-Century Studies* 27 (2002): 93–112.

––. *Rhetoric and the Origins of Medieval Drama.* Ithaca-London: Cornell University Press, 1992.

Erler, O. Das "Mystère de Saint Denis." Marburg, 1896.

Faber, Frederick W. *Histoire du théâtre français en Belgique depuis son origine jusqu'à nos jours; d'après des documents inédits reposant aux archives générales du royaume.* 5 vols. Bruxelles: Olivier, 1878–80.

Faivre, Bernard. "Le dit et le joué." Dans Bordier, éd. *Le Jeu théâtral, ses marges, ses frontières.* Paris: Champion, 1999. 193–200.

Fallandy, Yvette. "A Reexamination of the Blessed Virgin in the *Miracles de Nostre Dame par personnages.*" *Philological Quarterly* 43 (1964): 20–26.

Faral, Edmond. *Les Jongleurs en France au moyen âge.* Paris: Champion, 1910.

Foley, Mary F. "Two Versions of the Flood: the Valenciennes Twenty-Day Play and the *Mystère de la Passion* of Mons." *Tréteaux* 2 (1980): 21–38.

Forkert, F. *Beiträge zu den Bildern aus dem altfranzösischen Volksleben auf Grund der Miracles de Nostre Dame par personnages.* Heidelberg: Niemeyer, 1901.

Fourman, J. "Über die Sprache des *Mystère de S. Bernard de Menthon* mit einer Einleitung über seine Überlieferung." *Romanische Forschungen* 32 (1913): 625–747.

––. *Über die Überlieferung und den Versbau des Mystère de S. Bernard de Menthon.* Erlangen, 1911.

Fournier, Édouard. *Le Théâtre Français avant la Renaissance.* Paris, 1872.

Foxton, Cynthia. "Hell and the Devil in Medieval French Drama." Dans Jane H. M. Taylor, ed. *Dies Illa. Death in the Middle Ages.* Liverpool: Cairns, 1984. 71-79.

—. *The Devil and the Diableries in the French Passion Play.* Ph.D., Edinburgh University, 1985 (thèse inédite).

Frank, Grace. "Critical Notes on the *Palatine Passion.*" *Modern Language Notes* 36 (1921): 193-204.

—. "Erasures in the Cangé MSS 819-820." *Romance Philology* 12 (1958-59): 240-43.

—. "Popular Iconography of the Passion." *Publications of the Modern Language Association of America* 46 (1931): 333-40.

—. "The Authorship of *Le Mystère de Griselidis.*" *Modern Language Notes* 51 (1936): 217-22.

—. "The *Palatine Passion* and the Development of the Passion Play." *Publications of the Modern Language Association of America* 35 (1920): 464-83.

—. "Vernacular Sources and a French Passion Play." *Modern Language Notes* 25 (1920): 257-69.

—. *The Medieval French Drama.* Oxford: Clarendon Press, 1954.

Franke, E. *Untersuchungen über das Mystère de la Conception.* Greifswald, 1909.

Fuzellier, E. "La Représentation du *Mystère de Saint Pierre et de Saint Paul* à Aix en 1444." *Mélanges Cohen.* Paris: Champion, 1950. 185-90.

Gailly de Tourines. "Une représentation du *Mystère de la Passion* à Mézières en 1531." *Revue d'Histoire Ardennaise* 10 (1903): 65-77.

Gallagher, Edward J. "Sources and Secondary Characterization in the Sainte-Geneviève *Passion Nostre Seigneur.*" *Neuphilologische Mitteilungen* 79 (1978): 173-79.

Gangler-Mundwiller, Dominique. "Les Diableries nécessaires: le rôle des scènes diaboliques dans l'action des Mystères de la Passion." Dans *Mélanges de littérature Jeanne Lods.* Paris: E.N.S.J.F., 1978. 249-68.

Geister, O. *Die Teufelszene in der Passion d'Arras und der Vengeance.* Greifswald, 1914.

Giese, H. *La Passion de Jésus Christ jouée à Valenciennes en 1547.* Greifswald, 1905.

Ginter, K. *La Société médiévale dans le théâtre du XIVe siècle (Miracles de Nostre Dame par personnages).* Thèse inédite, Nanterre, 1969.

Girardot, A. de. "Le *Mystère des Actes des Apôtres* joué à Bourges en 1536." *Annales Archéologiques* 13–14 (1853–54).

——. éd. *Le Mystère des Actes des Apôtres représenté à Bourges en avril 1536, publié d'après le manuscrit original.* Paris, 1854.

Giraud, M. *Composition, mise en scène et représentation du Mystère des Trois Doms.* Lyon: Perrin, 1848.

Giraud, Yves. *La Vie Théâtrale dans les provinces du Midi: Actes du IIe Colloque de Grasse, 1976.* Tübingen-Paris: Éditions Place, 1980.

Giry, A. "Notes sur l'influence artistique du Roi René." *Revue Critique d'Histoire et de Littérature,* vols. 45 et 46. Paris, 1875.

Giuliano, Paula. *Arnoul Gréban, The Mystery of the Passion: The Third Day (Translated into English).* Asheville, NC: Pegasus Press, 1996.

Glutz, Rudolf. *Les Miracles de Nostre Dame par personnages.* Berlin: Deutsche Akademie der Wissenschaften zu Berlin, 1954.

Gomperz, S. "La Justice et l'écriture. Transcendance et soumission dans le *Mystère de la Passion* d'Arnoul Gréban." *La Licorne* (1976): 73–93.

Goodman, Hadassah P. *Original Elements in the French and German Passion Plays.* Bryn Mawr: Bryn Mawr College, 1951.

Gosman, Martin et R. Walthaus. *European Theatre 1470–1600: Traditions and Transformations.* Groningen: Forsten, 1996.

Gosselin, E. "Simple note sur les anciens théâtres à Rouen du XVIe au XVIIIe siècle." *Revue de Normandie* 2 (1863): 139–45; 195–203; 232–41; 358–62; 436–44.

——. *Recherches sur les origines et l'histoire du théâtre à Rouen avant Pierre Corneille.* Rouen, 1868 (extrait de la *Revue de la Normandie,* 1867–68).

Gouvenain, L. de. "Le théâtre à Dijon (1422–1790)." *Mémoires Communales de la Côte d'Or* 9 (1885–88): 239–407.

Gros, Gérard. "L'Avocate et sa vocation: Étude sur la dramatisation d'une *propriété* mariale dans l'*Advocacie Nostre Dame*." Dans Bordier, éd. *Le Jeu Théâtral, ses marges, ses frontières*. Paris: Champion, 1999. 125–40.

——. "Du registre de confrérie à l'anthologie mariale (étude sur la conception du manuscrit Cangé. Paris: BNF, mss fr. 819–820)." Dans Daniel Poirion, éd. *Styles et Valeurs. Pour une histoire de l'art littéraire au Moyen Âge*. Paris: SEDES, 1990. 75–100.

——. "Étude sur les rondels des *Miracles de Nostre Dame par personnages*." Dans *Fêtes de la Renaissance* 3. Paris: CNRS, 1975. 547–53.

——. "Le Texte narratif au seuil de la dramatisation: l'exemple de l'*Advocacie Nostre-Dame*." Dans Bordier, éd. *Économie du Dialogue dans l'Ancien Théâtre Européen*. Paris: Champion, 1999. 53–68.

——. "Étude sur la deuxième journée du *Mystère de la Passion* joué à Jaillon (Piémont)." *Bulletin Philologique et Historique du comité des travaux historiques et scientifiques* 1 (1960): 501–11 (Paris: Imprimerie Nationale, 1961).

——. *Étude sur le Mystère de l'Antéchrist et du Jugement de Dieu, joué à Modane en 1580 et 1606, et fragment de la première journée*. Chambéry: Imprimeries réunies, 1962.

Guessard, François et de Certain, ed. *Le Mistere du Siège d'Orléans*. Documents inédits sur l'Histoire de France 7. Paris: Imprimerie impériale, 1862.

Guillaume, P. "Le rôle du Primus Minister du *Mystère provençal de Saint André*." *Revue des Langues Romanes* 21 (1896): 113–16.

Gussenhoven, Frances. "The Serpent with a Matron's Face: Medieval Iconography of Satan in the Garden of Eden." Dans *European Medieval Drama* 4 (2000): 207–30.

Guyon, G. "La Justice pénale dans le théâtre religieux du XIVe siècle: les *Miracles de Nostre Dame par personnages*." *Revue historique de droit français et étranger* (1991): 465–86.

Ham, Edward B. "The Basic Manuscript of the Marcadé *Vengeance*." *Modern Language Review* 29 (1934): 405–20.

Hamblin, Vicki. "Lire les didascalies du *Siege d'Orleans*: conventions théâtrales ou tradition commémorative?" Dans Bordier, éd. *Langues, Codes et Conventions de l'ancien théâtre*. Paris: Champion, 2002. 93–100.

——. "Le *Siege d'Orleans*: procession, simulacre, mystère." Dans Bordier, éd. *Le Jeu théâtral, ses marges, ses frontières*. Paris: Champion, 1999. 165–78.

Hamon, A. *Un Grand Rhétoriqueur poitevin: Jean Bouchet*. Paris: Champion, 1901.

Happé, Peter. "Performing Passion Plays in France and England." Dans *European Medieval Drama* 4 (2000): 57–76.

——. "Procession and the Cycle Drama in England and Europe." *European Medieval Drama* 6 (2002): 31–48.

Harris, John W. *Medieval Theatre in Context: An Introduction*. London: Routledge, 1992.

Hashim, James. "Notes Towards a Reconstruction of *Le Mystère des Actes des Apôtres* as Presented at Bourges, 1536." *Theatre Research International* 12 (1972): 29–73.

Hécart, C. *Recherches historiques, bibliographiques, critiques et littéraires sur le théâtre à Valenciennes*. Paris: Hécart, 1816.

Heers, Jacques. *Fêtes, jeux et joutes dans les sociétés d'Occident à la fin du Moyen Âge*. Montréal-Paris: Vrin, 1971.

Heffernan, Thomas J., and E. A. Matter. *The Liturgy of the Medieval Church*. Kalamazoo: MIP, 2000.

Heinze, Paul. *Die Engel auf der mittelalterlichen Mysterienbühne Frankreichs*. Diss. Greifswald, 1905.

Helmich, Werner. *Die Allegorie im französischen Theater des 15. und 16. Jahrhunderts*. Tübingen: Niemeyer, 1976.

Hénault, M. *La Représentation d'un Mystère de la Passion à Valenciennes au XVIe siècle (1547)*. Valenciennes, 1890.

Henrard, Nadine. "*Amis et Amile*: de la geste à la scène." *Le Moyen Âge* 96 (1990): 463–77.

—. "Zebel, Zélomi, Salomé, Anastasie. Les figures des sages-femmes de la Nativité dans la littérature du Moyen Âge." Dans *Jeux de la Variante. Mélanges offerts à Anna Drzewicka*. Cracovie: Viridis, 1997. 208-19.

—. "La *Passion d'Augsbourg*: un texte dramatique occitan?" Dans Nadine Henrard, P. Moreno, et M. Thiry-Stassin, éd. *Convergences Médiévales: épopée, lyrique, roman: Mélanges offerts à Madeleine Tyssens*. Bruxelles: De Boeck Université, 2001. 243-56.

—. *Le Théâtre religieux médiéval en langue d'oc*. Geneva: Droz, 1998.

Henry, Albert. "Mystères joués à Namur aux XVIIe et XVIIIe siècle." *Annales de la Société Archéologique de Namur* 41 (1934): 87-118.

Henshaw, M. "The Attitude of the Church Towards the Stage at the End of the Middle Ages." *Medievalia et Humanistica* 7 (1952): 3-17.

Herelle, G. "Les théâtres ruraux en France (langue d'oïl et langue d'oc) depuis le XIVe siècle à nos jours." Dans *Annexe aux Études sur le théâtre basque*. Paris: Champion, 1930.

Hess, H. *Studien zum Mistere du Viel Testament*. Frankfurt, 1936.

Hess, Rainer. *Das romanische geistliche Schauspiel als profane und religiöse Komödie, 15. und 16. Jahrhundert*. Munich: Fink, 1965.

Higgins, Sydney et F. Paina, éd. *European Medieval Drama 1997*. Camerino: Università degli Studi di Camerino, 2000. (Within *European Medieval Drama 1-3*: 1997-99.

Higman, F. *Piety and the People: Religious Printing in French 1511-1551*. Aldershot: Scolar Press, 1996.

Hillard, D. "La *Destruction de Jérusalem* en bande dessinée (Paris, vers 1515)." *Bulletin du Bibliophile* (1996): 302-40.

Hindley, Alan. "Acting Companies in Late Medieval France." Dans A. Hindley, ed. *Drama and Community: People and Plays in Medieval Europe*. Turnhout: Brepols, 1999. 78-98.

—. ed. *Drama and Community: People and Plays in Medieval Europe*. Turnhout: Brepols, 1999.

—. "Histoire locale du théâtre français: Moyen Âge et Renaissance." *Le Moyen Français* 35-36 (1994-95): 129-59.

—. "Preaching and Plays: The Sermon and the Late Medieval French Moralities." *Moyen Français* 42 (1998): 71–85.

Hinrichs, B. *Le Mystère de Saint Rémi. Manuskript der Arsenalbibliothek zu Paris, 3364, nach Quellen, Inhalt und Metrum untersucht.* Diss. Greifswald, 1907.

Hippe, M. *Le Mystère du Roy Advenir par Jehan du Prier.* Greifswald, 1906.

Histoire du théâtre en Anjou du Moyen Âge à nos jours: Actes du Colloque d'Angers. Dans *Revue d'Histoire du Théâtre* 43–44 (1991–92).

Hoffmann, M. *Die Magdalenszenen im geistlichen Spiel des Mittelalters.* Münster, 1933.

Hosley, R. "Three Kinds of Outdoor Theatre before Shakespeare." *Theatre Survey* 12 (1971): 1–33.

Houville, G. d.' "La mondanité et la conversion de Marie-Madeleine de Jehan Michel." *Revue des Deux Mondes* 20 (1934): 427–30.

—. "Le *Vrai Mystère de la Passion* d'Arnoul Gréban." *Revue des Deux Mondes* 34 (1936): 198–201.

Huard, A. "Le théâtre orléanais à travers les âges jusqu'à la fin du XVIIIe siècle." *Société d'Agriculture . . . d'Orléans. Mémoires*, série 3, 3 (1903): 181–273.

Hüe, Denis. "De la *disputatio* à l'*effusio*." Dans Bordier, éd. *Économie du Dialogue.* Paris: Champion, 1999. 69–88.

—. "*Griselidis* et sa mise en scène." Dans Bordier, éd. *Le Jeu Théâtral, ses marges, ses frontières.* Paris: Champion, 1999. 141–64.

Huguenin, J.-F. *Les Chroniques de la ville de Metz: 900–1552, recueillies, mises en ordre et publiées pour la première fois, par Huguenin . . . éditées par S. Lamort, enrichies du plan de Metz et des attaques dirigées contre cette ville par Charles-Quint en 1552.* Metz: Lamort, 1883.

—. *Les Chroniques de Metz.* Metz, 1838.

Hurlbut, Jesse. "The Sound of Civic Spectacle: Noise in Burgundian Ceremonial Entries." Dans Clifford Davidson, ed. *Material Culture and Medieval Drama.* Kalamazoo: MIP, 1999. 127–40.

Jacquot, A. "Notes pour servir à l'histoire du théâtre en Lorraine." *Réunion des Sociétés Savantes des Beaux-Arts des Départements* 16 (1892): 561–85.

Jacquot, J. et E. Konigson, éd. *Le Lieu théâtral à la Renaissance.* Paris: CNRS, 1968.

Jaroszewska, Teresa. *Le Vocabulaire du théâtre de la Renaissance en France (1540–1585): contribution à l'histoire du lexique théâtral.* Lodz: Wydawnictwo Uniwersytetu Lodzkiego, 1997.

—. "Le lexique théâtral français à l'époque de la Renaissance." *Zeitschrift für romanische Philologie* 116 (2000): 438–55.

Jeanroy, A. "Notes critiques sur la *Passion de Semur.*" *Revue des Langues Modernes* 49 (1906): 220–29.

—. "Sur quelques sources des Mystères de la Passion." *Romania* 35 (1906): 365–78.

—. "Les Quarante *Miracles de Nostre Dame par personnages.*" Dans Le *Théâtre religieux en langue française jusqu'à la fin du XIVe siècle* (extrait de *l'Histoire Littéraire de la France*, vol. 39). Paris: Imprimerie Nationale, 1959): 169–258.

Jensen, Hans C. *Die 'Miracles de Nostre Dame par personnages': untersucht in ihrem Verhältnis zu Gautier de Coincy.* Heidelberg: Niemeyer, 1892.

Jodogne, Omer. "La Structure des mystères français." *Revue Belge de Philologie et d'Histoire* 42 (1964): 827–42.

—. "La Tonalité des mystères." Dans *Studi in Onore di Italo Siciliano, Biblioteca dell'Archivum Romanicum* 86, 1 (1966): 581–92.

—. "Le Caractère de Jean Molinet." Dans *La Renaissance dans les Provinces du Nord.* Paris: Centre National de la Recherche Scientifique (CNRS), 1956.

—. "Le *Miracle de Saint Nicolas et d'un juif.*" Dans *Mélanges de Linguistique romane et de philologie médiévale offerts à M. Maurice Delbouille.* 2 vols. Gembloux: Duculot, 1964. II, 313–28.

—. "Le souci du peuple dans les mystères français." *Études Classiques* 37 (1969): 338–50.

—. "Le théâtre au moyen âge: recherches sur l'aspect dramatique des pièces." Dans Sandro Sticca, ed. *The Medieval Drama.* Albany: State University of New York Press, 1972. 1–21.

—. "Le théâtre médiéval et sa transmission par le livre." *Research Studies* 32 (1964): 63–75.

—. "Marie-Madeleine pécheresse dans les Passions médiévales." Dans *Scrinium Lovaniense; Mélanges historiques Étienne van Cauwenbergh.* Louvain: Publications Universitaires, 1961. 272–84.

—. "Recherches sur les débuts du théâtre religieux en France." *Cahiers de Civilisation Médiévale* 8 (1965): 1–24; 179–89.

—. "Trois vies romancées dans la *Passion* de Jean Michel." *Revue des Langues Vivantes* 11 (1945): 8–21; 65–73; 110–20.

Josselin, M. "La Formation de deux troupes de comédiens français à Chartres en 1549." *Bibliothèque de l'École des Chartes* 89 (1928): 456–58.

Jullien, F. "Le Théâtre à Aix depuis son origine jusqu'en 1854." *Annales de la Société d'études provençales* (1908): 203–17; 249–80.

Jung, Marc-René. "Jacques Milet et son Épitre Épilogative." Dans *Mélanges Rychner, Travaux de Linguistique et Littérature* 16 (1978): 241–58.

—. "La Mise en scène de la *Destruction de Troye la Grant.*" Dans *Atti del IV Colloquio della SITM.* Viterbo, 1984. 563–80.

—. *La Légende de Troye en France au Moyen Âge.* Basel: Francke, 1996.

Kail, A. "Note sur un passage de la *Vengeance Jhesucrist* d'Eustache Marcadé." *Revue des Études Juives,* 4e série, 1 (1962), 339–407.

Keller, Hans-Erich. "Pour une réhabilitation des *Miracles de Nostre Dame par personnages*: à propos du *Miracle d'une Femme que Nostre Dame garda d'estre arse.*" *French Forum* 12 (1987): 133–45.

Kelson, J. H. "The Serventois in the Cangé Manuscript." *Philological Quarterly* 47 (1968): 506–12.

Kerdaniel, E.-L. *Un auteur dramatique du XVe siècle: André de La Vigne.* Paris: Champion, 1923.

Kipling, Gordon. "Fouquet, St. Apollonia, and the Motives of the Miniaturist's Art: A Reply to Graham Runnalls." *Medieval English Theatre* 19 (1997 [1999]): 101–20.

—. "Theatre as Subject and Object in Fouquet's *Martyrdom of St. Apollonia.*" *Medieval English Theatre* 19 (1997): 26–80.

Kneisel, Adolf. *Das Mystere de la Passion en rime franchoise (Textproben von journées I–X)*. Greifswald: J. Abel, 1906.

Knight, Alan E., ed. *The Stage as Mirror: Civic Theatre in Late Medieval Europe*. Cambridge: Brewer, 1997.

—. "Beyond Misrule: Theater and the Socialization of Youth in Lille." *Research Opportunities in Renaissance Drama* 35 (1996): 73–84.

—. "Cyclicity in Medieval French Drama." Dans Sarah Sturm-Maddox and D. Maddox, ed. *Transtextualities: Of Cycles and Cyclicity in Medieval French Literature*. Binghampton: MRTS, 1996. 179–94.

—. "Drama and Society in Late Medieval Flanders and Picardy." *Chaucer Review* 14 (1980): 379–89.

—. "Editing the Unique Manuscript: the Case of the Lille Plays." Dans *Text: Transactions of the Society for Textual Scholarship* 5 (1991): 145–55.

—. "Faded Pageant: the End of the Mystery Plays in Lille." *Journal of the Mid-West Modern Language Association* 29 (1996): 3–14.

—. "France." Dans Eckehard Simon. *The Theatre of Medieval Europe: New Research in Early Drama*. Cambridge: Cambridge University Press, 1991. 151–68.

—. "Processional Theatre and the Rituals of Social Unity in Lille." Dans Alan Hindley, ed. *Drama and Community: People and Plays in Medieval Europe*. Turnhout: Brepols, 1999. 99–109.

—. "Processional Theatre in Lille in the Fifteenth Century." Dans Jean-Claude Aubailly, éd. *Le Théâtre et la Cité dans l'Europe Médiévale. Fifteenth-Century Studies* 13 (1988): 347–58.

—. "The Bishop of Fools and His Feasts in Lille." Dans *Festive Drama: Papers from the Sixth Triennial Colloquium of the International Society for the Study of Medieval Theatre*, ed. Meg Twycross. Cambridge: Brewer, 1996. 157–66.

—. "The Enacted Narrative: from Bible to Stage in Late-Medieval France." *Fifteenth-Century Studies* 15 (1989): 233–44.

—. "The Image of the City in the Processional Theater of Lille." *Research Opportunities in Renaissance Drama* 30 (1988): 153–65.

—. "The Roman 'Saints' Plays of Lille." *Medieval English Theatre* 19 (1997): 15–25.

—. "The Sponsorship of Drama in Lille." Dans Rupert Pickens, ed. *Studies in Honor of Hans-Erich Keller: Medieval French and Occitan Literature and Romance Linguistics*. Kalamazoo: MIP, 1993. 275–85.

—. "The Stage as Context: Two Late Medieval French Susanna Plays." Dans Knight, ed. *The Stage as Mirror: Civic Theatre in Late Medieval Europe*. Cambridge: Brewer, 1997. 201–16.

—. "Uses of Rhetoric in Medieval French Drama." In Norris J. Lacy and J. C. Nash, ed. *Essays in Early French Literature presented to Barbara M. Craig*. York, SC: French Literature Publications, 1982. 73–80.

—. *Aspects of Genre in Late Medieval French Drama*. Manchester: Manchester University Press, 1983.

Koeppen, Bernhard. *Die beiden Valencienner Passionen in ihrem Verhältnis zu den Quellen*. Greifswald: J. Abel, 1911.

Konigson, Elie, éd. *Figures Théâtrales du Peuple*. Paris: CNRS, 1985.

—. "Mythes des origines et romans familiaux dans les derniers Mystères de la Passion français." *Revue d'Histoire du Théâtre* 24 (1972): 121–30.

—. "Religious Drama and Urban Society in France at the End of the Middle Ages." Dans James Redmond, ed. *Drama and Society*. Cambridge: Cambridge University Press, 1979. 23–36.

—. "Structures élémentaires de quelques fictions dramatiques dans les *Miracles par personnages* du manuscrit Cangé." *Revue d'Histoire du Théâtre* 29 (1977): 105–27.

—. *L'Espace théâtral médiéval*. Paris: CNRS, 1975.

—. *La Représentation d'un Mystère de la Passion à Valenciennes en 1547*. Paris: CNRS, 1969.

Koopmans, Jelle. "Jeux d'Apôtres virtuels? Un exemplaire du *Mystère des Actes des Apôtres* annoté du XVIe siècle." Dans Martin Gosman et R. Walthaus, ed. *European Theatre 1470–1600: Traditions and Transformations*. Groningen: Egbert Forsten, 1996. 31–42.

—. "Le *Mystère de Saint Sébastien*: scénographie et théorie des genres." *Fifteenth-Century Studies* 16 (1990): 143–56.

—. *Le Théâtre des Exclus au Moyen Âge: hérétiques, sorcières et marginaux*. Paris: Imago, 1997.

—. "Les démunis en scène: satire ou utopie, répression ou contestation?" Dans *Les Niveaux de vie au moyen âge*, éd. Jean-Pierre Sosson et al. Louvain-la-Neuve: Bruyland-Académie, 1999. 123–39.

—. "Théâtre du monde et monde du théâtre." Dans Bordier, éd. *Le Jeu théâtral, ses marges, ses frontières*. Paris: Champion, 1999. 17–36.

Kraatz, K. *Untersuchung über le Mystère de la Conception de la BN Réserve Yf 1604*. Greifswald: Reineke, 1906.

Krause, Kathy. "The Dramatization of the Heroine in the *Miracles de Nostre Dame par personnages*." *European Medieval Drama* 3 (1999 [2001]): 161–76.

Kruse, Kurt. *Jehan Michel: Das "Mystère de la Passion Jesu Christ joué à Paris et Angiers" und sein Verhältnis zu der Passion von Arnoul Gréban und zu den beiden Valencienner Passionen*. Diss. Greifswald: Reineke, 1907.

Kunstmann, Pierre. "L'Édition électronique: le cas des *Miracles de Nostre Dame par personnages*." Dans *Le Moyen Français: Le Traitement de texte*. Textes réunis par Claude Buridant. Strasbourg: Presses Universitaires, 2000. 115–22.

—. "L'édition électronique: le cas du théâtre religieux." Dans *Le Théâtre français des années 1450–1550. État actuel des recherches*. Textes réunis par Olga Anna Duhl. Dijon: Centre de Recherches Le Texte et l'Édition, Université de Dijon, 2002. 63–69.

L'Instructif de la Seconde Rethorique, préface du *Jardin de Plaisance et Fleur de Rethorique*, publié par Antoine Vérard en 1501. Eugénie Droz et A. Piaget, éd. 2 vols. Paris: SATF, 1910 et 1924.

La Langue, le texte, le jeu: Perspectives sur le théâtre médiéval. Giuseppe Di Stefano et R. Bidler, éd. Dans *Le Moyen Français* 19 (1988).

La Littérature Populaire aux XVe et au XVIe siècles, dans *Réforme Humanisme Renaissance* 11 (1980). Actes du colloque de Goutelas (1979).

Lagrave, Henri, C. Mazouer et M. Regalado, ed. *La Vie Théâtrale à Bordeaux: des origines à nos jours*, vol. 1: *Des origines à 1789*. Paris: CNRS, 1985.

Lalou, Elisabeth. "Les Cordonniers metteurs en scène des mystères de saint Crépin et saint Crépinien." *Bibliothèque de l'École des Chartes* 143 (1985): 91–115.

—. "Réflexions sur cérémonie, cérémonial et jeu." Dans Bordier, éd. *Le Jeu Théâtral, ses marges, ses frontières*. Paris: Champion, 1999. 115–24.

—. "Les rolets de théâtre, étude codicologique." *Théâtre et Spectacles Hier et Aujourd'hui: Moyen Âge et Renaissance*. Paris: Éditions du Comité des travaux historiques et scientifiques, 1991. 51–71.

—. "Le théâtre et les spectacles publics en France au Moyen Âge. État des Recherches." Dans ibid., 9–33.

—. "Les Tortures dans les mystères: théâtre et réalité." Dans *Spectacle in Early Theatre: England and France*. *Medieval English Theatre* 16 (1996): 37–50.

—. et D. Smith, "Pour une typologie des manuscrits de théâtre médiéval." Dans Jean-Claude Aubailly, éd. *Le Théâtre et la Cité dans l'Europe Médiévale*. *Fifteenth-Century Studies* 13 (1988): 569–79.

Langley, Frederick W. "Community Drama and Community Politics in Thirteenth-Century Arras: Adam de la Halle's *Jeu de la Feuillée*." Dans Alan Hindley, ed. *Drama and Community*. Turnhout: Brepols, 1999. 57–77.

Langlois, E. "Jean Molinet, auteur du *Mystère de S. Quentin*." *Romania* 22 (1893): 552–53.

Laurent, P. "Une fête au pont de Nièvre à Nevers il y a 500 ans." Dans *Mélanges historiques Niverno-Ardennais*. Paris: Champion, 1915. 18–20.

Lazar, Moshe. "Enseignement et spectacle: la *disputatio* comme *scène à faire* dans le drame religieux du Moyen Âge." *Scripta Hierosolymitana* 19 (1967): 126–51.

—. "La Dramatisation de la matière biblique dans le *Mistere du Viel Testament* (*Joseph et ses frères*)." Dans *Mélanges offerts à Rita Lejeune*. 2 vols. Gembloux: Duculot, 1968. II, 1433–51.

—. "Les Diables, serviteurs et bouffons: répertoire et jeu chez les comédiens de la troupe infernale." *Tréteaux* 2 (1978): 51–69.

—. "Satan and Notre Dame: Characters in a Popular Scenario." Dans Norris Lacy, ed. *A Medieval French Miscellany*. Lawrence: University of Kansas Publications, 1972. 1–14.

Lazard, Madeleine. "Un ordonnateur de mystères au XVIe siècle: le procureur poitevin Jean Bouchet." Dans *Études sur Étienne Dolet: le théâtre au XVIe siècle, le Forez, le Lyonnais et l'histoire du livre: publiées à la mémoire de Claude Longeon*. Geneva: Droz, 1993. 139–50.

Le Briz-Orgeur, Stéphanie. "À la recherche d'une écriture dramatique: conventions du dialogue dans quelques mystères": résumé de la thèse de doctorat soutenue en 1998, dans *Perspectives Médiévales* 25 (1999): 54–57.

—. "Le *Mystère de la Passion* d'Arnoul Gréban: un atelier du dialogue." Dans Giuseppe Di Stefano et R. Bidler, ed. *La Recherche: bilan et perspective*. 2 vols. I: *Moyen Français* 44–45; II: *Moyen Français* 46–47. Montréal: CERES, 2000. 327–46.

—. "Quand le silence fait parler de lui" (les Mystères de la Passion). Dans Bordier, éd. *Économie du Dialogue*. Paris: Champion, 1999. 211–26.

—. "Les Monologues d'hésitation dans la *Passion* d'Arnoul Gréban." Dans Bordier, éd. *Langues, Codes, et Conventions*. Paris: Champion, 2002. 149–66.

Le Roy, O. *Études sur les Mystères*. Paris: Hachette, 1837.

Lebègue, Raymond. "Du théâtre savant au théâtre populaire: le drame religieux médiéval et ses prolongements populaires." Dans *Actes du VIe Congrès national de la Société française de littérature comparée*. Paris: Didier, 1965. 75–84.

—. "Jean Molinet et la *Passion* de Valenciennes." *Romania* 59 (1933): 438–47.

—. "L'évolution du théâtre dans les provinces du nord." Dans F. Lesure, éd. *La Renaissance dans les provinces du nord*. Paris: CNRS, 1956. 117–26.

—. "La *Passion* d'Arles." *Romania* 58 (1932): 434.

—. "La *Passion* d'Arnoul Gréban." *Romania* 60 (1934): 218–31.

—. "La Survivance des personnages des mystères français." Dans *Studi in onore di Carlo Pellegrini*. Turin: Società editrici internazionale, 1963. 205–16.

—. "La vie d'un ancien genre dramatique, le mystère." *Helicon* 2 (1939): 216–24.

—. "Persistance, altération, disparition des traditions dramatico-religieuses en France." Dans Jean Jacquot, éd. *Dramaturgie et Société: XVIe et XVIIe siècles*. Paris: CNRS, 1968. 247–52.

—. "Quelques Survivances de la mise en scène médiévale." Dans *Mélanges Cohen*. Paris: Nizet, 1959.

—. *Études sur le théâtre français*. 2 vols. Paris: Nizet, 1978. I: "Les fonctions de la quadruple rime chevauchante," 24–28; "Le problème du salut dans les tragédies protestantes," 29–42; "Le diable dans l'ancien théâtre religieux," 43–52; "Les personnages de la mythologie dans la *Passion* de Jean Michel," 55–59; II: "La vie dramatique à Rouen de François Ier à Louis XIII," 85–112.

—. *La Tragédie française de la Renaissance*. Paris: Champion, 1954.

—. *La Tragédie religieuse en France*. Paris: Champion, 1929.

—. *Le Mystère des Actes des Apôtres*. Paris: Champion, 1929.

Lebert, C. "Le théâtre à Meaux aux XVe, XVIe et XVIIe siècles." *Bulletin Historique et Philologique* (1955–56): 18–19.

Leboucq, N. *Fêtes populaires au XVIe siècle dans les villes du Nord de la France et particulièrement à Valenciennes*. Douai: Crépin, 1871.

Lecocq, Georges. *Histoire du théâtre en Picardie depuis son origine jusqu'à la fin du XVIe siècle*. Paris: Menu, 1880.

Ledieu, A. "Abbeville en liesse: réjouissances et fêtes publiques au XVe siècle." *Mémoires de la Société d'Émulation d'Abbeville*, IVe série, 12 (1889–90).

Lefèvre, L. *Fêtes Lilloises du XIVe au XVIe siècle*. Lille: Lefebvre-Ducrocq, 1902.

—. *L'Histoire du théâtre de Lille depuis ses origines à nos jours*. 5 vols. Lille: Lefebvre-Ducrocq, 1901–1907.

Lepage, H. "Étude sur le théâtre en Lorraine et sur Pierre Gringore." *Mémoires de la Société des Sciences, Lettres et Arts de Nancy* (1848): 187 et seq.

Levy, B. "Du Fabliau à la farce" [discute les farces dans les mystères]. *Reinardus* 15 (2002): 97–100.

Lhotte, G. *Le Théâtre à Douai avant la Révolution*. Douai: Crépin, 1881.

—. *Le Théâtre à Lille avant la Révolution*. Lille: Daniel, 1881.

Lifschitz-Golden, Manya. *Les Juifs dans la littérature française du moyen âge (mystères, miracles, chroniques)*. New York: Columbia University, 1935.

Lindner, G. *Die Henker und ihre Gesellen in der altfranzösischen Mirakel- und Mysteriendichtung.* Greifswald: Reineke, 1902.

Lintilhac, E. *Histoire Générale du Théâtre en France.* 5 vols. Paris: Flammarion, 1904–11.

Loewald, Sharon. *Les Figures Féminines dans certains Mystères de la Passion en France au Moyen Âge.* Villeneuve d'Ascq: Presses Universitaires du Septentrion, 2001.

—–. "Quatre figures féminines apocryphes dans certains Mystères de la Passion en France." *Fifteenth-Century Studies* 28 (2003): 173–83.

Lohmann, Wilhelm. *Untersuchungen über Jehan Louvets zwölf Mysterien zu Ehren von Notre Dame de Liesse.* Greifswald: Reineke, 1900.

Longeon, Claude. "Le Théâtre au Puy-en-Velay au XVIe siècle." Dans *Mélanges offerts à Georges Couton.* Lyon: Presses Universitaires de Lyon, 1981. 23–34.

Longtin, Mario. "Conventions de lecture: l'exemple de la pausa dans le Mystère de sainte Barbe en cinq journées." Dans Bordier, éd. *Langues, Codes et Conventions.* Paris: Champion, 2002. 83–92.

Lottin, Denis. *Recherches sur les théâtres à Orléans.* Orléans: Jacob, 1836.

Louandre, François. *Histoire d'Abbéville.* Abbéville: A. Alexandre, 1883–84.

Lucken, C. "La cuisine du diable et l'hospice du saint: *Le Mystère de Saint Bernard de Menthon.*" Dans Bernard Laurioux et L. Moulinier-Brogi, éd. *Scrivere il Medioevo: Lo spazio, la santità, il cibo. Un libro dedicato ad Odile Redon.* Rome: Viella, 2001. 277–91.

Luedtke, Hélène. *Les Croyances religieuses au Moyen Âge en France d'après les pièces du théâtre sérieux des XIIe, XIIIe et XIVe siècles.* Lausanne: Imprimeries réunies, 1911.

Lynn, Thérèse B. "Pour une réhabilitation d'Ève." *French Review* 48 (1975): 871–77.

Maas, P. M. *Étude sur les sources de la Passion du Palatinus.* St. Maarten: Tiel, 1942.

Macini, Valentino. "Public et espace scénique dans le théâtre du moyen âge." *Revue d'histoire du théâtre* 7 (1965): 387–403.

Macon, G. "Note sur le *Mystère de la Résurrection* attribué à Jean Michel." *Bulletin du Bibliophile*, 1898. Pages?

Magnin, C. "Rapport sur quelques extraits de comptes municipaux relatifs aux dépenses faites pendant les XIVe, XVe et XVIe siècles, pour des représentations de jeux de personnages à Lille et à Douai." *Bulletin du Comité de la langue, de l'histoire et des arts de la France* 2 (1853–55): 119 et seq.

Mandach, André de. "Comment éditer un mystère inséré dans un texte biblique? Le *Jeu des trois rois* de Herman de Valenciennes." *Fifteenth-Century Studies* 13 (1988), 597–613.

Marcel, L. "Une représentation dramatique à Langres en 1377." *Nouvelle Revue de Champagne et de Brie*, 1925. Pages?

Marshall, M. "*Theatre* in the Middle Ages: Evidence from Dictionaries and Glosses." *Symposium* (1950): 1–39; 366–89.

Marsy, Comte de. "Les Origines tournaisiennes des tapisseries de Reims." *Travaux de l'Académie Nationale de Reims* 89 (1886–87): 339–99.

Martin, Toni. "Novel Aspects of Pilate in Jean Michel's *Mystère de la Passion*." *Fifteenth-Century Studies* 16 (1990), 177–88.

Mathieu, Michel. "Le personnage du marchand de parfums dans le théâtre médiéval en France." *Le Moyen Âge* 74 (1968): 39–71.

Mazouer, Charles. "Abraham du *Mistere du Viel Testament* à l'*Abraham Sacrifiant* de Théodore de Bèze." *Réforme Humanisme Renaissance* 44 (1997): 55–64.

—. "La Dérision dans les mystères." Dans *Rire des dieux*. Bordeaux: Presses Universitaires, 2000. 73–83.

—. "Dieu, Justice et Miséricorde dans le *Mistere du Viel Testament*." *Le Moyen Âge* 91 (1985): 53–73.

—. "L'eschatologie chrétienne dans le théâtre médiéval." Dans *La Fin des temps. Eidôlon* 58 (2001): 43–52.

—. "L'Histoire d'Abraham dans le *Mistere du Viel Testament*." Dans *Jeux de la Variante. Mélanges offerts à Anna Drzewicka*. Cracovie: Viridis, 1997. 220–30.

—. "Les Machines de théâtre." Dans *L'Invention au XVIe siècle*. Bordeaux: Presses Universitaires de Bordeaux, 1987. 197–218.

—. "La prédication populaire et le théâtre au début du XVIe siècle." Dans Bordier, éd. *Le Jeu Théâtral, ses marges, ses frontières.* Paris: Champion, 1999. 79–90.

—. "Rire et religion dans le théâtre médiéval." *Humoresques* 12 (2000): 131–42.

—. *Le Théâtre français du Moyen Âge.* Paris: SEDES, 1998.

—. *Le Théâtre français de la Renaissance.* Paris: Champion, 2002.

—. "Théâtre et société à Bordeaux jusqu'à la fin du XVIe siècle." Dans *La Vie théâtrale dans les provinces du Midi.* Tübingen-Paris: Niemeyer, 1980. 73–88.

—. "Vingt ans de recherches sur le théâtre du XVIe siècle. Première partie: Le Théâtre sérieux." *Nouvelle Revue du Seizième Siècle* 16 (1998): 301–25.

—. "Vingt ans de recherches sur le théâtre du XVIe siècle. Deuxième partie: le théâtre comique, spectacles de la cour, théâtre scolaire." *Nouvelle Revue du XVIe Siècle* 16 (1998): 301–25.

McKean, Mary F. *The Interplay of Realistic and Flamboyant Elements in the French Mystères.* Washington: Catholic University of America Press, 1959.

Mélicocq, A. "De l'art dramatique au moyen âge: les artistes dramatiques de Béthune." *Annales Archéologiques de Didron* 8 (1847): 155–64; 269–74.

—. "Du théâtre au XVIe siècle à Béthune." *Bulletin de la Société de l'Histoire de France* 7 (1843): 108–109; 349–50.

—. "Jeux de personnages représentés par les sociétés de rhétorique de Lille, à Courtrai, Ypres, Tournai, Malines." *Messagier des Sciences Historiques* (1856): 347–50.

—. "Les artistes dramatiques des provinces de la Flandre et de l'Artois aux XIVe, XVe et XVIe siècles." *Mémoires de la Société des Antiquaires de la Morinie* 20 (1886–87): 343–454.

—. "Les sociétés dramatiques du nord de la France et du midi de la Belgique aux XIVe, XVe et XVIe siècles." *Archives historiques et littéraires du nord de la France et du Midi de la Belgique.* 3e série 6 (1857): 5–38.

Mellot, J. "A propos du théâtre liturgique à Bourges au Moyen-Âge et au XVIe siècle." Dans *Mélanges . . . offerts à Gustave Cohen*. Paris: Champion, 1950.

Ménage, René. "La mesnie infernale dans la *Passion* d'Arnoul Gréban." Dans *Le Diable au Moyen Âge. Doctrine, problèmes moraux, représentations*. Aix-en-Provence/Paris: Champion (CUERMA), 1979. 331-49.

Meredith, Peter, et J. Tailby, ed. *The Staging of Religious Drama in Europe in the Later Middle Ages: Texts and Documents in English Translation*. Kalamazoo: MIP, 1983.

Mermier, Guy R. "The *Mystère de Saint Sébastien*: Structure and Psychology of an *Exemplum*." *Fifteenth-Century Studies* 3 (1980), 115-46.

Metais, C. "Notes sur les mystères représentés à Tours pendant le moyen âge." *Bulletin de la Société de Touraine* 8 (1892): 23 et seq.

Meyer, B. *Die Sprache des Mistere du Viel Testament*. Heidelberg: Niemeyer, 1907.

Meyer, H. *Die Predigten in den Miracles de Nostre Dame par personnages*. Berlin: Schmidt, 1911.

Meyer, P. "Fragment d'un mystère du XVe siècle." *Romania* 31 (1902): 103-106.

—. "Les Légendes hagiographiques." *Histoire Littéraire de la France* 33 (date?), 337-446.

Micha, Alexandre. "La Femme injustement accusée dans les *Miracles de Nostre Dame par personnages*." Dans *Mélanges Cohen*. Paris: Nizet, 1950. 85-92.

Mokross, K. *Weitere Studien über das Mystère de la Passion en rimes franchoises (journées XI-XV)*. Greifswald, 1908.

Moralités Françaises: Réimpression facsimilé de vingt-deux pièces allégoriques imprimées aux XVe et XVIe siècles; introduction de Werner Helmich. Geneva: Éditions Slatkine, 1980.

Morice, Émile. *Histoire de la mise en scène depuis les mystères jusqu'au Cid*. Paris: Librairie française, allemande et anglaise, 1836.

Mosselmans, N. "Les villes face au prince–importance réelle de la cérémonie d'entrée sous le règne de Philippe le Bon." Dans *Villes et campagnes au Moyen Âge. Mélanges Georges Despy*. Liège: Éditions du Perron, 1991. 533–48.

Mostert, Wilhelm. *Das Mystère de S. Genis, seine Quelle und seine Interpolatoren*. Diss. Bonn, 1894.

Muir, Lynette. "The Fall of Man in the Drama of Medieval Europe." *Studies in Medieval Culture* 10 (1977): 121–31.

—. "The Saint Play in Medieval France." Dans Clifford Davidson, ed. *The Saint Play in Medieval Europe*. Kalamazoo: MIP, 1986. 123–80.

—. "Apocryphal Writings and the Mystery Plays." Dans Gari R. Muller, ed. *Le Théâtre au Moyen Âge*. Montréal: L'Aurore, 1981. 79–83.

—. "Aspects of Form and Meaning in the Biblical Drama." Dans D. A. Trotter, ed. *Littera et Sensus. Essays on Form and Meaning in Medieval French Literature presented to John Fox*. Exeter: Exeter University, 1989. 109–23.

—. *The Biblical Drama of Medieval Europe*. Cambridge: Cambridge University Press, 1995.

—. "European Communities and Medieval Drama." Dans Alan Hindley, ed. *Drama and Community*. Turnhout: Brepols, 1999. 1–17.

—. "Further Thoughts on the Tale of the Profaned Host." *Early Drama, Art, and Music Review* 21 (1999): 88–97.

—. "The Mass on the Medieval Stage." *Comparative Drama* 23 (1989–90): 314–30.

—. "Résurrection des Mystères: Medieval Drama in Modern France." *Leeds Studies in English* 29 (1998): 235–47.

—. "Playing God in Medieval Europe." Dans Knight, ed. *The Stage as Mirror: Civic Theatre in Late Medieval Europe*. Cambridge: Brewer, 1997. 25–50.

—. "*Les Prophètes du Christ*, cent ans après." Dans *Mélanges de littérature Jeanne Lods: Du moyen âge au XXe siècle*. Paris: E.N.S.J.F., 1978. 447–58.

—. "René d'Anjou and the Theatre in Provence." *European Medieval Drama* 3 (1999 [2001]): 57–72.

—. "Le Théâtre hennuyer à la fin du moyen âge." Dans *De la Représentation du Mystère de Valenciennes de 1547 à la post-modernité*. *Lez Valenciennes* 24 (1998): 31–40.

—. "The Trinity in Medieval Drama." *Comparative Drama* 10 (1976): 116–29.

Müller, L. *Das Rondel in den französischen Mirakelspielen und Mysterien des XV. und XVI. Jahrhunderts*. Marburg: N. G. Elwert, 1884.

Müller, P. *Studien über drei dramatische Bearbeitungen der Alexius-Legende*. Berlin, 1888.

Nagler, A. M. *A Source Book in Theatrical History*. New Haven and London: Yale University Press, 1959.

—. *The Medieval Religious Stage: Shapes and Phantoms*. New Haven and London: Yale University Press, 1976.

Neumann, W. *Die letzte Journée des Mystères de la Passion von Arnoul Gréban in der Handschrift von Troyes in ihrem Verhältnis zur übrigen Überlieferung*. Greifswald: Reineke, 1905.

Noomen, Willem. "Pour une typologie des personnages des *Miracles de Nostre Dame par personnages*." Dans *Mélanges de linguistique et de littérature offerts à Lein Geschiere*. Amsterdam: Rodopi, 1975. 71–89.

—. *Étude sur les formes métriques du Mistère du Viel Testament*. Amsterdam: Rodopi, 1962.

Oakshott, Jane. "The Arras Miniatures: Inadmissible Evidence?" *Early Drama, Art, and Music Review* 14 (1992): 64–73.

Oldörp, B. *Untersuchungen über das Mystère "La Vengeance Nostre Seigneur."* Greifswald: Kunike, 1907.

Otto, H. *Kritische Studien über das anonyme Jeu Saint Loÿs, roy de France*. Greifswald: Kunike, 1897.

Pansier, P. "Les Débuts du théâtre à Avignon." *Annales d'Avignon et du Comtat Venaissin* 6 (1919): 10–13.

Paoli, G. "Taverne et théâtre au Moyen Âge." Dans *Théâtres et spectacles hier et aujourd'hui*. Avignon: CTHS, 1991. 73–82.

Pares, J. "Représentations théâtrales à Aups (Var)." *Revue d'Histoire du Théâtre* 3 (1951): 411-12.

Parfaict, les frères Claude et François. *Histoire du théâtre françois*. Paris: Chez P. G. Le Mercier et Saillant, 1734. Amsterdam, 1734-49 (15 vols.); Paris, 1745-49 (15 vols.). Geneva: Slatkine Reprints, 1967.

Paris, L. *Le Théâtre à Reims depuis les Romains jusqu'à nos jours*. Reims, 1885.

—. *Toiles peintes et tapisseries de la ville de Reims ou la mise en scène du théâtre des Confrères de la Passion*. 2 vols. Reims: Brulant, 1843.

Paris, Paulin. "La mise en scène des mystères." *Journal général de l'instruction publique et des cultes*. 30 mai et 13 juin, 1855.

Parmentier, J. *L'Assomption de Nostre-Dame*. Paris: Crapelet, 1839.

Pas, J. de. "Mystères et jeux scéniques à Saint-Omer aux XVe et XVIe siècles." *Mémoires de la Société des Antiquaires de la Morinie* 31 (1913): 345-77.

Patzer, L. "The *Miracles de Nostre Dame par personnages* and the Fourteenth Century." *Modern Language Notes* 20 (1905): 44-48.

Payen, Jean-Charles. "Théâtre médiéval et culture urbaine." *Revue d'Histoire du Théâtre* 35 (1983): 233-50.

Pein, E. *Untersuchungen über die Verfasser der Passion und der Vengeance Jhesucrist*. Greifswald: Kunike, 1903.

Penn, Dorothy. *The Staging of the 'Miracles de Nostre Dame par personnages' of MS Cangé*. New York: Columbia University, 1933.

Perrin, A. "Les Moines de la Basoche." *Mémoires et Documents publiés par la Société Savoisienne d'histoire et d'archéologie* 9 (1865): pages ?

Petit de Julleville, Louis. *Les Comédiens en France au Moyen Âge*. Paris: Cerf, 1889.

—. *Histoire du théâtre en France: Les Mystères*, 2 vols. Paris: Hachette, 1880.

—. *Répertoire du théâtre comique en France au Moyen Âge*. Paris: Hachette, 1886.

Pflaum, H. "Les scènes de Juifs dans la littérature dramatique du moyen âge." *Revue des Études Juives* 89 (1930): 111-34.

Picot, Émile. "Fragments inédits de Mystères de la Passion: la *Passion d'Amboise*." *Romania* 19 (1890): 264–82.

Piétresson de Saint-Aubin, P. "La *Passion de Notre Seigneur Jésus-Christ*, mystère inédit du XVe siècle." *Bibliothèque de l'École des Chartes* 85 (1924): 310–22.

Pinto-Mathieu, Elisabeth. "Visions du corps et conscience du péché dans les Passions médiévales." Dans *Apogée et Déclin*. Paris: Presses de l'Université de Paris–Sorbonne, 1993. 237–48.

Piolin, Paul. *Recherches sur les mystères qui ont été représentés dans le Maine*. Angers: Cosnier et Lachèse, 1858.

––. *Le Théâtre chrétien dans le Maine au cours du Moyen Âge*. Maniers: Fleury et Dangin, 1891.

Planche, Alice. "Du tournoi au théâtre en Bourgogne. Le Pas de la Fontaine des Pleurs à Chalon-sur-Saône, 1449–1450." *Le Moyen Âge* 81 (1975).

Plesch, Véronique. "*Étalage Complaisant?* The Torments of Christ in French Passion Plays." *Comparative Drama* 28 (1994–95): 458–85.

––. "Killed by Words: Grotesque Verbal Violence and Tragic Atonement in French Passion Plays." *Comparative Drama* 33 (1999): 22–55.

––. "The Staging of a Late Medieval Passion Play." Dans Clifford Davidson, ed. *Material Culture and Medieval Drama*. Kalamazoo: MIP, 1999. 75–102.

––. "Walls and Scaffolds: Pictorial and Dramatic Passion Cycles in the Duchy of Savoy." *Comparative Drama* 32 (1998): 252–90.

––. "*Ludus Sabaudiae*: Observations on Late Medieval Theater in the Duchy of Savoy." *Early Drama, Art, and Music Review* 21 (1998): 1–21.

Port, C. "Documents sur le théâtre à Angers et sur le véritable auteur du *Mystère de la Passion*." *Bibliothèque de l'École des Chartes*. Cinquième série, 2 (1861): 69–80.

––. *Le Théâtre à Doué (Maine-et-Loir)*. Angers: Cosnier, 1895.

Pottier, L. *La Vie et Histoire de Madame Sainte Barbe. Le Mystère joué à Laval en 1493 et les peintures de Saint Martin-de-Connée*. Laval: Goupil, et dans la *Revue Historique et Archéologique du Maine* 50 (1901): pages?

Poupé, E. "Documents relatifs aux représentations scéniques en Provence du XVe au XVIIe siècle." *Bulletin Philologique et Historique jusqu'en 1715* (1920).

Quedenfeld, G. *Die Mysterien des heiligen Sebastian, ihre Quellen und ihr Abhängigkeitsverhältnis.* Marburg, 1895.

Quéruel, Danielle. "Fête et théâtre à Reims à la fin du XVe siècle." Dans *"Et c'est la fin pour quoy sommes ensemble": Hommage à Jean Dufournet. Littérature, histoire et langue du Moyen Âge.* Ed. Jean-Claude Aubailly. 3 vols. Paris: Champion, 1993. 1171–86.

Raimbault, M. "Notes sur le théâtre religieux médiéval en Bourgogne." *Revue d'Histoire de l'Église de France* 57 (1972): pages?

——. "Une représentation théâtrale à Aix en 1444." *Revue des Langues Romanes* 67 (1935): 263–74.

Rastall, Richard. "The Construction of a Speaking Tube for Late Medieval Drama." *European Medieval Drama* 4 (2000): 231–44.

Réau, Louis. *Iconographie de l'Art Chrétien.* 3 vols. Paris: P. U. F., 1958.

Recueil des Chroniqueurs du Puy-en-Velay. 3 vols. I et II, *Le Livre de Podio* d'Estienne Mège ou Médicis, éd. A. Chassaing; III, *Les Chroniques de Burel.* Le Puy-en-Velay, 1874.

Revol, Thierry. "Drames liturgiques latins du XIIIe siècle: vêtements liturgiques ou costumes de théâtre?" Dans Bordier, éd. *Le Jeu Théâtral.* Paris: Champion, 1999. 37–64.

Rey-Flaud, Henri. *Le Cercle Magique.* Paris: Gallimard, 1973.

——. *Pour une Dramaturgie du Moyen Âge.* Paris: Presses Universitaires de France, 1980.

Reyff, Simone de. "Quelques aspects du dialogue dans le *Mystère de l'Institucion de l'Ordre des Freres Prescheurs.*" Dans Bordier, éd. *Économie du Dialogue.* Paris: Champion, 1999. 89–114.

Ridoux, C. "Du *Palatinus* à la *Passion* d'Angers; quelques exemples de réécriture dans les mystères." *Lez Valenciennes* 9 (1984): 13–23.

Ritch, J. "Confrontation entre les théâtres français et anglais du moyen âge à partir de *The N-town Cycle* et *Le Mystère de la Passion* d'Arnoul Gréban: la composition du drame médiéval ou une mentalité sans copyright." *Hier et Aujourd'hui: Points de vue sur le moyen âge anglais*. Nancy: Publications de l'Asssociation des Médiévistes Anglicistes de l'Enseignement Supérieur 21, 1997. 57–73.

—. "Le rôle du jubé dans la *Résurrection de Jésus-Christ*, pièce de Maître Eloy Du Mont." *Memini. Travaux et documents publiés par la Société des études médiévales du Québec* 3 (1999): 155–70.

—. "Notice Biographique sur Maître Eloy Du Mont dict Costentin et son *Livre de la Louenge de la Mort Corporelle*." *Bibliothèque d'Humanisme et Renaissance* 57 (1995): 401–406.

Rittaud-Hutinet, Jacques. *Des Tréteaux à la scène. Le Théâtre en Franche-Comté du Moyen Âge à la Révolution*. Besançon: Cêtre, 1988.

Robert, U. "Les origines du théâtre à Besançon." *Mémoires de la Société des Antiquaires de France* 59 (1900): 60–76.

Rousse, Michel. "Jonglerie dans le théâtre des mystères." Dans Anne Sancier et P. Servet, éd. *Les Genres insérés dans le théâtre*. Lyon: Université Jean Moulin, 1998. 13–29.

—. "L'acteur au moyen âge, Xe–XIIIe siècle: vers l'intériorisation du jeu." Dans *L'Acteur et son métier*. Dijon: Éditions Universitaires de Dijon, 1997.

—. "Le dialogue dans le développement du théâtre." Dans Bordier, éd. *Économie du Dialogue*. Paris: Champion, 1999. 19–32.

—. "Mystères et farces à la fin du moyen âge." Dans *Laboratoire d'études théâtrales de l'Université de Haute-Bretagne. Études et Documents* 1 (1978): 3–21.

—. "Le Théâtre et les Jongleurs." *Revue des Langues Romanes* 95 (1991): 1–14.

Roussineau, Gilles. "La Représentation du *Mystère de Saint Vincent*, joué à Angers en 1471." *Revue d'Histoire du Théâtre* 43 (1991): 27–42.

Roy, Bruno. "La liturgie et l'édition des farces: le cas de *Frère Guillebert*." Dans Bordier, éd. *Le Jeu Théâtral*. Paris: Champion, 1999. 65–78.

Roy, Émile. *Études sur le théâtre français du XIVe et du XVe siècle: Le Jour du Jugement, mystère français sur le grand schisme, publié pour la première fois d'après le manuscrit 579 de la Bibliothèque de Besançon, et les mystères de la Bibliothèque Sainte Geneviève.* Paris: Bouillon, 1902.

—. *Le Mystère de la Passion en France du XIVe au XVIe siècle. Étude sur les sources et le classement des mystères de la Passion.* Dijon: Damidot Frères, 1903–04. (Slatkine Reprints, Geneva, 1974.)

Runnalls, Graham A. "The Manuscript of the *Miracles de Nostre Dame par personnages.*" *Revista de Portugal* 22 (1968–69): 15–22.

—. "The *Miracles de Nostre Dame par personnages*: a Study of the Erasures in the Manuscript, and the Dates of the Plays and the 'serventois.'" *Philological Quarterly* 49 (1970): 19–29.

—. "A Newly-Discovered Fourteenth-Century Play? *Le Mystère de Saint Christofle.*" *Romance Philology* 24 (1971): 464–77.

—. "An Actor's Rôle in a French Morality Play." *French Studies* 42 (1988): 398–407.

—. "The Book Market in Early Sixteenth-Century France." *Early Book Society Newsletter*, second series, 1 (1996): 3–5.

—. "The Catalogue of the Tours Bookseller and Antoine Vérard." *Pluteus* 2 (1984): 163–74.

—. "The Catalogue of the Tours Bookseller and Late Medieval French Drama." *Le Moyen Français* 11 (1982): 112–28.

—. "La Circulation des textes des mystères à la fin du moyen âge: les éditions de la *Passion* de Jean Michel." *Bibliothèque d'Humanisme et Renaissance* 58 (1996): 7–33.

—. "Civic Drama in the Burgundian Territories in the later Middle Ages." *Revue Belge de Philologie et d'Histoire* 78 (2000): 409–22.

—. "Le commerce des mystères imprimés: le cas du *Mystère de l'Assomption.*" Dans Bordier, éd. *Le Jeu Théâtral, ses marges, ses frontières.* Paris: Champion, 1999. 179–92.

—. "La Compilation du *Mistère du Viel Testament*: le *Mystère de Daniel et Susanne.*" *Bibliothèque d'Humanisme et Renaissance* 57 (1995): 345–67.

—. "Deux hommes de théâtre du début du XVIe siècle." *Revue d'Histoire du Théâtre* 48 (1996): 391–406.

—. "Drama and Community in Late Medieval Paris." Dans Alan Hindley, ed. *Drama and Community*. Turnhout: Brepols, 1999. 18–33.

—. "Émile Picot's Fichier: an Under-Used Source of Information." *Tréteaux* 4 (1982): 15–20.

—. "L'Évolution des mystères français: du geste à la parole?" *Théâtre Opéra Ballet* 1 (1995): 11–23.

—. "The Evolution of a Passion Play: *La Passion de Semur*." *Le Moyen Français* 19 (1988): 163–202.

—. "Form and Meaning in Medieval Drama." Dans D. A. Trotter, ed. *Littera et Sensus: Essays on Form and Meaning in Medieval French Literature Presented to John Fox*. Exeter: University of Exeter, 1989. 95–107.

—. "Jean Fouquet's *Martyrdom of St. Apollonia* and the Medieval French Stage." *Medieval English Theatre* 19 (1997 [1999]): 81–100.

—. "Jean Louvet, compositeur de mystères et homme de théâtre parisien 1536–1550." *Bibliothèque d'Humanisme et Renaissance* 62 (2000): 561–89.

—. "*Judith et Holofernès*: mystère religieux ou mélodrame comique?" *Le Moyen Âge* 95 (1989): 75–104.

—. "Langage de la parole ou langage du geste? Le *Mystère de Saint Laurent*." Dans *Langues, codes et conventions*. Éd. Jean-Pierre Bordier. Paris: Champion, 2002. 121–34.

—. "The Linguistic Dating of Middle French Texts with Special Reference to the Theatre." *Modern Language Review* 71 (1976): 757–65.

—. "Le Livre de Raison de Jacques Le Gros et le Mystère de la Passion joué à Paris en 1539." *Romania* 118 (2000): 138–93.

—. "*Mansion* and *lieu*: Two Technical Terms in Medieval French Staging." *French Studies* 35 (1981): 385–93.

—. "Medieval Actors and the Invention of Printing in Late Medieval France." *Early Drama, Art, and Music Review* 22 (2000): 59–80.

—. "The Medieval Actors' Rôles Found in the Fribourg Archives." *Pluteus* 4–5 (1986–87): 5–67.

—. "Medieval French Drama: A Review of Recent Scholarship. Part 1A." *Research Opportunities in Renaissance Drama* 21 (1978): 83–90.

—. "Medieval French Drama: A Review of Recent Scholarship. Parts 1B and 1C." *Research Opportunities in Renaissance Drama* 22 (1979): 111–36.

—. "Medieval Trade Guilds and the *Miracles de Nostre Dame par personnages*." *Medium Aevum* 39 (1970): 257–87.

—. "Monologues, dialogues et versification dans le *Mystère de Judith et Holofernès*." Dans Bordier, éd. *Économie du Dialogue*. Paris: Champion, 1999. 115–40.

—. "Le *Mystère de la Passion* de Châteaudun de 1510: les acteurs." Dans *"Et c'est la fin pour quoy sommes ensemble"*: *Hommage à Jean Dufournet. Littérature, histoire et langue du Moyen Âge*. 3 vols. Paris: Champion, 1993. 1245–53.

—. "Le *Mystère de la Passion* joué à Châteaudun en 1510: le *Compte* de Jehan Brebier." *Fifteenth-Century Studies* 18 (1991): 201–10.

—. "Mystère 'représentation théâtrale': histoire d'un mot." *Revue de Linguistique Romane* 64 (2000): 321–45.

—. "Les Mystères à Paris et en Île-de-France à la fin du Moyen Âge: l'apport de six actes notariés." *Romania* 119 (2001): 113–69.

—. *Les Mystères dans les provinces françaises (en Savoie et en Poitou, à Amiens et à Reims)*. Paris: Champion, 2003.

—. *Les Mystères Français Imprimés*. Paris: Champion, 1999.

—. "Les Mystères de la Passion en langue française: tentative de classement." *Romania* 114 (1996): 468–516.

—. "Le Mystère français: un drame romantique?" Dans Maria Chiabò et F. Doglio, éd. *Esperienze dello Spettacolo Religioso nell'Europa del Quattrocento*. Rome: Torre d'Orfeo Éditrice, 1993. 225–44.

—. "The *Mystère de Sainte Venise*: a Recently-Discovered Late Medieval French Mystery Play." *Tréteaux* 1 (1978): 77–87.

—. "Mysteries' End in France: Performances and Texts." *European Medieval Drama* 3 (1999 [2001]): 201–209.

—. "An Odd Couple: Fiacre and Veronica: Two Saints, Two Printed Plays and One Parisian Confraternity." Dans Nadine Henrard, P. Moreno, et M. Thiry-Stassin, éd. *Convergences Médiévales: Mélanges offerts à Madeleine Tyssens.* Bruxelles: De Boeck Université, 2000. 431–39.

—. "Quatre fragments de manuscrits de Mystères de la Passion." Dans *Miscellanea di Studi Romanzi: offerta a Giuliano Gasca Queirazza.* Alessandria: Edizioni dell' Orso, 1988. 911–18.

—. "The 'Procès de Paradis' Episode in Vérard's Version of the *Mystère de la Vengeance.*" Dans Maria Chiabò, F. Doglio et M. Maymone, éd. *Atti del IV Colloquio della SITM.* Viterbo, 1984. 25–34.

—. "René d'Anjou et le théâtre." *Annales de Bretagne et des Pays de l'Ouest* 88 (1980): 157–80.

—. "Repas fictifs, repas réels: le rôle des banquets et de l'alimentation dans les mystères français." Dans Emmanuelle Rassart-Eeckhout et al., éd. *La Vie matérielle au moyen âge. L'apport des sources littéraires, normatives et de la pratique.* Louvain-la-Neuve: Université Catholique de Louvain, 1997. 205–16.

—. "Sponsorship and Control in Medieval French Religious Drama: 1402–1548." *French Studies* 51 (1997): 257–66.

—. "The Staging of André de la Vigne's *Mystère de Saint Martin.*" *Tréteaux* 3 (1981): 68–79.

—. "Le Théâtre à Montferrand au moyen âge." *Le Moyen Âge* 85 (1979): 465–94.

—. "Le Théâtre à Paris et dans les Provinces à la fin du moyen âge: le *Mystère de Saint Crespin et de Saint Crespinien.*" *Le Moyen Âge* 82 (1976): 517–38.

—. "Le Théâtre en Auvergne au moyen âge." *Revue d'Auvergne* 97 (1983): 69–93.

—. "The Theatre in Paris at the End of the Middle Ages: *Le Mystère de Saint Denis.*" Dans *Mélanges Jeanne Wathelet-Willem.* Liège: Association des Romanistes de l'Université, 1978–79. 619–35.

—. "Towards a Typology of Medieval French Play Manuscripts." Dans Philip E. Bennett et G. A. Runnalls, ed. *The Editor and the Text*. Edinburgh: Edinburgh University Press, 1990. 96–113.

—. "Two Manuscripts, 13000 Lines of Text, and Still Not Half the Play: the Mystery of the *Mystère de Saint Denis*." Dans William C. McDonald et G. Mermier, ed. *The Medieval Text: Methods and Hermeneutics. A Volume of Essays in Honor of Edelgard E. DuBruck. Fifteenth-Century Studies* 17 (1990): 351–62.

—. "Un siècle dans la vie d'un mystère: *Le Mystère de Saint Denis*." *Le Moyen Âge* 97 (1991): 407–30.

—. "Were They Listening Or Watching? Text and Spectacle at the 1510 Châteaudun Passion Play." *Medieval English Theatre* 16 (1994): 25–36.

—. "When is a *mystère* not a *mystère*? Titles and Genres in Medieval French Religious Drama." *Tréteaux* 2 (1980): 23–28.

—. *Études sur les Mystères*. Paris: Champion, 1998.

Sadron, P. "Les Associations permanentes d'acteurs au moyen âge." *Revue d'Histoire du Théâtre* 4 (1952): 220–31; 6 (1954): 81–?

—. "Les plus anciens comédiens français connus." *Revue d'Histoire du Théâtre* 7 (1955): 38–43.

—. "Notes sur l'organisation des représentations théâtrales en France au moyen âge." Dans *Mélanges Cohen*. Paris: Nizet, 1959. 205–18.

Sainte-Beuve, Charles A. "Le *Mystère du Siege d'Orleans* ou de Jeanne d'Arc, et à ce propos de l'ancien théâtre français." *Nouveaux Lundis* 3 (1891). Paris: Calmann-Lévy. 352–418.

Samaran, Charles. "Le rôle de S. Simon (Archives des Alpes de Haute Provence, Digne, C* 852)." *Romania* 31 (1902): pages ?

—. "Les rôles du prologue d'un *Jeu de S. Nicolas*." *Romania* 51 (1925): 191–97.

Santucci, Monique. "Le merveilleux *Mystère de Saint Bernard de Menton*." Dans *Aspects du classicisme et de la spiritualité: Mélanges en l'honneur de Jacques Hennequin*. Ed. Alain Cullière. Paris: Klincksieck, 1996. 595–607.

Schaab, Otto. *Studien über den Teil der Auferstehung Christi der beiden Valencienner Passionen, welcher über die Auferstehung Christi handelt.* Greifswald: Reineke, 1909.

Schoell, Konrad. "Le Théâtre historique au XVe siècle." Dans *Études sur la culture européenne au Moyen Âge et à la Renaissance. En hommage à André Lascombes.* Éd. Michel Bitot, R. Mullini, and P. Happé. Tours: Publications de l'Université François Rabelais, 1996. 189–96.

Schnell, H. *Über den Abfassungsort der Miracles de Nostre Dame par personnages. Ausgaben und Abhandlungen aus dem Gebiete der romanischen Philologie* 53 (Marburg: N. G. Elwert, 1886).

——. *Untersuchungen über die Verfasser der Miracles de Nostre Dame par personnages. Ausgaben* etc. (see above) # 33 (Marburg: N. G. Elwert, 1885).

Schreiner, H. *Weitere Studien über die erste Valencienner Passion.* Greifswald: Reineke, 1907.

Schuker, T. *Madness in French Medieval Plays.* PhD (thèse inédite), Berkeley, 1979.

Schulze, Helga. "Martyrdom as an Act of Fortitude: Theme and Structure in the *Mystère de Saint Quentin.*" *Romania* 98 (1977): 398–409.

Schumacher, H. "Les éléments narratifs de la *Passion d'Autun.*" *Romania* 37 (1908): 571–93.

Schwarz, W. "Prologue and Nativity Scenes from *Le Mystère de la Passion de Notre Seigneur Jesus Christ* by Arnoul Gréban, Organist of Notre Dame, 1450–1456." *University of California Chronicle* 33 (1931): 257–66.

Seefeldt, P. *Studien über die verschiedenen mittelalterlichen dramatischen Fassungen der Barabaralegende nebst Neudruck des ältesten Mystère Français de Sainte Barbe.* Greifswald: Reineke, 1908.

Serrigny, E. *La Représentation d'un Mystère de Saint Martin à Seurre en 1496.* Dijon: Lamarche, 1888.

Servet, Pierre, éd. *Le Théâtre au début de la Renaissance. Réforme Humanisme Renaissance* 44 (1997).

——. "Défense et Illustration du *Mystère de la Résurrection* d'Angers, 1456." *Revue d'Histoire du Théâtre* 43 (1991): 16–26.

—. "D'un héros l'autre: l'homme de guerre et le saint dans la *Vie de Sainct Christofle* de Chevalet (Grenoble 1530)." Dans *PRISMA* 15/2 (1990): 283-97.

—. "L'insertion épique dans les mystères hagiographiques: la *Vie de Sainct Christofle* de Chevalet." Dans Anne Sancier et P. Servet, éd. *Les Genres insérés dans le théâtre*. Lyon: Université Jean Moulin, 1998. 31-45.

—. "Le personnage de la Vierge dans les Mystères." Dans *Imagines Mariae: Représentations du personnage de la Vierge dans la poésie, le théâtre et l'éloquence entre le XIIe et le XVIe siècles*. (Études recueillies par Christian Mouchel.) Lyon: Presses Universitaires de Lyon, 1999. 79-125.

—. "La *Résurrection* abrégée (inédite) d'Éloy Du Mont, dit Costentin: mystère ou tragédie?" *Nouvelle Revue du Seizième Siècle* 9 (1991): 15-40.

—. "La Séduction du diable dans les mystères religieux du XVe siècle." Dans E. Ramos, éd. *El Arte de la Seducción en el mundo románico medieval y renacentista*. Valencia: Universitat de Valencia, 1995. 310-21.

—. "Note sur l'attribution à Jean Du Prier du *Mystère de la Résurrection* d'Angers." *Romania* 112 (1991): 187-201.

Shiley, R. "La Chapelle in the *Miracle de la mère du pape*, the Sixteenth Play of the *Miracles de Nostre Dame par personnages*." *Modern Language Notes* 18 (1943): 493-97.

Simon, Eckehard, ed. *The Theatre of Medieval Europe: New Research in Early Drama*. Cambridge: Cambridge University Press, 1991.

Skey, Miriam A. "Herod the Great in Medieval European Drama," *Comparative Drama* 13 (1979): 330-64.

Smith, Darwin. "La Question du *Prologue* de la *Passion* ou le rôle des formes métriques dans la *Creacion du Monde* d'Arnoul Gréban." Dans Bordier, éd. *L'Économie du Dialogue dans l'Ancien Théâtre Européen*. Paris: Champion, 1999. 141-67.

—. "Le jargon franco-anglais de Maître Pathelin." *Journal des Savants* (1989): 259-76.

—. "Les manuscrits de théâtre; introduction codicologique à des manuscrits qui n'existent pas." *Gazette du Livre Médiéval* 33 (1998): 1-10.

Smith, Darwin et E. Lalou. "Pour une typologie des manuscrits de théâtre médiéval." Dans *Le Théâtre et la Cité. Fifteenth-Century Studies* 13 (1988): 569-79.

Sorel, Alexandre. *Notice sur les mystères représentés à Compiègne au Moyen Âge.* Compiègne: Elder, 1873.

Soyer, J. "Une dispute entre acteurs du *Mystère de la Passion* joué à Orléans en l'année 1400." *Bulletin de la Société Archéologique et Historique de l'Orléanais* 24 (1940): 54-55.

Southern, Richard W. *The Medieval Theatre in the Round.* London: Faber, 1975.

Stadler-Honnegger, M. *Étude sur les Miracles de Nostre Dame par personnages.* Paris: Champion, 1926 (Geneva: Slatkine Reprints, 1975).

Stein, H. "Arnoul Gréban, poète et musicien." *Bibliothèque de l'École des Chartes* 79 (1918): 142-46.

Stone, Donald, Jr. *French Humanist Tragedy.* Manchester: Manchester University Press, 1974.

Stratman, Carl. *Bibliography of Medieval Drama*, 2nd edition. New York: Unger, 1972.

Streblow, E. *Le Mystère de Semur.* Greifswald: Reineke, 1905.

Strumpf, R. *Die Juden in der mittelalterlichen Mysterien- Mirakel- und Moralitatenliteratur Frankreichs.* Heidelberg: Niemeyer, 1920.

Stuart, D. *Stage Decoration in France in the Middle Ages.* New York: Columbia University Press, 1910.

Subrenat, Jean. "Jésus et Joseph dans les mystères du XVe siècle: Une curieuse relation 'père-fils.'" Dans *Les Relations de parenté dans le monde médiéval,*" *Senefiance* 26 (1989): 549-64.

——. "Ève repentante et pardonnée. Une expérience spirituelle originale dans le drame religieux français du XVe siècle." Dans Maria Chiabò et F. Doglio, éd. *Esperienze dello Spettacolo Religioso nell'Europa del Quattrocentro.* Rome: Torre d'Orfeo Éditrice, 1993. 199-224.

—. "La Terre aux premiers jours d'après les *Passions* du XVe siècle." Dans Bernard Guidot, éd. *Provinces, régions, terroirs au Moyen Âge: de la réalité à l'imagination*. Nancy: Presses Universitaires de Nancy, 1993. 59–70.

—. "La vie quotidienne des petites gens et sa représentation dans les Passions du XVe siècle." Dans *Les Niveaux de vie au moyen âge*, éd. Jean-Pierre Sossons et al. Louvain-la-Neuve: Bruyland-Académie, 1999. 317–39.

Surdel, Alain-J. "Amour, mariage et transgressions dans les légendes et les mystères hagiographiques." Dans *Amour, mariage et transgressions au moyen âge*. Éd. Danielle Buschinger and A. Crépin. Göppingen: Kümmerle, 1984. 73–91.

—. "Les Représentations de la mort dans le théâtre religieux du XVe siècle et des débuts du XVIe siècle." Dans Gilles Ernst, éd. *La Mort en toutes lettres*. Nancy: Presses Universitaires de Nancy, 1983. 11–23.

—. "Mystère hagiographique et vie profane: la guerre dans la *Vie et Passion de Monseigneur Sainct Didier* de Guillaume Flament." Dans Danielle Buschinger, éd. *La Littérature d'inspiration religieuse: théâtre et vies des saints* (Colloque d'Amiens). Göppingen: Kümmerle, 1988. 203–13.

—. "Temps humain et temps divin dans la *Legenda Aurea* et dans les mystères dramatiques." Dans Yvonne Bellanger, ed. *Le Temps et la durée dans la littérature au Moyen Âge et à la Renaissance*. Paris: Nizet, 1986. 85–102.

—. "Typologie et stylistique des locutions sentencieuses dans le *Mystère de Saint Didier de Langres* de Guillaume Flament (1482)." Dans *Richesse du Proverbe*, 2 vols. Vol. 1: *Le Proverbe au Moyen Age*. Lille: Presses Universitaires de Lille, 1984. 145–59.

Taillandier, A.-H. "Notice sur les Confrères de la Passion." Paris: Fournier s.d., et dans la *Revue Rétrospective* 4 (date ?): 31.

Taylor, Jane H. M., ed. *Dies Illa: Death in the Middle Ages*. Liverpool: Cairns, 1984.

Tellier, Soeur M. "Quelques Nouvelles Sources des *Miracles de Nostre Dame par personnages*." *Les Lettres Romanes* 12 (1957): 127–42.

Thiboust, J. *Relation de l'ordre de la triomphante et magnifique monstre du mystère des SS. Actes des Apostres par Jacques Thiboust*. Labouvrie-Bourges: Manceron, 1838.

Thiry, Claude. "Une avocate inspirée? Procula dans quelques *Passions* françaises." *Le Moyen Français* 11 (1982): 54–88.

Thomas, A. "Fragments de farces, moralités, mystères, etc. (B.N. n.a.f. 10660)." *Romania* 38 (1909): 177–95.

——. "Le Mystère de la Passion à Saint-Flour en 1425." *Romania* 21 (1892): 425–27.

——. "Notice Biographique sur Eustache Marcadé." *Romania* 35 (1906): 583–90.

——. "Le Théâtre à Paris et aux environs à la fin du XIVe siècle." *Romania* 22 (1893): 606–11.

Tinnius, F. *Studium über das Mystère de Saint Clément*. Greifswald: Reineke, 1909.

Tivier, M. *Étude sur le Mystere du Siege d'Orleans et sur Jacques Milet, auteur présumé de ce mystère*. Paris: Thorin, 1868.

Touber, Anton H. "Dramatising the Visual." *European Medieval Drama* 5 (2002): 99–112.

Traver, Hope. *The Four Daughters of God*. Philadelphia: J. C. Winston, 1907.

Tribout de Morembert, Henri. *Le Théâtre à Metz du Moyen Âge à la Renaissance*. Paris-Metz: Publication de la Société de l'Histoire du Théâtre, 1952.

Trotter, D. A. ed. *Littera et Sensus: Essays on Form and Meaning in Medieval French Literature Presented to John Fox*. Exeter: University of Exeter, 1989.

Truchet, F. "Le théâtre en Maurienne au XVIe siècle. *Le Mystère de l'Antéchrist et du Jugement*." *Congrès de la Société Savoisienne* 12 (1894): 135–58.

Tuaillon, George. "Le *Mystère de saint Antoine* (Névache 1503)." Dans *La Pierre et l'écrit. Évocations* 1995–96. City? Publisher? 35–60.

——. "Le Théâtre Religieux en Maurienne au XVIe siècle et la situation linguistique dans les Alpes." Dans *Histoire Linguistique de la Vallée d'Aoste du Moyen Âge au XVIIIe siecle*. Vallée d'Aoste, 1985. 178–84.

—. "Le Théâtre religieux en Maurienne et dans le Val de Suse: *L'Histoire de Monseigneur Saint Sébastien*, la *Dioclétiane* de Lanslevillard et la *Dioclétiane* de Chaumont." *Mémoires de l'Académie de Savoie*, 8e série. 1 (2000): 239–59.

—. "Saint Sébastien dans le théâtre religieux de Maurienne et de la Vallée de Suse." *Actes de la Conférence Annuelle sur l'Activité Scientifique du Centre d'Études Francoprovençales: Le Théâtre Populaire dans les Alpes Occidentales*. Vallée d'Aoste: Assessorat de l'Éducation et de la Culture, Bureau Régional pour l'Ethnologie et la Linguistique, 1999. 101–16.

Tydeman, William. *The Theatre in the Middle Ages*. Cambridge: Cambridge University Press, 1978.

—, ed. *The Medieval European Stage: 500–1550*. Cambridge: Cambridge University Press, 2001.

Vallet de Viriville, A. "Notice d'un mystère par personnages représenté à Troyes vers la fin du XVe siècle." *Bibliothèque de l'École des Chartes*. Première série, 3 (1841–42): 448–74.

Van den Wildenberg-De Kroon, Conny. "Die Gestalt des Wirtes in den deutschen und französischen mittelalterlichen Oster- und Passionsspielen." *Amsterdamer Beiträge zur älteren Germanistik* 30 (1992): 149–57.

—. "Joseph ein Tölpel? Zur Josephgestalt in den Weihnachtsszenen des spätmittelalterlichen deutschen und französischen Dramas." *Amsterdamer Beiträge zur älteren Germanistik* 33 (1990): 127–37.

—. "Zur Aufführungs- und Lesefunktion deutscher und französischer Spiele im Mittelalter." *Amsterdamer Beiträge zur älteren Germanistik* 34 (1991): 143–51.

Veltrusky, Jarmila F. "La mondanité de Marie-Madeleine: beauté, joie, péché." Dans Maria Chiabò et F. Doglio éd. *Esperienze dello Spettacolo Religioso nell'Europa del Quattrocentro*. Rome: Torre d'Orfeo, 1993. 269–81.

—. "Chants, paroles et jeux de scène dans le *Jeu d'Adam*." *Théâtre Opéra Ballet* 2 (1996): 31–54.

—. "Dramatic Characters and Composite *Dramatis personae*." *Theatre Survey* 35 (1994): 19–32.

—. "L'Apothiquaire dans le théâtre religieux du moyen âge." Dans *Création Théâtrale et Savoir Scientifique en Europe*, éd. I. Mamczarz. Paris: Klincksieck, 1992. 153–67.

Vimont, D. "La Confrérie de la Passion et les origines du théâtre français à la Trinité et à l'Hôtel de Bourgogne." *Bulletin de la Société de l'Histoire de Paris et de l'Île de France* (1940): 49–55.

Vince, Ronald W. *A Companion to the Medieval Theatre*. New York: Greenwood Press, 1989.

———. *Ancient and Medieval Theatre: A Historiographical Handbook*. Westport, CT: Greenwood Press, 1984.

Vingqvist, H. *Étude sur la langue du Mistère de Saint Adrien*. Diss. Lund, 1909.

Vitale-Brovarone, A. "Devant et derrière le rideau: mise en scène et *secretz* dans le cahier d'un régisseur provençal du moyen âge." Dans Maria Chiabò, F. Doglio, et M. Maymone, éd. *Actes du IVe Colloque de la SITM (Viterbo, 1983)*. Viterbo, 1983. 453–64.

———. "Il quaderno di segreti d'un regista provenzale del medioevo: Note per la messa in scena d'una Passion." *Pluteus Testi* 1 (1984): pages ?

Vitz, Evelyn B. "La liturgie dans les Mystères de la Passion—et les mystères en tant que liturgie." Dans Giuseppe Di Stefano et R. Bidler, ed. *La Recherche: bilan et perspective*. Montréal: Éditions CERES, 2000. 591–608.

Voigt, L. *Die Mirakel der Pariser Hs 819, welche epische Stoffe behandeln, auf ihre Quellen untersucht*. Leipzig, 1883.

Voragine, Jacobus de. *La Légende Dorée: Édition critique, dans la révision de 1476 par Jean Batallier, d'après la traduction de Jean de Vignay (1333–1348) de la "Legenda aurea" (c.1261–1266)*, ed. Brenda Dunn-Lardeau. Paris: Champion, 1997.

———. *The Golden Legend*, translated by William G. Ryan. 2 vols. Princeton: Princeton University Press, 1993.

Wadsworth, Randolph L. Jr. "The *bourreaux* in Arnoul Gréban's *Mystère de la Passion*." *Revue de Littérature Comparée* 44 (1970): 499–509.

Warning, Rainer. "On the Alterity of Medieval Religious Drama." *New Literary History* 10 (1979): 265–92.

———. "Ritus, Mythos und geistliches Spiel." *Poetica* 3 (1970): 211–39, et dans Manfred Fuhrmann, ed. *Poetik und Hermeneutik*. 5 vols. Munich: Fink, 1970. Vol. 5, 83–114.

—. *Funktion und Struktur. Die Ambivalenzen des geistlichen Spiels*. Munich: Fink, 1974.

Warren, G. "Les diables dans la *Passion* d'Arnoul Gréban." *Chimères* 15 (1981): 9–25.

Wickham, Glynne. *Early English Stages: 1300–1660*. 4 vols. London, 1959–72.

—. *The Medieval Theatre*. London: Weidenfeld and Nicolson, 1974.

Wieck, H. *Die Teufel auf der mittelalterlichen Mysterienbühne Frankreichs*. Marburg: Hirschfeld, 1887.

Wilkins, James D. "Corps et biens: The Body as Currency in Fifteenth-Century *Mystères de la Passion*." *Fifteenth-Century Studies* 24 (1998): 254–72.

Wilkins, N. "Music in the Fourteenth-Century *Miracles de Nostre Dame par personnages*." *Musica Disciplina* 28 (1974): 39–75.

Wilmotte, Maurice. "L'élément comique dans le théâtre religieux." Dans *Études Critiques sur la tradition littéraire en France*. Paris: Champion, 1909. 93–126.

Witt, Elizabeth A. *Contrary Marys in Medieval English and French Drama*. New York: Peter Lang, 1995.

Wright, J. G. *Study of the Themes of the Resurrection in the Medieval French Drama*. Bryn Mawr: Bryn Mawr College, 1935.

Wright, Stephen K. "The Destruction of Jerusalem: An Annotated Checklist of Plays and Performances, ca. 1350–1620." *Research Opportunities in Renaissance Drama* 41 (2002): 131–56.

—. "History of an Audience: Eustache Marcadé's *La Vengance [sic] Jhesucrist* in the Light of Reception Theory." *Fifteenth-Century Studies* 12 (1987), 195–207.

—. *The Vengeance of our Lord: Medieval Dramatizations of the Destruction of Jerusalem*. Toronto: Pontifical Institute of Mediaeval Studies, 1989.

Yates, Frances. "Dramatic Religious Processions in Paris in the Sixteenth Century." *Annales musicologiques: Moyen Âge et Renaissance* 2 (1954): 215–71.

Young, Karl. "Observations on the Origin of the Medieval Passion Play." *Publications of the Modern Language Association of America* 25 (1910): 309–54.

—. *The Drama of the Medieval Church.* 2 vols. Oxford: Oxford University Press, 1933. Repr. Clarendon, 1962.

Zumthor, Paul. *Le Masque et la Lumière: La Poétique des Grands Rhétoriqueurs.* Paris: Éditions du Seuil, 1978.

Graham A. Runnalls: g.a.runnalls@ed.ac.uk
University of Edinburgh

Jesse Hurlbut: jesse_hurlbut@byu.edu
Brigham Young University

The Cleveland 'St. John the Baptist,' Attributed to Petrus Christus, and Philip the Good's Triumphal Entry into Bruges (1440)

Mark Trowbridge

In 1979, the Cleveland Museum of Art acquired a small, well-preserved panel of *St. John the Baptist* (fig. 1), its composition suggesting that it was once the right wing of a triptych.[1] Temporarily ascribed to the circle of Jan van Eyck, the panel was later (and more precisely) attributed by several critics to Petrus Christus. Principal among these scholars was Maryan Ainsworth, who advocated including such an ascription in the 1994 catalogue for the retrospective of Christus's work to be housed at the Metropolitan Museum in New York; for instance, she noted the work's "similarities in technique and execution" to other paintings by that artist. Ainsworth also dated Cleveland's panel shortly after Christus's 1444 arrival in Bruges, at a time when his work was most Eyckian in character;[2] dendrochronological analysis, undertaken in a symposium accompanying the New York exhibition, affirmed such a date.[3]

Significant aspects of the Cleveland *Baptist* are reminiscent of Eyckian prototypes. The central figure combines features from the two St. Johns as they appeared on the exterior of Jan and Hubert van Eyck's celebrated polyptych in Ghent (fig. 2). The Cleveland *Baptist*'s pose, bearing, and indicating gesture (referencing the *Agnus Dei*) derive from his counterpart in Ghent, and his slight turn of the shoulder, cock of the head, and right arm drawn further from the lamb as indicated object seem to come from the Ghent Evangelist's pose as well. Less significant details of the Cleveland *Baptist* might also be traceable to the workshop of Jan van Eyck: Anne Lurie has noted that the sweet woodruff in the lower left corner was quite rare in fifteenth-c. paintings, yet it appeared around the female martyrs in the *Ghent Altarpiece*,[4] and behind the angel's wing in New York's Friedsam *Annunciation*, the latter also recently reattributed to Christus.[5]

Eyckian elements in the Cleveland *Baptist* must have been inspired by the painting's likely milieu, Bruges, and may have been specifically requested by clients there.[6] Jean Wilson has written about that city's "culture of display": how persons associated with the Burgundian court emulated ducal cultural practices, only to find these imitations adopted by aspiring Brugeois further down the social ladder. As Wilson notes, such practices helped lead to an art-buying population who valued replicas as highly as original works, a clientele fueling their "particular desires for specific types of images."[7] On the other hand, the Cleveland panel's Eyckian appearance was also a choice made by its painter, perhaps motivated by Christus's own attempts to cater to such a clientele. Working for an open market rather than for commission, and aware of existing patterns of patronage, Christus would be well served by emulating the style of Bruges's most famous painter. This study will investigate another way that Christus may have tried to accommodate the tastes of Bruges clients: in the Cleveland panel he also sought to evoke a procession in Bruges's recent history, one that lay rooted in the city's cultural identity. The dramatized pageant welcoming Duke Philip the Good back to the city in 1440 was a procession headed by the figure of St. John the Baptist.

In the Cleveland acquisition, Christus's *St. John the Baptist* stands alone in a wilderness. While this pose is common for saints depicted in altarpiece wings of Netherlandish paintings, that particular composition immediately evokes one of the better-known moments from the saint's *vita*: his prayers and sermons vocalized in the Judean wilderness, as recounted in Matthew 3, 1–2. This moment is certainly what Christus intends to portray; though the saint's figure dominates the foreground of the composition, the artist depicts the verdant wilderness with the utmost precision, making the setting as important for the composition as the saint who inhabits it.[8] Landscape details, particularly the flowers, help specify the Baptist's preaching in the wilderness; Ainsworth discusses the flowering strawberries, to which the Baptist's left foot points, an image signifying "a noble soul in humble surroundings," and the blooming plantains, just right of the Baptist's left hip, plants which thrive even along roads and pathways. Also called *Wegerich*, a German term meaning "right way," the plant symbolizes the way the prophet prepared for Christ, reminding viewers of the Baptist's words from the wilderness.[9] The remote character of the St. John's surroundings is carefully established by the walled city (fig. 3), which the artist relegates to the background, seen behind the figure's right shoulder. There the fortified gate serves to emphasize the distance of civilization, with the saint separated from the city by a darkened forest, wherein two figures converge along a lonely path. This remote city ostensibly represents Jerusalem, but the artist has translated it, like the Judean desert landscape described in scripture, into something more local, so that it closely resembles contemporary Bruges.

The Cleveland composition belongs to a fairly standard image depiction of a full-length Baptist standing alone in the wilderness. Most versions come from the vicinity of Bruges, no surprise to the art historian, when one considers the importance of that city's Hospital of St. John, and the activity of its members in buying works of art. These comparable acquisitions include another *Baptist* by Christus (destroyed, ex-Berlin, fig. 4), one by Hans Memling (Paris, Louvre, fig. 5), two by Gérard David (New York, Metropolitan Museum, fig. 6, and Madrid, El Escorial), and two by the Master of the St. Lucy Legend (Minneapolis, fig. 7, and Upton House). Fewer standing Baptists can be found outside Bruges, although they do exist: a panel in Granada attributed to Albert van Ouwater of Haarlem, for example, or the right wing of the *Perle van Brabant* altarpiece by Dirk Bouts of Louvain (Munich, Alte Pinakothek, fig. 8).[10] All variations on this theme share certain qualities: the lush, forested landscape, often replete with rugged hills and rocky outcrops behind the saint; a path, winding through these hills and trees, signifying the *way* the prophet prepares for the Lord. Still, the standing Baptists vary enough in pose and gesture to suggest that they do not come from a single prototype, with Christus's Cleveland version resembling only van Eyck's earlier Ghent grisaille (fig. 2) and, to a much lesser degree, David's later New York wing (fig. 6).[11]

Just as the Baptist's pose differs in these many examples, so too do the backgrounds; most lack the city depicted in the Cleveland image (including David's otherwise similar version), their artists striving, it seems, to emphasize the saint's solitude rather than his distance from civilization. A tiny city sits beside the water far behind Bouts's *Baptist*, and a slightly more prominent town is perched upon a hill in Memling's Louvre version, but neither of these municipalities has the fortified gate and bridge seen behind Cleveland's saint. Only the Lucy Master's Minneapolis panel (fig. 7) has such a gate, complete with two round battlements seen flanking the opening, as well as a crenellated bridge. Still, that painting's gate differs from Cleveland's, the artist adding an extra set of fortified towers on the bridge, and omitting the spires atop the main battlements.

The cityscape in the Cleveland *Baptist* may also help confirm its attribution to Christus. Similar civic fortifications — walls and turrets of faded brick or sandstone, surmounted by blue-slated roofs and spires — appear in works central to that artist's oeuvre, including his autograph *Annunciation* and *Nativity* in Berlin (fig. 9), the signed Groeningemuseum's *Nativity* (fig. 10), and the Metropolitan Museum's *Lamentation* of the Mother of Christ.[12] While these comparisons are admittedly inconclusive as evidence for Christus's authorship of the Cleveland panel, they show the consistency of that panel's background within the artist's oeuvre. This brief tour of Christus's cityscapes also indicates the importance of the gate in the Cleveland *Baptist*. In his other works, Christus's cities are far smaller and less substantial as parts of the compositions; the town only becomes equally significant in his Copenhagen *St. Anthony and Donor* (fig. 11), also the city most resembling Cleveland's background. In the Copenhagen *St. Anthony*, the city's prominence is due to the artist's intent to specify it as Bruges, a symbol — like the coat of arms — denoting the donor's social standing. The *Baptist*'s city is no less intended to specify Bruges, and I argue that it is also no less tied to civic status, as important to its owner as the town and arms were to the donor accompanied by *St. Anthony*.[13]

The city gate in the Cleveland *Baptist* may have been included because it recalls a dramatized version of the saint in the wilderness: the people of

Bruges mounted the scene during a recent triumphal entry of Duke Philip the Good of Burgundy, a major event playing a significant role in Bruges's sense of identity. In 1440, Philip returned to the city after a prolonged absence; the people of Bruges had revolted against him in 1437, barring the city gates behind him. The uprising had been primarily economic: as Philip battled England in Calais, the Hanseatic League, ever important to Bruges's economy, departed the city, after several Hanseatic merchants, suspected of harboring English loyalties, were killed in nearby Sluis. Bruges's economic dissatisfaction with Philip's rule led the city to assert greater independence, using its militia — recently returned from Calais — to intimidate and dominate cities in the surrounding region.

When Philip came to quell the uprising in May 1437, the people of Bruges drove him and his delegation from their city, killing the officer who led the Duke's retreat.[14] Furious, Philip immediately retaliated, returning well armed with his own troops, and quickly subjugating the town by force; by March 1438, Bruges had surrendered. For the nearly three years that followed, the Duke imposed various and oppressive sanctions upon the city, restricting its control over the surrounding region, limiting the privileges of its guild members, and imposing prohibitive fines. It was not until December 1440 that Philip would finally reconcile with Bruges, and he returned on the third Sunday of Advent to forgive the city, or so its inhabitants desperately hoped.

In order to help inspire Philip's pardon, the city greeted him with more than twenty dramatized tableaux, staged along a processional route leading down the Langestraat, through the Market, concluding at the Ducal Palace (see the map in the Appendix).[15] The first drama, on a platform erected outside the city's *Kruispoort* (labeled #1 on the map), presented John the Baptist praying in the wilderness. A fine description of the entry can be found in the *Excellente cronike van Vlaenderen*, published in 1531, whose text relied on earlier eyewitness reports:

> Item, first a forest was organized at the Kruispoort, standing constructed in wood on four wheels, like a bush all green, and in it stood the personage of John the Baptist, clad in a rough hide, bare armed and belted as it befitted him. And this was led before the procession all the way to the court of the prince, and before the bush was written [in Latin]: "Hear the voice crying in the wilderness, preparing the way for the Lord." This was a symbol for the arrival of our formidable Lord [Philip], and that every effort should be made to welcome him.[16]

Not by coincidence, Philip had heard the Baptist's same words that very morning during mass, as the gospel reading from the Advent liturgy: more than simply recalling the Duke's recent experience, the inscription on the stage was intended to invite Philip's active identification with Christ, part of the city's overall plan to win the Duke's forgiveness.[17]

The actor (of St. John) continued to prepare the way for the Duke during the entire procession, leading him through the gate, and serving as his guide for the forthcoming tableaux. A second chronicle recounts that after entering Bruges, the Baptist actually spoke (in Latin), "shouting to all people in the street where he was led: 'Prepare the way for the Lord!' — all the way to the Duke's court."[18] By presenting to Philip the various religious scenes the Duke would encounter, the dramatized Baptist effectively played the role that saints do in art, functioning like the St. John who introduced Philip the Good's grandfather, Philip the Bold, as reflected on the portal of the chapel in Dijon's Chartreuse de Champmol, perhaps helping to inspire Bruges's choice to welcome the Duke in 1440.[19]

Each scene in the procession continued to encourage viewers to accept Philip's ongoing identification with Christ. The Baptist led the Duke to a Tree of Jesse (labeled #6 on the map), this timeworn symbol for the divine right to rule now applied directly to Philip, the Duke equated with Christ the king. Philip's identification with the Savior was sustained by the many prophets he met, each reciting verses about rejoicing on the Lord's Day (labeled numbers 3, 5, and 7), and by Christ himself, on a stage before the Dominican Cloister (labeled #11), where Philip saw the Savior tell Zacchaeus that salvation had come that day, the very day that the Duke had come to Bruges. Elsewhere, Philip encountered the city of Bruges, erected in miniature on the Molenbrug (labeled #12), before which King David played his harp, a combination suggesting the symbolic link between Bruges and Jerusalem, common in the fifteenth century. As the actor playing David sang "of the mercies of the lord forever," figures singing "Noel" directly to Philip appeared from the model city's rooftops.[20] Still other stages symbolized the city as worthy of such mercy, either penitent before Christ, as Mary Magdalen was (#9), or joyful at his arrival, as the shepherds were at the Nativity (#10). Each reference, far from being subtle, reiterated the link between the advent of Christ and the return of the Duke: both had come to bring grace, Christ to all of humankind, and Philip specifically to Bruges, or so the city fathers anticipated.

The Baptist remained on hand at each tableau, exhorting Philip to adopt Christ's role, and, by so doing, forgive the city. At the end of the pageant, the Duke saw Christ in a final pair of productions, a *Resurrection* on the Market Square (# 21), and a *Transfiguration* at the entry to his Ducal Palace (# 22), the latter inscribed with Christ's words from the Resurrection, "Behold I am with you unto the end of the age."[21] Again the Baptist's presence helped underscore the significance of these two dramas: Philip was to see himself as Christ *resurrected* to power, remaining *with the city* and residing in his Bruges palace.

Bruges's efforts were largely successful: although Philip would maintain the itinerant nature of his court, he did welcome the city back to his fold; more importantly, he eased his sanctions of the past three years. Bruges's success was so notable that other towns would employ similar tactics to curry the Duke's favor after their own rebellions: Lille in 1453; Mons in 1455; and most famously Ghent in 1458, when that town's citizens used dramas to stress Philip's Christ-like nature and the city's penitence, ten years after the onset of their rebellion and following five years of ducal sanctions.[22]

Christus's Cleveland *Baptist* evokes particular aspects of its 1440 theatrical counterpart: that dramatic tableau was erected just outside the city gates, a foliate wilderness from which the Baptist directly addressed his audience.[23] While most painted Baptists share the forested setting, the Cleveland version is one of the few which has St. John directly speaking to the audience, with his head and shoulders squared to the viewer. Cleveland's panel is also characterized by the prominence given to the background city, rare among other versions of this scene: this town, surrounded by water, is dominated by a fortified bridge, like Bruges's once-barred gates, now seen as open and teeming with traffic. Although meant to represent Jerusalem, the scene city still seems intended to specify Bruges, its gate closely resembling Bruges's eight medieval portals, erected toward the end of the fourteenth century.

The fortified gate in the Cleveland panel resembles Bruges's sandstone *Kruispoort*, before which the dramatized Baptist stands (fig. 12). That edifice, erected in 1401–1402 by Jan van Oudenaarde and Maarten van Leuven, has been often and heavily restored. Its original appearance is known through various sixteenth-c. depictions of the city; most famous is a detail from Marcus Gheeraerts's huge etched map of the city, commissioned by Bruges in 1562 (fig. 13). Despite illustrating the opposite side of the *Kruispoort*, many of Gheeraerts's etched details concur with the gate painted by Christus: the rounded towers flanking the opening, the machicolated upper story between those towers, the crenellated bridge leading over the canal, the many conical spires crowning the structure (hand-colored blue, like the Cleveland gate, in an impression of Gheeraerts's map in Bruges's *Steinmetzkabinet*), even the proximity of a windmill. Yet, Cleveland's painting does not replicate the exact profile of Bruges's *Kruispoort*; rather, it is an amalgam of all Bruges's gates. Furthermore, Christus did not depict the *Kruispoort* decorated, as it certainly was for the 1440 entry, just as it would be in 1515, for the royal entry of the future Emperor Charles V. In an illustration of the latter event (fig. 14), the *Kruispoort* again departs from the one depicted later by Gheeraerts, just as Christus's gate had before, despite ostensibly recording Charles V's entry into the city.

Recent theories might explain Christus's departure from visual accuracy; in spite of the renowned interests of Netherlandish painters in detailing the particulars of their everyday world, when it came to architecture, artists often employed details to evoke rather than specify locations or contexts. Craig Harbison discusses the inaccurate cityscapes confounding scholars who look to situate Netherlandish paintings in a given locale.[24] More reminiscent than exacting, Harbison argued that these painted buildings often allude to locations without specifically documenting them; I contend that the gate in the Cleveland *Baptist* makes just such an allusion. Christus includes details sufficient to remind its viewers of Bruges and its *Kruispoort*, yet the artist, like most masters in fifteenth-c. Netherlands, was not compelled to detail either city or gate exactly.

Likewise, particulars in Christus's *Baptist* are sufficient to allude to that figure's counterpart from Philip's 1440 triumphal entry, even though the artist does not resort to an exact portrait of that tableau — a point I will return to at the conclusion of this study. Here it is important to note that viewers would have drawn easy connections between this painted *Baptist* and the enacted saint who had recently greeted Philip, especially during a period when, as Max Martens has noted, "the city was slowly recovering from the dramatic political events it had witnessed between 1436 and 1440."[25] Long after the Duke's triumphal entry, the citizens of Bruges would have remembered the Baptist at the city gate and his role as their spokesperson in a production that garnered Philip's forgiveness and led to the town's renewed economic success. In a manner similar to the panel's Eyckian style, the allusion to a significant part of Bruges's history and identity may have been requested by a patron entrenched in what Wilson called that city's "culture of display."[26] Whatever the case, these elements certainly helped to assure ready acceptance of Christus's work among a broad clientele.

Understanding what might be painted allusions to late-medieval stages requires some discussion of the importance such dramas held for their audience, and how this significance may have helped inspire patronage of, or interest in, such pictures. Philip's 1440 entry was just one exemplification of dramatized production in which Bruges vested its interests. Like most Netherlandish centers, the city also mounted an annual *ommegang*, the Procession of the Holy Blood, in which dramatized carts traveled through the city, re-enacting scenes at specified points along the route.[27] Philip's entry was a variation on this scheme, with the stages stationary and the audience moving from scene to scene. The relationship between the annual procession and Philip's triumphal entry was even closer, with the city's reusing dramas from the *ommegang*, including its Nativity, as well as one of its most spectacular stages, the towering Tree of Jesse.

Biblical scenes had been part of the Holy Blood Procession since the first dramas were introduced in 1396, when a "ghesellen van den spele" was paid to impersonate the "twelve apostles and four evangelists."[28] This production continued annually, and over the next half decade Bruges introduced plays that came to comprise two primary sequences: five scenes centered around Christ's Infancy (the Tree of Jesse, Annunciation, Nativity, King Herod, and the Adoration of the Magi), and another series depicting His Passion which included the City of Jerusalem mentioned above, and an Agony in the Garden, referred to in the archives as a "Hovekine," the latter production mounted each year by the city's painters' guild.[29]

Bruges's introduction of plays into its Procession was an expression of a wide interest in biblical street theater that first flowered in most regional centers around the year 1400, many focusing on similar themes.[30] These mystery plays enthralled the people of the Low Countries, with literally thousands of dramas recorded in the fifteenth and sixteenth centuries, a multitude of productions contributing to what drama historian Theo de Ronde called a "theatrical life" characterizing the fifteenth-c. Netherlands.[31]

Like processions in other Netherlandish centers, Bruges's had begun as a more simple, though no less important, religious festival. Its *ommegang* focused on the public display of a famed relic of Christ's blood, delivered from Jerusalem in the twelfth century, and ushered around the city as early as 1303. Already in 1310, Pope Clement IV granted indulgences to any who attended Bruges's Procession, and in 1331 the city elevated the relic upon a dais, ensuring that none would miss it, or the papal pardon that attended its viewing.[32] Such religious implications played no small role in the Procession's growing popularity and would have aided the devotional impact of the scenes that came to accompany the relic after 1396.[33] Even before the dramas became a staple of the spectacle, the event had developed into an occasion for civic leaders to vaunt their town before invited visitors, and Bruges took many steps to insure the presence of foreign dignitaries at its spectacles, issuing invitations every year after 1331.[34] The fame of Bruges's Procession was further spread when it sent its skilled theatrical artisans to other cities, either to assist in local processions, or to witness the latest developments in dramatic arts as mounted by those towns.[35]

The city's pride in its plays is confirmed by the reuse of the *ommegang* dramas for Philip's triumphal entry in 1440; with its civic life on the line, the town appropriated many scenes from Procession to Entry. The city would continue to rely upon its annual pageantry to impress the Burgundian court. After 1460 the annual dramas in the Procession of the Holy Blood became infrequent; Bruges staged them a mere ten times in the final four decades of the fifteenth century, but each time its leaders were in attendance.[36]

In these crucial contexts, Bruges's repeated reliance upon its most popular productions serves as a potent reminder of the significance which mystery plays held for that city's sense of identity. Any painting that sought to evoke such dramas would only have benefited from such importance, becoming more desirable both as status symbol and as potent votive object. Christus's allusion to one of those plays helps to clarify our understanding of patronage in the fifteenth century, shedding light on how audiences perceived the works. Bruges clients may have desired paintings with dramatic overtones, hoping that such connections to the mystery plays — and by extension to the miraculous, indulgencing relic of the Holy Blood — might enhance the *St. John* panel's efficacy as a vehicle for prayer.

However, despite relying on religious imagery, Christus's Cleveland panel makes reference to a spectacle primarily secular in tone. As such, Petrus's *Baptist*, regardless of its modest size, would have become a signifier of the city itself, and an aspect important for local consumption or for export trade. Though Christus did not yet reside in Bruges in 1440, on coming to the city, the immigrant artist would have become familiar with the local dramas and aware of the importance his new neighbors vested in those productions. Not only did the event loom large in Bruges's history, the city's artists had been responsible for all its theatrical decorations. Bruges's municipal accounts paid the "painters of the city and the sculptors of the Carmersstraat" twice, first for their materials, and again for making and delivering their work.[37] The artists may even have helped enact the dramas: the accounts list a separate payment to a group of performers who "staged the histories on the stages through all the streets, from our aforementioned formidable lord's court to the Kruispoort, for the costs and difficulties that they had on the day that our eminent lord entered."[38] Although the municipal accounts did not identify these performers, the twenty-two different representations welcoming would have required a large group indeed, probably comprising anyone in Bruges skilled in theatrical presentations. Certainly, the members of the painters' guild would have been included, since they had staged an Agony in the Garden play in the Procession of the Holy Blood for more than forty years and came to supervise all of Bruges's processional dramas after 1445.[39]

Correlations between Christus's *Baptist* and the 1440 entry help clarify aspects of the artist's early practice: his Cleveland panel relies upon religious imagery and makes reference to a secular civic spectacle. As such, his *Baptist*, despite its modest size, would have become a potent signifier of Bruges itself, and an aspect important for local consumption or export trade. The painting's theatrical allusions render a portrait of the young artist as a very astute businessman. On arriving in Bruges, Christus not only gained inside access to the workshop of Jan van Eyck, inheriting some of that artist's clientele, but Petrus also shrewdly mined local theatrical traditions employed by the painters' guild in the service of the city, thus helping to insure that his works would have as wide an audience as possible in his newly adopted market.

Connections to theatrical productions helped to explain Christus's early years in Bruges and aspects of fifteenth-c. patronage, but, in conclusion, the nature of the relationship between art and drama in his *St. John the Baptist* is equally important to historians of both fields and illuminates a long-standing problem in studying connections between the two visual media. Interplay between art and theater did occur: some of the century's greatest artists — Robert Campin, his pupils Rogier van der Weyden and Jacques Daret, plus Hugo van der Goes, and Petrus Christus — were recorded as working in conjunction with dramatized processions. Despite this circumstance, stages never appear as such in Netherlandish panel paintings (of the fifteenth century) by those artists or others. The conclusions drawn here regarding Cleveland's *St. John the Baptist* suggest that this lack of accurate depictions (i.e., stages) may not have been a problem for contemporary audiences looking to draw connections between the two media, and need not remain so for modern historians. As mentioned before, painters, in the Cleveland panel and elsewhere, may have sought to evoke rather than to specify theatrical conventions and events in order to enhance the secular and/or spiritual value of their works. Despite the absence of late-medieval stages in these paintings, scholars can still utilize the visual conventions of late-medieval theater for a fuller understanding of how images functioned in that society. When audiences confronted scenes in paintings, the onlookers' experience with the same topics in theater would form the critical arsenal the viewers used to interpret and understand meaning in the visual arts. Mining the rich tradition of theatrical performances reveals much information on how viewers may have understood images and provides a fuller picture of what we might call an early Netherlandish "period eye."[40]

Stations of the Procession in Bruges. Map of Bruges by Marcus Gheeraerts, 1562 (digital manipulation copyright of the author):

1. Outside the Kruispoort: John the Baptist in the Wilderness
2. Inside the Kruispoort: Job on the Dung Heap
3. Corner of Langestraat and Peperstraat: Four Prophets with Scrolls
4. Hospital of St. Aubert, on the Langestraat: Sacrifice of Abraham
5. Corner of Langestraat and Rodestraat: Four Prophets with Scrolls
6. Corner of Langestraat and Ooievaarstraat: Tree of Jesse
7. Corner of Langestraat and Vulderstraat: Four Prophets with Scrolls
8. Corner of Langestraat and Kerseboomstraat: Esther Elected among Women
9. Corner of Langestraat and Bilkske: Esther and Ahasuerus
10. Dominican Cloister, on Langestraat: Nativity, with the Annunciation to the Shepherds
11. Dominican Cloister, on Langestraat: St. Dominic and the Virgin, with Zacchaeus at the Entry into Jerusalem

12. On the Molenbrug: King David and the City of Bruges
13. Corner of Hoogstraat and Boomgaardstraat: Three Acts of Mercy (Hungry, Thirsty, Naked)
14. Corner of Hoogstraat and Ridderstraat: Three Acts of Mercy (Stranger, Prisoner, Sick)
15. On Hoogstraat, leading to Burg: Last Act of Mercy (Dead)
16. On Hoogstraat, leading to Burg: God the Father, with Woman Kneeling at His Feet
17. On Hoogstraat, at Entrance to the Burg: Story of Joachim, in Three Scenes
18. In the Burg: Castle Fountain, with Woman Urinating Wine
19. At the Prison, in the Burg: Peter Freed from Prison
20. On Breidelstraat, at Exit from the Burg: Fountain
21. In the Markt, at the Raashuis: Resurrection, with Christ and St. Christopher
22. On Geldmuntstraat, at Entrance to Ducal Court: Transfiguration.

Appendix: Itinerary of Philip's 1440 entry into Bruges

Map: Marcus Gheeraerts, *Map of Bruges*. Bruges, City Archives

Fig. 1: Jan van Eyck, (immediate circle of) *John the Baptist in a Landscape*, c.1440. Copyright Cleveland Museum of Art. Leonard C. Hanna, Jr. Fund, 1979.80.

Fig. 2: Jan and Hubert van Eyck, *Ss. John the Baptist and John the Evangelist*. Detail from the exterior of the *Ghent Altarpiece*, 1432. Cathedral of St. Baafs, Ghent. Photo copyright IRPA–KIK, Brussels.

Fig. 3: City gate. Detail of figure 1.

Fig. 4 (left): Petrus Christus, *St. John the Baptist*, c.1460–65.
Formerly Kaiser-Friedrich Museum, Berlin (destroyed).

Fig. 5 (right): Hans Memling, *St. John the Baptist*, c.1480.
Paris, Musée du Louvre, inv. RF 1453.

Fig. 6 (left): Gérard David, *St. John the Baptist*. Left wing of a triptych, c.1485–90. New York, The Metropolitan Museum of Art. Michael Friedsam Collection, 1931 (32.100.40b).

Fig. 7 (right): Master of the St. Lucy Legend, *St. John the Baptist*, left wing of the triptych. The Lamentation with St. John and St. Catherine, c.1490. Minneapolis Institute of Arts, Bequest John R. Van Derlip Fund in Memory of Ethel Morrison Derlip 35.7.87.

Fig. 8 (left) : Dirk Bouts, *St. John the Baptist*, left wing of the *Perle van Brabant Altarpiece*, c.1470–80. Munich, Alte Pinakothek, Inv. Nr. WAF 77.

Fig. 9(right): Petrus Christus, *Nativity*, 1452. Staatliche Museen zu Berlin, Preussischer Kulturbesitz, Gemäldegalerie. Photo: Jörg P. Anders.

Fig. 10: Petrus Christus, *Nativity*, detail of cityscape, c.1452. Bruges, Groeninge Museum. Photo copyright IRPA–KIK, Brussels.

Fig. 11: Petrus Christus, *St. Anthony and a Donor*, c.1450.
Copenhagen, Statens Museum for Kunst.

Fig. 12: Kruispoort, Bruges (photograph copyright of the author).

Fig. 13: Marcus Gheeraerts, Kruispoort and vicinity,
detail from *Map of Bruges*, 1562.

Fig. 14: Kruispoort, from Remy du Puys, *La tryumphante et solomnelle entrée faicte sur le nouvel et joyeux advenement de treshault . . . prince Monsieur Charles prince hespaignes Archiduc dautirce . . . en sa ville de Bruges lan mil. V cens et XV le xviii jour d'avril après Pasques.*
Paris: Gilles de Gourmont, 1515.

Notes

[1] This article was presented in shorter form at the 2001 College Art Association Conference in Chicago. The study originally formed part of my dissertation "Art and *Ommegangen*. Paintings, Processions, and Dramas in the Late-Medieval Low Countries" (Diss., Institute of Fine Arts, New York University, 2000), which I am currently reworking for publication with a fellowship from the Metropolitan Museum of Art. I wish to thank Maryan Ainsworth of the Metropolitan Museum and Ann Roberts of Lake Forest College for reading drafts of the current work and graciously offering their advice.

[2] Maryan W. Ainsworth, ed., *Petrus Christus. Renaissance Master of Bruges* (New York: Metropolitan Museum of Art, 1994): 84.

[3] "dendrochronological": concerning the science of dating events, intervals of time, and variations in environment in former periods by study of the sequence of and differences between *rings of growth in trees and aged wood*. Of the panels from the van Eyck/Christus group analyzed, only Jan van Eyck's *Madonna in a Church* (1437, Berlin) came from a tree that was felled earlier, between 1316-22, as compared to the Cleveland panel, from 1364-70. See: Peter Klein, "Dendrochronological Findings of the Van Eyck/Christus Group," 149-66 in *Petrus Christus in Renaissance Bruges. An Interdisciplinary Approach.* ed. Maryan W. Ainsworth (New York: Metropolitan Museum of Art, 1995): 153.

[4] Alison T. Lurie, "A Newly Discovered Eyckian *St. John the Baptist in a Landscape*," *Cleveland Museum of Art Bulletin* 68 (1981): 86-109 (91). In the 1998 Metropolitan Museum catalogue, Della Sperling further discusses the symbolism of this plant: also known as "lady's bedstraw," it alluded to the bed where Mary would give birth to Christ. See *From Van Eyck to Bruegel. Early Netherlandish Painting in the Metropolitan Museum of Art*, ed. M. W. Ainsworth and Keith Christiansen (New York: Metropolitan Museum of Art, 1998): 102.

[5] Ainsworth, *Renaissance Master*, 117.

[6] Such a request may have been the case even for works destined for foreign export; for one example of this inspiration, see Stephanie Buck, "Petrus Christus's Berlin Wings and the Metropolitan Museum's Eyckian Diptych," 65-84 in Ainsworth, ed. *Christus in Renaissance Bruges*.

[7] Jean Wilson, *Painting in Bruges at the Close of the Middle Ages: Studies in Society and Visual Culture* (University Park: Pennsylvania State University Press, 1998): 6.

[8] Such interest in natural details is uncommon in the work of Christus, and is one of the arguments used to argue for an alternative attribution (Ainsworth and Christiansen, *Van Eyck to Bruegel*, 102). Still, Ainsworth noted that Christus was quite able to render the scene with the exactitude seen in the Cleveland panel, and did so in one of his better-documented works, the *Madonna of Jan Vos* (*Renaissance Master*, 81); elsewhere, Della Sperling affirmed that the Cleveland *Baptist* and the Friedsam *Annunciation* were "certainly by the same artist" (in Ainsworth and Christiansen, ed., *Van Eyck to Bruegel*, 100).

[9] Ainsworth, *Renaissance Master*, 80; and Lurie, "Eyckian *St. John*," 91.

[10] To this list of Netherlandish Baptists can be added (1) images depicting the Baptist standing in an interior, mostly by Hans Memling (two in London, and one each in Lübeck and Vienna); (2) seated Baptists, like those painted by Geertgen tot Sint Jans (Berlin) and Memling (Munich and Bruges); (3) a kneeling Baptist by the Master of the

Morrison Triptych (where?); (4) images where the saint accompanies the Virgin and/or other saints, as in four depictions by the Master of the St. Ursula Legend (Brussels, Champaign IL, Hamburg, and London); and (5) images where the saint accompanies a donor, such as David's Sedano triptych and Memling's diptych for Jean du Cellier (both in Paris, Musée du Louvre). This group purposely overlooks images narrating other events from the Baptist's life, such as Memling's large altarpiece for the St. Jans Hospitaal in Bruges, and David's *Baptism* triptych for Jean de Trompes (both in Bruges, at the St. Jans Hospitaal and Groeningemuseum respectively).

[11] On the other hand, Memling's many versions of the Baptist seem to share a common inspiration with only slight modifications; for example, his two seated Baptists (Munich and Bruges), and his four images of that saint in an interior (see note 10).

[12] Similar fortified bridges and gates can be found only in the background of Robert Campin's Dijon *Nativity*, and in two altarpiece wings by Rogier van der Weyden, one depicting St. Veronica, from the *Crucifixion* triptych in Vienna, and the other, interestingly enough, behind a half-length *St. John the Baptist*, from the Bracque triptych in Paris, Musée du Louvre.

[13] The gate's importance is obvious when the Cleveland composition is compared with Christus's other *Baptist*; cf. fig. 4.

[14] See Maximilian P. Martens, "Bruges During Petrus Christus's Lifetime," 3–14 (3) in Ainsworth, *Renaissance Master*.

[15] On the 1440 spectacle, see Gordon Kipling, "The Idea of Civic Triumph: Drama, Liturgy and the Royal Entry in the Low Countries," *Dutch Crossing* 22 (1984): 60–83; and Martens, "Artistic Patronage in Bruges Institutions, Ca. 1440–1482" (Diss., University of California, Santa Barbara, 1992): 125–35.

[16] My translation of the following original text in Middelnederlands language (both at once Flemish and Dutch):

> Item alder eerst was gheordonneirt ter Cruyspoorte een foreest, staende ghetemmert [fol. 107] up .iiij. wielen ghelijk een busch al groene, daer inne dat stont een personaegie van Sint Jan Baptiste, ghecleeet [sic] met eenen ruden velle, den aermebloot, ende ghegort als daer toe diende. Ende dit wort voor die processie ghevoert tot den hove toe vanden prinche, ende voor den busch so stont ghescreven: "Ego vox clamantis in deserto, parate viam domini." Ende was een bediet dat onse gheduchte heere quam, ende dat hem elck bereet soude maken om hem te ontfanghene (*Dits die excellente cronike van vlaenderen beghinnende van Liederick Buc den eersten frestier tot den laetsten, die door haer vrome feyte, namaels Graven van Vlaendren ghe maect worden, actervolghende die rechte afcomste der voorseiden graven, tot desen onsen luchtichste hooch gheboren Keyser Karolo, altijt vermeeerderde des rijcx gheboren te Ghendt* [Antwerp: Vorsterman, 1531]: fols. 106v–107).

The Baptist appeared in a similar capacity in Arnoul Gréban's *Passion* of 1452, where he delivered sermons and instructed the audience on how to prepare for Christ's arrival. See Edelgard DuBruck, "Changes of Taste and Audience Expectation in Fifteenth-Century Religious Drama," *Fifteenth-Century Studies* 6 (1983): 59–91. For more on theatrical characters that directly address the audience, see Clifford Davidson, "The Realism of the York Realist and the York Passion," *Speculum* 50 (1975): 270–83 (275); Jörg O.

Fichte, *Expository Voices in Medieval Drama: Essays on the Mode and Function of Dramatic Exposition* (Nuremberg: H. Carl, 1975): 27; and Hans-Jürgen Diller, "Theatrical Pragmatics: The Actor-Audience Relationship from the Mystery Cycles to the Early Tudor Comedies," in *Drama in the Middle Ages. Comparative and Critical Essays. Second Series*, ed. Clifford Davidson and John H. Stroupe (New York: AMS Press, 1991): 321-29 (322).

[17] Kipling, "Civic Triumph," 63-64.

[18] . . . welc personagie van Sente Janne vorseidt gine van der vorseider poorten eene goede spacie vore minen hardden gheduchten heeren tot in sijn hoff, roupende over al in de straten, daer by dore was lydende tot den volcke: "Parate viam Domino." (*Kronyk van Vlaenderen, van 580 tot 1467*, ed. Constant Philippe Serrure and Philip Marie Blommaert, 2 vols. [Ghent: D. J. Vanderhaeghen-Hulin, 1839-40 {2, 107}]).

[19] Interestingly, the pose and style of Cleveland's saint have also been compared to Claus Sluter's saint: Ainsworth, *Renaissance Master*, 78.

[20] Item ter muelenbrugghe was ghemaect een stede van schilderye, die welcke beteckende die stede van Brugghe. Ende daer in sadt die coninck David spelende up een harpe, ende daer stont ghescreven boven synen hoofde. "Misericordias domini in eternum cantabo." Ende huyter stede quamen vele maechdehens chierlick toe ghemaect, roupende yeghen onsen gheduchtegen here ende prinche: "Noel noel noel!" (*Excellente cronike*, fol. 107v.).

[21] Item voor tcalchuys was eene staegie, daer up dat ghetoocht was die resurrectie van onsen here in levende personen, aerdich toe ghemaect, ende daer stont ghescreven. Ecce ego vobiscum sum usqz ad consummationem seculi. Twelcke beteekende dat once ghenadighe heere, midts synder ghenade ende ontfermherticheyt metter stede van Brugghe wesen wilde ende blijven teeweghen daghen (*Excellente cronike*, fol. 108v.).

[22] On Lille, see Alan E. Knight, "The Image of the City in the Processional Theater of Lille," *Research Opportunities in Renaissance Drama* 30 (1988): 153-65. For Mons, see Gustave Cohen, *Le théâtre français en Belgique au moyen âge* (Brussels: La Renaissance du Livre, [1953]): 78; and Dagmar Eichberger, "The *Tableau Vivant*: An Ephemeral Art Form in Burgundian Civic Festivities," *Parergon* 6a (1988): 37-64 (43). On Ghent's rebellion and Philip's subsequent triumphal entry, see Jeffrey Chipps Smith, "Philip the Good's Triumphal Entry into Ghent in 1458," 258-68 in *'All the World's a Stage': Art and Pageantry in the Renaissance and Baroque*, ed. Barbara Wisch and Susan Scott Munshower (University Park: Pennsylvania State University Press, 1990); and Elizabeth Dhanens, "De blijde inkomst van Filips de Goede in 1458 en de plastische kunsten te Gent," *Actum Gandavi. Zeven bijdragen in verband met de oude kunst te Gent* (Academiae Analecta. Mededelingen van de Koninklijke Academie voor Wetenschappen, Letteren en Schone Kunsten van België [1987]: 55-89).

[23] See Albertine Clément-Hemery, *Histoire des fêtes civiles et religieuses, des usages anciens et modernes, de la Belgique méridionale (les Flandres, le Hainaut, le Brabant, etc.) et d'un grand nombre de villes de France* (Avesnes: Viroux, 1846): 27-29; Jozef de Baets, O.P., "De 'Toog' der Gentse rederijkers van 1458," *Koninlijke souvereine hoofdkamer van rhetorica 'De Fonteine' te Gent. Jaarboek* 9 [2nd ser. 1], 1959: 33-40 (40); and Martens, "Artistic Patronage," 128.

[24] Craig Harbison, "Fact, Symbol, Ideal: Roles for Realism in Early Netherlandish Painting," 21-34 in Ainsworth ed., *Christus in Renaissance Bruges*.

[25] Martens, "Petrus Christus, a Cultural Biography," 15–24 (15) in Ainsworth, *Renaissance Master*.

[26] Wilson (above, note 7), *Painting in Bruges*, 6.

[27] On this staging technique, see Arthur C. Cawley, "Pageant Wagon Versus Juggernaut Car," *Research Opportunities in Renaissance Drama* 13–14 (1970–71): 204–209; Meg Twycross, "The Flemish *Ommegang* and its Pageant Cars," *Medieval English Theatre* 2 (1980): 15–41; and Hubert Soly, "Openbare feesten in Brabantse en Vlaamse steden, 16de–18de eeuw," in *Het openbaar initief van het gemeenten in België. Historische grondslagen (Ancien Régime)* (Brussels: Crédit Communal de Belgique, 1984): 605–20.

[28] Louis Gilliodts-van Severen, *Inventaire des archives de la ville de Bruges: inventaire des chartes, première série*. 7 vols. (Bruges: E. Gaillard, 1871–78), 4: 468–70; and Leo van Puyvelde, "Het ontstaan van het modern toneel in de oude Nederlanden. De oudste vermeldingen in de rekeningen," *Verslagen en mededeelingen der Koninklijke Vlaamsche Academie voor Taal- en Letterkunde* (1922): 909–52 (918, 928).

[29] The "hovekine," the diminutive form of *Hof* or garden, was certainly Christ's Agony in the Garden; the scene was first added in 1397 (*Stadsrekeningen* [Municipal Account Books] *Brugge* 1396–97, fol. 92, item 1). See Antoon Viaene, "Het 'Spel van den hovekin,'" *Biekorf* 42 (1936): 113–18; and Martens, "Artistic Patronage," 141–45. The Annunciation first appeared in 1398, to be accompanied in 1399 by the "stede van Jherusalem" and the Adoration of the Magi, referred to as "de offrande van den drien coninghen" (*Stadsrekeningen Brugge* 1397–98, fol. 98v, item 3; *Stadsrekeningen Brugge* 1398–99, fol. 92v, item 4). The Tree of Jesse was added in 1401, with a "kindsbedde, met koning Herodesse" (a Nativity with a King Herod scene) the following year (*Stadsrekeningen Brugge* 1400–1401, fol. 105, item 7; *Stadsrekeningen Brugge* 1401–1402, fol. 115v, item 6). These items are cited in Gilliods-van Severen, *Inventaire*, 3: 401–402 and 423; 4: 469–70; see also Leo van Puyvelde, *Over vermoedelijken invloed van toneelvoorstellingen op de schilderkunst in de XIVe en XV euw* (Antwerp: Vlaamsch taal- en geschiedkundig congres, 1913): 11; and van Puyvelde, "Ontstaan," 918, 928.

[30] Louvain first dramatized its annual procession in the early 1390s; Antwerp's processional plays began in 1398, and Tournai dramatized its *ommegang* in 1408, while Ypres seems to have led all cities in this regard, mounting its first dramas in 1383. Finally, Brussels established a group of rhetoricians in 1401, perhaps coinciding with the onset of its annual processional dramas, the companies producing these plays (tableaux) often forming the kernel of what would become later *rederijkerskamers*. For more on this phenomenon around 1400, see Appendix 6 of my dissertation, "Art and Ommegangen," 304–308.

[31] See *Het tooneelleven in Vlaanderen door de eeuwen heen* (Bruges: Davidsfonds, 1930). Leo van Puyvelde claimed to have compiled more than two thousand records of such plays; see *Schilderkunst en toneelvertooning op het einde van de Middeleeuwen: een bijdrage tot de kunstgeschiedenis van de Nederlanden* (Ghent: A. Siffer, 1912): 62.

[32] See Gilliodts-van Severen, *Inventaire*, 2: 428, 430.

[33] The history of the ritual only underscores its religious importance. In 1311, a confraternity devoted to the relic of the Holy Blood was established, its membership reserved for elite members of Bruges society (Gilliodts-van Severen, *Inventaire*, 1: 303; 2: 422–25 and 430–31). In 1312 the procession began to be illuminated by torch and candlelight, and three years later to be accompanied by musicians (Gilliodts-van Severen, *Inventaire*,

2: 426-27); by 1351 the ceremony was marked by a fortnight of solemn proceedings (*Inventaire*, 2: 432). In the early fifteenth century the Bishop of Tournai began to assist in the Procession, bringing his status to the *ommegang* first in 1413-14 (*Inventaire*, 4: 468), and in 1418-19 the Procession was upgraded to "Majus triplex festum" (*Inventaire*, 2: 338-39), coinciding with the first entry of Philip the Good into Bruges (Kipling, "Civic Triumph," 70). It should be added that the Procession's importance was also secular: after 1381 the city's twelve arms appeared along the parade route, repainted annually for the event (*Inventaire*, 2: 412).

[34] Gilliodts-van Severen, *Inventaire*, 2: 429. Bruges's practice may have been inspired by an event in 1330, when Philip VI of France granted safe conduct to those traveling to Tournai's Procession, including a delegation from Bruges. Since such a decree was necessary, foreign attendance in Bruges may well have dropped in previous years (numbers are not available, but there are few archival mentions of the ceremony between 1316 and 1330), and the city clergy and magistrate may have realized that invitations had become necessary, and that, with Philip's decree, pilgrims would once again be safe.

[35] In 1465-66, Bruges sent its official city-rhetorician, Antonis de Roovere, to Lier to write three plays; see Antonin van Elslander, "Letterkundig leven in de Bourgondische tijd. De rederijkers," *Koninklijke souvereine hoofdkamer van rhetorica 'De Fonteine' te Gent. Jaarboek* 18 [2nd ser. 10] (1968): 61-78 (71). Artisans also came to Bruges to help with its initial theatrical endeavors: Janne van Hulst and Janne van Ghend were the first individuals mentioned by name in connection with Bruges's plays, in 1396-97. See Gilliodts-van Severen, *Inventaire*, 3: 401-402 and 423; 4: 469-70; van Puyvelde, *Invloed van toneelvoorstellingen*, 11; and van Puyvelde "Ontstaan," 918, 928.

Other cities sent skilled artisans to work on their neighbors' productions. Brussels dispatched its municipal painter, Rogier van der Weyden, to nearby Nivelles in 1441 to paint a dragon used in the town's annual procession: see Elizabeth Dhanens, *Rogier van der Weyden. Revisie van de documenten* (Brussels: AWLSK, 1995): 102. Josef Duverger suggested that Rogier's followers as city painters, Vrancke van der Stockt and Jan and Cornelis Schernier, completed similar tasks; see: *Brussel als kunstcentrum in de XIVde en XVde eeuw* (Antwerp: De Sikkel, 1935): 12. Brussels also sent its first *rederijker*, Collin Caillieu, and his successor, Jan Smeken, to other cities; see Alexandre Henne and Alphonse Wauters, *Histoire de la ville de Bruxelles*, 3 vols. (Brussels: Perichon, 1845), 1: 272; and Duverger, *Kunstcentrum*, 11, 13.

[36] The plays only appeared in the processions mounted in 1463, 1468, 1469, 1472, 1478, 1479, 1481, 1484, and 1486. I have just prepared two articles on the participation of artist/dramatists in Bruges's Procession of the Holy Blood, studies which discuss this issue at greater length.

[37] Item gheghevan van finen ghesleghenen goude, van finen ghesleghenen zelvere ende van foelgen ende anderen dinghen twelke al verbezicht was bi den scildders vander stede ende bi den beildescrivers vander Carmer strate omme de spelen ende ystories die achter strate ghemaect waren. . . . Item gheghevan den voorseiden scilders ende den beildescrivers van der Carmers strate vorseiden met haren cnapen van haren dachhueren ende over diversche stoffe bi hemlieder ghelevert (*Stadsrekeningen Brugge* 1440-41, fol. 93v, item 1).

[38] Item gheghevan allen den persoonen die de ystorien speilden ende tooghen up de stallagen al de straten duere van ons voorseiden gheduchts heeren hove tot der Crusspoorte over haerlieder costen ende moeynessen die zy hadden upten

dach van ons gheduchten heeren incommene (*Stadtsrekeningen Brugge* 1440–41, fol. 94, item 2).

[39] The painters' guild was specified in municipal accounts each year after 1398 (*Stadsrekeningen Brugge* 1397–98, fol. 95v, item 5), and the painter Jan van Ghend had led the group that performed the debut version in 1397 (*Stadsrekeningen Brugge* 1396–97, fol. 92v, item 1). After 1445 the painters' guild was the only group regularly mentioned in connection with any drama in the Procession of the Holy Blood (*Stadsrekeningen Brugge* 1444–45, fol. 58v, item 10).

[40] Michael Baxandall, *Painting and Experience in Fifteenth-Century Italy: A Primer in the Social History of Pictorial Style* (Oxford and New York: Oxford University Press, 1972).

Metropolitan Museum of Art

Book Reviews

Ashley, Kathleen, and Pamela Sheingorn, ed. *Interpreting Cultural Symbols: Saint Anne in the Late-Medieval Society*. Athens and London: The University of Georgia Press, 1990. Pp. 243. 64 b. & w. illustrations.

This handsome-looking paperback shows a painting by an anonymous Swabian artist of c.1500 on the front cover, a work located at the Philadelphia Museum of Art which represents the *Holy Kinship*, i.e., St. Anne's extended family of twenty-three members, who include, besides Anne, Mary, and Jesus, also John the Baptist, St. Servatius and seven apostles (Anne's grandsons). The book contains an introduction of sixty-eight pages by the editors, which provides the well-researched historical development of St. Anne's cult. Six articles by various contributors follow, studies which reflect Kalamazoo papers of 1988 and treat art and literature on the subject of St. Anne in western Europe. Interpreted within their political, historic, economic, and social contexts, these essays if read with the introduction in mind complement each other by providing a complete overview of when, why, where, how, and by whom the artwork and the texts were produced. The writings focusing on the St. Anne legend and art are trying to provide, for the first time in English, a comprehensive survey: the appearance of the saint in art and drama, the commissioning by individuals and groups, such as brotherhoods and nuns, and the saint's life borne out in folklore, history, and popular piety (*Volksfrömmigkeit* in German).

St. Anne's Feast Day is July 26. She has been the patron saint for mothers because she is not only Mary's mother but the grandmother of Jesus; although part of Mary's life, Anne is not specifically mentioned in the New Testament. Her own life and cult are apocryphal, and therefore the Church fathers, popes, philosophers, and theologians constantly criticized and forbade any writing and art representing her life. As early as the twelfth century, reformers contested the Holy Kinship, the three marriages of Anne (*trinubium*), the three Marys (her children), and Anne's Immaculate Conception. So, at times, only the nuclear family of four members was allowed to be portrayed: Anne, Mary, Jesus, and Joseph.

With the Reformation and the Council of Trent (1545-63), the Holy Kinship as a subject of the art and the cult of St. Anne disappeared along with the cults of all the other saints, at least for Protestants. Until then, in spite of church councils' decrees against St. Anne's veneration, as well as objections voiced by theologians, philosophers, and popes, the cult became widespread, influential, and popular. Numerous churches, cloisters, and brotherhoods adopted St. Anne as their patron saint. Her Feast Day was a holiday, and many shrines and pilgrimages were dedicated to her relics in

Chartres, Apt, and Düren (for instance), while art work commissioned on her behalf included portrayals of the donors, whose likenesses appeared in holy scenes and came to replace some members of the Holy Kinship. St. Anne was usually portrayed as an old widowed woman, who wore a wide, long robe, and often had her arms extended outward in protection and blessing, though she seemed larger than other figures in *Holy Kinship* paintings, not unlike St. Ursula in her wide coat, whom Ashley and Sheingorn treated in an earlier study. In a recent publication, the two scholars collaborated again, this time about the child St. Foy's texts, signs, and history.

One way of orienting readers about the development of St. Anne's cult is to follow three important texts of her legend, discussed by popes and Church fathers, writings on which decrees depended for producing any art about St. Anne. Dated c. A.D. 150, the earliest document was written in Greek, stemming from Egypt or Syria, and called *Protevangelium of James*. Considered to have been omitted from the canonical Gospels, this text recounts the Immaculate Conception of Anne, who was chosen by God to bear Mary (in spite of Anne's old age), as revealed to her and to Joachim, her husband. The account specifies that at Mary's third birthday she was given into the care of priests in a temple (details reprinted in English in Ashley and Sheingorn's introduction, 53–57). These events were then reworked by Hieronymus in Latin (between 550 and 700), called later Pseudo-Matthew, known for having established Mary's perpetual virginity. The Holy Kinship was thus invented in western Europe by c.850, and, before the year 1000, Roswitha von Gandersheim based her *Maria,* an elegant poem in Latin distiches, on Jerome.

The problem of Anne's three marriages did not have much of an impact on her worship before the twelfth century, when Bernard de Clairvaux spoke up against the Feast Day of this saint because of the above impediment. Thomas Aquinas (1226–74) was opposed to recognizing her Immaculate Conception and the *trinubium*, and so was Johann von Freiburg, a Dominican. However, in the *Legenda Aurea* of about 1260 (the third important text), Jacobus de Voragine used a later version of *Pseudo-Matthew*, which included Anne's genealogy and the *trinubium*. As early as 1172, *The Three Songs of the Virgin* by Priester Wernher, based on *Pseudo-Matthew* as well, were accompanied by a full picture cycle.

The *Legenda Aurea*, the most influential text in European countries for all hagiographic matters, included St. Anne's life in the chapter "Nativity of the Virgin." Jean Gerson (1363–1424) supported both the Holy Kinship and the Immaculate Conception, and the Council of Basel proclaimed the latter as a dogma of faith in 1438. Visual expressions of the doctrine were configurations of Anne, Mary, and Jesus, the most famous depiction of which is undoubtedly Leonardo da Vinci's Renaissance painting of c.1510 in the Louvre. Yet, the controversy about St. Anne reappeared at the Council of Trent. Up to that point, all religious orders had accepted the doctrine of the Holy Kinship, especially the Carmelites (since the thirteenth century), as well as the brotherhood of the Carmelite cloister in Frankfurt am Main, who, after 1479, commissioned a large altar with sixteen paintings of St. Anne's life. Franciscans and Dominicans had approved the *trinubium* and the doctrine of Anne's Immaculate Conception at least one century before both became dogma.

The six essays following Ashley and Sheingorn's introduction cover a great wealth of material. The first three studies (by Francesca Sautman, Gail McMurray Gibson, and Kathleen Ashley) deal foremost with literature in France and England, while the other essays (by Roger J. Crum and David G. Wilkins, Pamela Sheingorn, and Myra D. Orth) showcase primarily art in Italy, Germany, and France. In the essay "In the Defense of Florentine Republicanism: Saint Anne and Florentine Art, 1343-1575," Crum and Wilkins offer their thesis; namely, that certain patrons (merchants, political groups, and the Medici) ordered that St. Anne be painted in Florence whenever the government was Republican; once, in 1343, the city was saved from an oppressive French ruler, Walter VI of Brienne, on St. Anne's Day. Even when the Republic was in danger, artwork was commissioned for the annual feast day.

Republicanism is the one motive for painting St. Anne given in the Crum/Wilkins essay, but this reviewer finds it convincing only in the case of paintings where other groups of the historic battle against the French are included. Considerations about dogmas, decrees, and doctrines seem to be deliberately omitted by these essayists; here, John the Baptist becomes simply the patron saint of Florence, rather than part of a *Holy Kinship* painting by Giovanni Maria Butteri (1575), where members of the Medici family replace the holy figures! For the authors, Leonardo da Vinci's painting of 1510 does not portray the Immaculate Conception, at least not exclusively. In my opinion the Medici's reason for ordering this painting in 1575 might be their opposing the Council of Trent's decree not to recognize either the *trinubium* or the Holy Kinship. The Immaculate Conception, however, was favored by Catholics, and paintings of Anne's Trinitarian family were still done during the seventeenth and eighteenth centuries.

Closely related to this essay is the one by Myra D. Orth, "'Madame Sainte Anne': The Holy Kinship, the Royal Trinity, and Louise of Savoy." After the military victories over Italy by the French King François I in 1515, the Medici pope had an alliance with France in 1516. Paintings arrived at the French court during 1517-18 from Florence, showing the Trinitarian group (St. Anne, the Virgin, and Christ), often with the infant St. John or his symbol, the lamb, as in Leonardo da Vinci's painting. Leonardo painted at the court in Amboise and died there in 1519; other works were by Raphael (Santi) and Andrea del Sarto.

At the same time, François's mother, Louise of Savoy, received the *Petit Livret fait à l'honneur de Madame Saint Anne*, an illustrated treatise written by a Franciscan and former tutor of the king, François Du Moulin. The text featured St. Anne's life and the Holy Kinship, but in a critical and ironic way, reflecting the viewpoint of a reformer. Another author, Jacques Lefèvre d'Étaples, contested the legends of Mary Magdalen and of St. Anne during 1517-18, in spite of the Sorbonne's censorship of his treatises. For a while, in the 1520s, biblical humanism was discussed and practiced in France, a trend which sanctioned the use of the Gospel Holy Family of four only (see above), and excluded other aspects of the St. Anne Legend. Du Moulin even appealed to Louise of Savoy in favor of Lefèvre by giving her the *Petit Livret* and implied that Louise was the head of the family (just like St. Anne, and Mary at the same time), while Christ "became" François I.

Orth continues by indicating that the model of the "Royal Trinity" in the paintings given to King François I and his Queen Claude, daughter of Anne of Brittany (who was devoted to St. Anne), does not quite seem to fit the royal family. Although the idea of dynasty is implied, I do not think that the paintings were meant to demonstrate that St. Anne had only one child, Mary, as the reformers wanted it, and that this idea can be concluded from the book for Louise of Savoy (as Orth sees it). Rather, the Florentine St. Anne paintings demonstrate the Immaculate Conception, and therefore a holy union between the three — Anna, Maria, and Jesus — according to the dogma of 1438 and in line with papal approval given in 1483. These paintings reflect the Catholic view and have nothing to do with the reformers in France, nor with the Republican government in Florence. Despite these criticisms, Orth's essay is well written.

Lefèvre stayed protected by the court and died in 1536 at the Nérac castle of Louise's daughter, Margarite de Navarre. Raphael's *Holy Family* for François I (1518), including Joseph, was a gift of the Medici, honoring the French dynasty. Around 1530, interest in the Reformation subsided in France, and eventually the whole country stayed Catholic.

Pamela Sheingorn, in her essay called "Appropriating the *Holy Kinship*: Gender and Family History," does not focus on one historical incident or on patronage, but she rather examines the different representational types of the *Holy Kinship* in art: illustrations, paintings, stained glass windows, engravings, and sculptures made in France, England, Germany, and Holland. By giving examples from c.1300 to c.1520, Sheingorn delineates a development embodied in style, as well as in family history. She points out that the *Kinship's* women saints are portrayed separately from their husbands early on, then depicted alone and holding a central position; eventually the men are included in the pictures, on balconies and in the background, and finally in the forefront, teaching the children to read. Sheingorn basically sees in this "development" a decrease of the women's role and status, and a certain emphasis on having children educated by men.

Whereas a tableau of ancestors in a French manuscript of c.1300 portrays everyone as young adults, including Anne and the seven grandchildren, on a Cologne painting of about 1420 the *Holy Kinship* is shown like a family gathering with Anne, the grandmother, and the grandchildren as babies. All the women are saints with halos, while as babies only Jesus and John the Baptist are surrounded by circles of light. In this painting, St. Anne is holding an open book, but she is not teaching the baby Jesus how to read. On a French miniature of c.1450, only St. Anne, her three daughters, and seven grandchildren are pictured, without halos and without men, like a genre-picture of everyday life. Although Sheingorn analyzes next a Dutch painting of an *Anna selbdritt* (Anne's Trinity) of 1510–15 from the National Gallery, chronologically the Dutch altar paintings of 1480–90 at the Walters Museum showing Anne, Mary, and Jesus in the middle, should have been explained first because they portray the Immaculate Conception, with Anne again holding an open book. As side panels, John the Baptist and St. Servatius, relatives of Anne, are depicted.

Continuing the doctrine of the Immaculate Conception however, the large Dutch painting of 1510–15 was created; the rendering shows Anne, Mary, and Jesus on a bench, Mary holding an open book, while Anne is keeping Jesus. I believe that here, as in the other paintings, the book is supposed to be the Bible and the scene demonstrates that these three persons are included in it, not that Jesus is being taught how to read, as Sheingorn seems to think. I also presume that God the Father is portrayed up above, exactly as in other paintings of this volume, where *Anna selbdritt* (149, 79, 39) is the subject, this concept indicating the Immaculate Conception for Anne and Mary, and not the paternal lineage.

In the Thuringian sculpture of the *Holy Kinship* (c.1510), Sheingorn sees, as a message, only a large family: according to the Reformation, "everyone should belong to a family" (185). However, this sculpture, with the men in the background and the women in front holding their babies, as well as having other children at their feet, becomes recognizable as a typical Catholic concept of the Holy Kinship, as it was allowed to be portrayed until the Council of Trent.

Paintings of the *Holy Family* expressing the Protestant view, with only Anne, Mary, Joseph, and Jesus, emerged at the same time, parallel to the *Holy Kinship*; for example, in an engraving by Hans Baldung Grien of 1511. The work by Lucas Cranach the Elder of c.1509, commissioned by Friedrich der Weise of Saxony, has the *Holy Family* at the center, with Mary holding an open book, and Anne keeping Jesus. On the balcony and on side panels, the men depicted have features resembling and combining those of the Emperor, his court chaplain, the painter, Friedrich der Weise, and his son Johann. In 1515, Emperor Maximilian commissioned a painting (copied by Bernhard Strigel), in which his family takes the place of the *Holy Kinship*; on the painting's backside, however, the *Kinship* itself is shown: the Emperor and his family probably wanted to demonstrate their support of the legend.

In another engraving by Lucas Cranach the Elder (1510) and a reissue after 1518 with a poem by Melanchthon, the *Holy Family* is again portrayed in the center (only Anne, Mary and Jesus have a halo), Anne holds an open book, and baby Jesus sits on Anne's lap. Although the six-year old cousins are taught to read on their first day of school, that does not mean, as Sheingorn assumes, that baby Jesus is being taught and that Joseph, who stands, as usual, aside from the group, is distracting him. Furthermore, the groupings of family units and of the three husbands of Anne do not necessarily indicate, as Sheingorn asserts, that the men are "taking over," but rather that they keep a respectful distance from the *Holy Family* in the center of the picture (in fact some might even have the features of reformers, like Erasmus of Rotterdam on the right, the husband of Mary Salome). The *Holy Family*, or rather Anne, Mary and Jesus, sit on a bench, while the other two Marys are on the floor with their infants. The same arrangement is shown as part of a *Holy Kinship* painting in an altarpiece at Münster of c.1520, where all persons are haloed, except for the father who stands behind the wall.

In 1519, Luther criticized brotherhoods for using saints' names, and during 1525 he rejected all legends about Mary and Anne; later, in 1543, he only accepted the Holy Family, St. Anne, and Elisabeth (mentioned in the Bible). In Nürnberg, a peace of religions was proclaimed during 1532; then, in 1555, all of Germany approved the Augsburg peace, so that Protestants and Catholics could coexist side by side. At the Council of Trent the reforms were agreed upon by all Catholics in Europe.

Briefly, the three literary essays in Ashley and Sheingorn's volume deal with patronage and popular piety for St. Anne in England and France. Gail McMurray Gibson's study "Saint Anne and the Religion of Childhood: Some East Anglian Texts and Talismans" explains that St. Anne's Day was formally allowed by Pope Urban VI in 1382 in honor of Queen Anne of Bohemia, her namesake. In East Anglian towns, where the N-Town cycle of mystery plays and the Saint Anne's Day plays of the Digby manuscript originated, in Suffolk and Norfolk, a text for a brotherhood of merchants exists, the *Robert Reynes of Acle Commonplace Book* of the fifteenth century, retelling the St. Anne genealogy and life according to the *Legenda Aurea*. Most importantly, Gibson tells us about the two families of Denston and Clopton, who have not only arranged to have their own stained glass windows in their respective churches, along with their tombs, but also commissioned an alabaster relief of a fourteenth-c. *Nativity* in Long Medford, where Mary is shown in her childbed. Gibson connects this sculpture to the legend of St. Anne, because women prayed to St. Anne to have a child and to deliver it by means of an easy birth. Katherine Clopton Denston, whose only child was called Anne, had commissioned the St. Anne's legend written by Osbern Bokenham (1392–1445), which alluded to Katherine's own life and included prayers on her behalf for a son. Bokenham wrote thirteen legends of women saints, texts which survived, were gathered in a manuscript after his death (1447), and published in 1938 under the title of *Legendary of Hooly Wummen*. Between the lines, in prologues and epilogues, Bokenham referred to his patrons and their history.

In the study by Kathleen Ashley, "Image and Ideology: Saint Anne in Late Medieval Drama and Narrative," three plays about Saint Anne of the late fifteenth and early sixteenth centuries are discussed. The Huy *Nativity* (near Lüttich / Liège) was written in French by a Carmelite nun: the play presents a visit to St. Mary by Anne and the other two Marys. Affective piety and female mysticism influence this ecclesiastical piece, where Anne is seen as a wise matriarch who instructs her daughters. In the N-Town cycle, conception and birth are themes of the *Mary Play*, and Anne represents godly wedlock, inspired by the *Legenda Aurea*. Apocryphal materials on the conception, nativity, and betrothal of the Virgin are included; there is no record of a performance; a lay religious guild may have commissioned the *Mary Play*. In the Digby manuscript of the *Candelmas Day and the Killing of the Children of Israel*, a comedy performed on Saint Anne's Day, the social context is a town festival in East Anglia, where St. Anne is not a character in the play but the patron of a guild.

The essay by Francesca Sautman, "Saint Anne in Folk Tradition: Late Medieval France," describes how popular piety in France transformed St. Anne's vita, calendar, and genealogy. *Volksfrömmigkeit* about the saint came to include intercessions during illnesses, especially those of children. Some ideas are founded on folk legends about St. Anne: she was the patron of carpenters and woodworkers because of a mystical connection to trees; as a child, she was abandoned, some people say, and raised in the wilderness by a deer. A widespread romance about St. Anne, in eight manuscripts of the thirteenth and fourteenth centuries, is *Le Roman de Saint Fanuel et de Sainte Anne et Nostre Seigneur et de ses Apostres*. Sautman also shows some images of *Saint Anne Trinitarian*, a woodcut of a sixteenth-c. Book of Hours, and a miniature of 1380, the *Nativity of the Virgin Mary* in a Franciscan Book of Hours and Missal.

Altogether this collection is a commendable presentation and analysis of every aspect of the St. Anne cult known to medievalists, based, in part, on previous studies in Europe (Beda Kleinschmidt's book of 1930, for example, quoted by every contributor to this collection: *Die heilige Anna: Ihre Verehrung in*

Geschichte, Kunst und Volkstum [Düsseldorf: Schwann]). In conclusion, Ashley and Sheingorn's excellent publication should be part of every university library.

Sibylle Jefferis, University of Pennsylvania

Baraz, Daniel. *Medieval Cruelty: Changing Perceptions, Late Antiquity to the Early Modern Period.* Ithaca: Cornell University Press, 2003. Pp. xi; 225.

Baraz investigates cruelty as a cultural issue, because medieval references on the subject occur in historical records, even though these remarks about cruelty vary in frequency and content over the period Baraz has chosen. First relatively obscure in writings, the topic of cruelty appears in various sources after the central Middle Ages (in philosophical texts, chronicles, and hagiography).

Types of cruelty are attributed to the "other" in the early Middle Ages (Vandals, Muslims, Vikings, Jews, and Mongols), while later the focus is on sexual cruelty and cannibalism. After connecting lexical references to cruelty, the author then links the term to irrational and "non-human" violence, viewed, for example, as judicial in cases of severity during the administration of law. Cruelty is intentional, while violence may not be so, Baraz specifies. The three principal forms of cruel behavior and suffering are evidenced in: punishment by the law, martyrdom, and descriptions of the "other." Baraz ends the volume with the sixteenth century, since cruelty comes to a peak in the 1500s, in his opinion; later on, "classical, medieval, and early modern categories were either borrowed, inverted, or expanded" (12).

Chapter one, called "Speculating on Cruelty, from Seneca to Montaigne," contains an overview of the entire book. (The footnote at the bottom of page 13 is not indicated in the text.) According to Aristotle, virtue can be expressed through two contrasting categories: *misericordia* and *crudelitas* (14); Seneca distinguishes between ethics of intention and ethics of action (15). For St. Augustine cruelty is primarily spiritual, not physical; hence, the bodily suffering of the martyrs is negligible to him. A turning point for the topic occurs with Thomas Aquinas (thirteenth century), who views the relation between body and soul: since the two entities are inseparable, as he explains, cruelty may be intentional or an accidental outcome of an action by a perpetrator. With Antoninus of Florence (1389–1459) the question of taking pleasure in cruelty (*irrational* cruelty) arises, which then becomes characteristic of early modern interpretations, as is shown by Montaigne, who does not provide a rigid definition, but conveys comparable ideas in his "On Cruelty," an essay mostly on irrational cruelty, a concept linked to Montaigne's Renaissance emphasis on the body. Seneca and Montaigne influence the English *revenge tragedy* (26) — as well as German baroque dramas describing the rise and fall of princely characters (the reviewer). Neither medieval secular nor canon law refers to cruelty.

Chapter two, "Late Antiquity — the Building Blocks of a Discourse," recalls that cruelty was an important cultural issue in the pagan era. In legal and political contexts cruelty was interpreted as excessive punishment or as violence by tyrants; during Christian times the two main negative discourses were tyranny and the cruelty of the "other" (heretics, barbarians). "The Early Middle Ages — An Age of Silence?" is the title of chapter three, an article which indicates that medieval sources do not refer to cruelty explicitly. There are some exceptions, however, for example in hagiographic material dealing with the Vikings ("others," designated thusly, are treated as cruel without ambiguity in martyrological texts); but even these descriptions of the martyrs' sufferings are done in a minimalist manner, Baraz continues. In early theater texts, *low* speech is excluded, and so are violence and cruelty, these exclusions reflecting a choice of style.

"The Central Middle Ages — A Renaissance of Cruelty," chapter four, showcases the increasing cultural preoccupation with cruelty that occurs during this time span. Alan of Lille paraphrases Seneca on the subject as seeing cruelty as a perversion of justice, the opposite of mercy, and *saevitia* becomes a ground for divorce. In this chapter Baraz discusses the martyrdom of William of Norwich, the murder of Thomas Becket, the Albigensian Crusade, and the Mongol conquests (where cannibalism is mentioned only in Western sources). William of Norwich is tortured and killed by the Jewish "other," while the Albigensians are persecuted as heretics by Christians; Becket's murder (described by sympathizers in an affective mode) happens in the context of English politics, and here Christians have become the "others."

Baraz's chapter five, "The Late Middle Ages — Manipulated Images and Structured Emotions," focuses on three cases of manipulation: the French conflict of the *Jacquerie* (an uprising of peasants and anti-aristocrats, in which all opponents describe themselves as "others"), as reported by Jean Froissart; the case of Pedro I of Castile, named both "the cruel" and "the just," a king excessive in his application of justice in order to manipulate his people; and the role of cruelty in the passion plays, this time exerted by the Jews against Christ, as emphasized by the *fatistes*' manipulation of viewers' emotions in the service of Christianity — as explained by Baraz.

Finally, in chapter six, the author views "The Early Modern Period — Cruelty Transformed" and establishes that the modern quantity and range of comments, and the interest in cruelty are noteworthy, as shown in wars of religion by both Catholics and Protestants, and in violence exerted upon American natives. Whereas late-medieval peasant rebellions remain local, the sixteenth-c. religious wars involve many regions of Europe and even affect the New World. Medieval massacres, sexual cruelty, and cannibalism continue to be used in reports, but their functions have now changed. The account of Simon of Trent's martyrdom as brought about by Jews (1475) appears in

Christian sources enhanced by affective spirituality emphasizing Christ's passion and culminating in the child's (Simon's) canonization in 1588. Early modern literature, as Baraz shows, is preoccupied with detailed descriptions of violence and bloodshed as well as images of cannibalism, the latter as reported from the New World (and some from the religious wars in Europe).

In conclusion, Baraz reminds us that the film *The Silence of the Lambs* (1991) links cruelty, cannibalism, and sex in a certain "subversiveness" (176): these modes of violence may be frowned upon, but the descriptions provide a certain "subversive pleasure" (ibid.). Five appendices are added here, as well as a glossary of Latin terms, a selected bibliography (eight pages), and an index (four pages, double columns). While the detail of this instructive and comprehensive book is interesting and fairly well written, the structure of the chapters is often disconcerting to the reader, as the author (in each chapter) proceeds from an initial outline to a more individualized report — which is concluded by yet another general outline. Missing in the bibliography are: Edelgard E. DuBruck, "Montaigne on Cruelty," *Michigan Academician* 11 (1979): 297–305; *Violence et contestation au moyen âge* (Paris: Éditions du C. T. H. S., 1990); Christiane Raynaud, *La Violence au Moyen Âge* (Paris: Le Léopard d'Or, 1990); Michel Porret, *Le Corps violenté: du geste à la parole* (Geneva: Droz, 1998); Christiane Raynaud, *"À la hache!" Histoire et symbolique de la hache dans la France médiévale (XIIIe–XVe siècle)* (Paris: Le Léopard d'Or, 2002); E. E. DuBruck and Yael Even, ed. *Violence in Fifteenth-Century Text and Image* (vol. 27 of *Fifteenth-Century Studies*) (Rochester: Camden House, 2002).

Edelgard E. DuBruck, Marygrove College

Brown, Cynthia J., ed. *Pierre Gringore. Oeuvres polémiques rédigées sous le règne de Louis XII.* Geneva: Droz, 2003. Pp. 376.

Voilà enfin que justice est faite à Pierre Gringore (c.1475–1538/39), un auteur qui attend depuis fort longtemps d'être reconnu et redécouvert, car le principal obstacle a été jusqu'aujourd'hui l'inaccessibilité de la plupart de ses oeuvres. L'édition des oeuvres complètes de Gringore entamée en 1858 par Charles d'Héricault, Anatole de Montaiglon et James de Rothschild n'a pas été achevée. En effet, à la fin du second volume publié en 1877 le troisième est déclaré sous presse, mais il ne paraîtra jamais. Charles Oulmont, quelques années plus tard, entreprend à son tour l'édition des oeuvres de Gringore, mais à nouveau sans mener à terme son projet. Oulmont n'en reste pas moins l'auteur de l'ouvrage le plus complet et le plus récent sur ce riche corpus, une étude qui date hélas de 1911: *La poésie morale, politique et dramatique à la veille de la Renaissance* (chez Champion). Depuis, rares ont été les contributions consacrées à Gringore, on peut citer l'ouvrage daté de Walter Dittmann (1923), mais celui-ci ne porte que sur les textes dramatiques de

Gringore. Il faut donc se contenter de brèves analyses ci et là et de quelques trop rares articles; on doit sans doute expliquer cet oubli par le fait que Gringore appartient à la génération des rhétoriqueurs. Ce volume s'inscrit en effet dans le cadre de la réhabilitation de ces poètes boudés par l'historiographie française, entreprise par Paul Zumthor avec la publication en 1978 du livre *Le masque et la lumière*; un courant qui profite à Gringore, même si cet auteur n'est pas à proprement parler un rhétoriqueur.

Alors pourquoi lire aujourd'hui Gringore? Les mérites de son oeuvre sont nombreux. Tout d'abord elle comporte plus de vingt-cinq textes et couvre un large éventail de genres; on y trouve à la fois des poésies qui ne diffèrent en rien de pamphlets politiques, des oeuvres morales et religieuses, des oeuvres théâtrales qui vont de la sottie au mystère, des projets d'entrées royales, des textes légers raillant les moeurs du temps et, pour finir, des traductions. Pour Brown, Gringore est l'un des écrivains français les plus importants du XVIe siècle (9): Montaiglon en faisait le successeur de Villon; en effet, Gringore offre un témoignage sans égal de son époque. Il appartient à divers cercles: il s'associe à la troupe des Enfants sans souci, et écrit aussi bien pour la ville de Paris que pour la confrérie des maçons et charpentiers; il est protégé par quelques seigneurs normands et fréquente les milieux de l'édition à Paris et à Lyon. Gringore est surtout réputé pour ses longs poèmes allégoriques moralisants, comme le *Chasteau de Labour* publié en 1499 qui connut plusieurs éditions et fut traduit en anglais dès l'année suivante, et pour ses pièces dramatiques, comme le fameux *Jeu du Prince des Sotz et de Mere Sotte*.

Cette pièce couronne plusieurs années d'activité théâtrale durant lesquelles Gringore s'était rendu célèbre sous le nom de Mère Sotte. Le texte doit sa persistante notoriété au fait qu'il conserve dans sa totalité tout un ensemble composé d'un cri, d'une sottie, d'une moralité et d'une farce. Outre les nombreuses éditions anciennes, le *Jeu* a été réédité par Alan Hindley en 2000 chez Champion, et pour ainsi dire entrera prochainement dans le canon littéraire puisqu'il sera inclus dans une anthologie en préparation dans la collection de la Pléiade.

Ces succès mis à part, Gringore peine à trouver un mécène. Il semble pourtant fort proche du pouvoir, puisque de nombreuses poésies écrites entre 1499 et 1513 (que l'on trouve dans le volume de Brown) servent les intérêts de la couronne et qu'il est à de nombreuses reprises engagé par les autorités municipales de Paris pour ses qualités de dramaturge et poète. Il participe en effet aux préparatifs de l'entrée de Philippe le Bon en 1501, de Georges d'Amboise en 1502, de la reine Anne de Bretagne en 1504, de la troisième épouse de Louis XII, Marie Tudor, en 1514, et encore en 1517 pour l'entrée de Claude de France.

Mais il doit attendre 1518 pour trouver un protecteur permanent en la personne d'Antoine de Lorraine. C'est sous ses auspices que Gringore se stabilise et s'affiche dès les premières violences de la Réforme comme fervent catholique. Lui qui avait si virulemment dénoncé les excès de l'Église (en particulier lors du conflit qui oppose Louis XII et Jules II) est paradoxalement le premier auteur français à dénoncer nommément le courant luthérien dans son *Blazon des Hérétiques* en 1524. Gringore est singulier pour bien d'autres raisons encore: signalons brièvement sa place dans l'histoire du livre. Cynthia J. Brown a montré dans son *Poets, Patrons, and Printers: Crisis of Authority in Late Medieval France* (Ithaca: Cornell University Press, 1995) que Gringore contrôlait de près l'impression de ses oeuvres et qu'il a su faire preuve d'un sens très aigu du commercial. En ceci il se distingue d'auteurs comme Jean Marot, ou Jean d'Auton, qui n'avaient pas du tout assimilé la révolution de l'imprimé et avaient laissé la majorité de leur oeuvre manuscrite. Il apparaît que pour Gringore, l'édition imprimée devance le manuscrit et qu'elle lui sert parfois curieusement de modèle. Mais cet auteur est aussi très sensible à la propriété littéraire et fait figure de pionnier; si l'on croit Brown il serait "le premier écrivain de langue française à obtenir un privilège d'auteur qui protégeait son oeuvre contre toute impression non autorisée pendant une période d'un an" (16).

Le volume de Cynthia J. Brown propose huit pamphlets politiques que Gringore ait composés pour attirer l'attention des autorités royales entre 1499 et 1513. Seuls trois de ces textes ont été réédités depuis l'édition de Montaiglon et, il faut l'avouer, dans des impressions peu accessibles, et qui égalent rarement le travail éditorial, philologique et linguistique que nous offre ici Brown. Chaque texte est précédé par une brève introduction comportant le résumé de l'oeuvre, le contexte historique, les traditions littéraires liées au genre du texte (rhétorique épidéictique, rhétorique exhortative, monologue dramatique, allégorie, moralité polémique, pièce comique), les questions de versification, la liste des éditions existantes ainsi que le justificatif de l'établissement du présent texte, le tout suivi d'un appareil de notes. L'ensemble est précédé par une introduction générale et clôt par une bibliographie, un index des noms propres et un glossaire. On y trouve les *Lettres nouvelles de Milan*, *La Piteuse complainte de la terre sainte*, *L'Entreprise de Venise*, *L'Union des Princes*, *L'Espoir de Paix*, *La Chasse du cerf des cerfz*, *Le Jeu du prince des sotz et Mere Sotte* (excepté la farce), et *L'Obstination des Suysses*. Ces textes intéresseront les littéraires et les historiens: ils traitent des campagnes italiennes de Louis XII, du conflit de la France et du Saint Siège et du rôle des mercenaires suisses. L'édition sera utile à tout ceux qui cherchent à mieux comprendre les années qui précèdent le règne de François Ier et la génération de la Pléiade. Il faut donc saluer le travail de Cynthia J. Brown en espérant que les prochains volumes ne tarderont pas, et aideront à faire redécouvrir et mieux connaître l'oeuvre originale de Pierre Gringore.

Nicole Hochner, The Hebrew University of Jerusalem

Di Stefano, Giuseppe, ed. *Boccace, 'Decameron,' traduction (1411–1414) de Laurent de Premierfait.* Montréal: Éditions CERES, 1998–1999. Pp. xxxi; 1238.

In the present volume, Giuseppe Di Stefano offers the reader a first edition of the first translation into French of the integral text of Giovanni Boccaccio's *Decameron* (1348–53). This monumental endeavor, having spanned a major portion of the editor's international career, contributes to the field of philology a work as important as his *Dictionnaire des locutions en moyen français* (CERES, 1991). The edition is an indispensable tool for the study of middle French idioms, as well as an invaluable document delineating Boccaccio's early diffusion and reception in France. Published under the titles of *Decameron, De Cameron, Le livre des Cent Nouvelles de Jehan Bocace de Certald* or *Prince Galeot,* the French translation of the Italian's popular collection of one hundred *novelle* was carried out by Laurent de Premierfait (d. 1418), a prominent, although understudied, late-medieval humanist.

In this edition, Di Stefano assumes the readers' familiarity with the cultural and literary aspects of the *Decameron.* Therefore, rather than providing information on such well-known issues as the socio-historical background, structure, narrative techniques, and major themes of the storytellers, the editor focuses on rendering as faithfully as possible the lexical characteristics of Laurent's translation, while also capturing the textual dynamics involved in the production and transmission of its manuscripts.

Di Stefano offers an extensively researched and richly documented critical apparatus, consisting of an informative introduction; a selective bibliography; and a meticulously elaborated, comprehensive list of variants. He discusses here several theoretical and methodological points of interest, such as the identity and literary activity of the translator; the production and transmission of the manuscripts and printed editions of the French *Decameron,* as well as the editorial procedures having guided the editor's treatment of Laurent's work. Equally compelling is the list of editorial challenges that a project of such magnitude and complexity has generated for Di Stefano.

The prefatory material provides valuable information on Laurent de Premierfait (d. 1418), known chiefly as a translator, although his poetic activity has also been of interest to scholars. It is intriguing that although this man's career as a translator was carried out under Charles VI, Laurent's major works, including the *Decameron* translation, were dedicated primarily to Jean, Duke of Berry, known as a generous patron of the letters. Among Premierfait's achievements are the first translation into French of Boccaccio's *De casibus virorum illustrium* (1400 and 1409), as well as Cicero's *De senectute* (1405) and *De amicitia* (1405 and 1416). The editor justifiably insists on Laurent's noteworthy contribution to the late-medieval French humanist tradition established by such pioneer translators of the classics as Nicolas Oresme and Pierre Bersuire (Di Stefano, ix–xi).

A collection of one hundred *novelle* told by seven noble ladies and three gentlemen having fled Florence (ravaged by the black plague in 1348), the *Decameron* enjoyed a widespread and lasting success, as attested by a considerable number of early modern translations into French, Spanish, German, and English (reviewer's note). While selected passages of the work were available in Petrarch's Latin rendering, it was Laurent de Premierfait's translation that assured the popularity of the integral text in France, a book serving as a literary model way into the sixteenth century (xxvii). Then, beginning in the year 1545, Laurent's text was abruptly displaced by a new translation executed by Antoine Le Maçon at the request of Marguerite, Queen of Navarre, who undertook to model her *Heptaméron* after Boccaccio's original work. Subsequently, Le Maçon's rendering became the exclusive source of all later editions (this translation will soon be available in Rose M. Bidler's edition). Di Stefano convincingly argues that it was hardly the alleged poor quality of Laurent's version that led to its fall into oblivion, as the publisher Étienne Roffet had stated in his preface to Le Maçon's new translation; rather, and paradoxically so, the "poor quality" was the result of a vigorous output of copies, imitations, and, from 1485 on, of printed versions which significantly altered the original text. Furthermore, within the context of the humanist debate over theory and practice of translation, a topic emerging in the sixteenth century, the rejection of Premierfait's text could be seen as a consequence of the humanist tendency to favor the *ad verbum* translation method (with full fidelity to the source), rather than the *sententia*-based approach focusing on content clarity (prevalent during the medieval period).

After the editor offers a thorough review of previous scholarship, his introduction provides an account of manuscript production, filiation, and transmission. In contrast to Carla Bozzolo (1973), who had based her classification of the fifteen extant manuscripts on a distinction between the presence or absence of the Griselidis story from the tenth day of the *Decameron*, Di Stefano establishes his corpus in light of the fact that all manuscripts are subject to continuous and significant changes in the transmission process. He distinguishes, however, between those modifications representing authorial interventions performed, for instance, under the pressure of a new patronage, and other less relevant scribal changes prompted primarily by textual inconsistencies. For example, a textual lacuna must have appeared in the original manuscript between days VIII and IX (as shown in MS BOD, see Di Stefano, 981, note 732), a circumstance which led to two different scribal solutions involving the *lancofiore* (Blancheflour) *novella* (VIII, 10).

A detailed analysis and comparison of all the manuscripts containing Premierfait's translation and an examination of Boccaccio's own Italian version of the text leads the editor to retain MS Vatican Pal. Lat. 1989 (VAT) as the archetype for his edition (xix). Di Stefano argues emphatically that VAT, copied between 1414 and 1420, is not only the closest in time to Premierfait's original translation but also the most faithful witness of this text. Both obvious and apparent errors have, however, been identified and explained in sufficient detail (xiii–xiv; e.g., *faire* instead of *foire*, 268). Moreover, four French manuscripts are included as control texts. Three French texts are presented in detail in the introduction: in addition to VAT, the MS Bodleian Douce 213 (BOD) dating from 1468–69, previously considered to be the best manuscript, and MS Paris BNF fr. 129 (BN2), dated c.1475. As for the Italian source texts of the *Decameron*, Di Stefano has chosen Vittore Branca's edition (1987), based on the MS Berlin Hamilton 90 (BOC), and another Italian text (Paris BNF it. 483: Pa1 — a copy of an early version produced at the time of the French translation), serving as a control text. Thus, a fine balance has been achieved between the traditional Bédierist editorial method promoting the best manuscript as the most faithful to the original text, and more recent editorial practices inspired by Paul Zumthor's *mouvance* theory (1979), which aims to offer a full but non-hierarchical (i.e., non-derivative) image of all witnesses (first copies?) of the original text (see Mary Speer, 1991).

Di Stefano's goal has been to provide an edition that renders the source text faithfully; ideally, his work would be the first variant of the translation, he believes (xxviii). However, the reality of the texts (source and translation) scarcely supports this prediction: neither the Italian source text nor the first French target rendering are known at the present time, and Di Stefano argues that the latter was indeed a rare manuscript circulating in clerical circles exclusively (xxiii). Even more puzzling is the fact that Laurent, having admitted to insufficient mastery of the Italian language (Prologue, p. 5), has felt compelled to use a Latin intermediary as the source of his translation. This Latin rendering was authored by Antonio d'Arruzo, a Franciscan monk, but it no longer exists; it took thus a great deal of philological acumen such as that of our editor to capture (guess?) the lexical characteristics of a text in regard to which none of the original versions is known. He has done so by analyzing specifically the case of loan words (calques), forms of lexical and syntactic replication that tend to dominate earlier translation practices and thus can be considered as partial indicators of authenticity. The calque feature is conspicuously exhibited in VAT, as shown by the example of the verb *mugir*: although inappropriately used in VAT to describe the howling of a lioness (a lesson rejected in both BN1 and BOD), this calque is derived from the Latin term *mugire*, which, for its part, is a loanword based on the Italian "mugghiar che pareva un leone" (VIII, 7 — to roar like a lion). Rather than representing a complicating factor in the fragmentary manuscript filiation, the Latin "filter" of the text (xxv), although hypothetical, proves, in cases such as this one, to be a reliable control for editing the original French translation. The bibliography has been selected so as to document with precision all the major points discussed in Di Stefano's introduction.

The integral text of VAT has been transcribed according to accepted editorial protocol, although even such basic graphic distinctions as those between "i" and "j," or "v" and "u," or adjectival and adverbial prefixes (e.g., "scestassavoir," p. 311, spelled as "cestassavoir" on xxxi) have been scrutinized by the editor with great care and precision. Typographical features, such as bold type and italics, have been used to distinguish between titles, introductory and concluding parts of the frame story, and the narrative material of each particular day, respectively. In addition to Boccaccio's prologue, the editor has included Laurent de Premierfait's own preface, preserved in two manuscripts other than VAT. The paratextual material provides valuable information about the translator, the issues of patronage, and collaboration, as well as significant theoretical points related to the translation process (1–6). It remains up to the reader, however, to grasp such rhetorical nuances as that between Boccaccio's primary, although not exclusive, concern for providing amusement for lovesick ladies (which reflects a medieval narrative courtly convention), and Laurent de Premierfait's reader-response awareness becoming evident as he targets a mixed audience and also seeks to outweigh the *delectare* principle by inscribing increased moral profit.

Editorial interventions, presented in brackets, were performed only when an error in VAT was obvious and a proposed correction seemed satisfactory (xxix). However, it has not always been possible to distinguish between errors due to lacunae or to inconsistencies of the scribes (e.g., "extendi," which is also spelled "extendit," 985), and those apparent errors prompted by the intricacies of the source text and lexical paucity of the target version (a helpful list of challenging terms is provided on xi). The use of Italian editions as control texts helped to identify these cases (see for instance 917, note 167).

Even though it is beyond the scope of this edition to provide an analysis of the grammatical features of Laurent de Premierfait's French translation, the less-initiated reader might have benefited from some comments on the reasons which led the translator to render rather indiscriminately the Italian gerund using the syntactical calque, which resulted in a plethora of terms such as "en lisend" (from "leggendo," 438), or the more current present participle "parlans" (from "ragionando," 305), as suggested by the control text (BOC). Moreover, the editor might have questioned whether de Premierfait succeeded in translating puns, such as "donde s'imbeccano" (where they feed), used by Boccaccio to describe "papere" (goslings), an extended metaphor for "women" (in order for Filippo Balducci to keep his son from untimely sexual desire — author's preamble to day IV, Di Stefano, 442).

Obviously, the translator of the Italian pun arrived at Middle French via Latin! These are minor details eliciting further inquiry.

In sum, we can only commend the editor for the excellent quality, erudition, precision, and linguistic wisdom documenting this rich undertaking. The present volume will serve for many years as a superb model for editorial projects involving translations of medieval texts. Furthermore, it will benefit the fields of cultural history and comparative literature given its concern with inter-vernacular appropriation of texts through the translation process; in addition, Di Stefano's work clarifies the status of the French language within the framework of vernacular tongues and Latin. Finally, by virtue of its role as a document about early modern humanism in general, the edition testifies to the continuing vitality and scientific value of the philological approach.

Olga Anna Duhl, Lafayette College

Duval, Frédéric, and S. Hériché-Pradeau, ed. *Guillaume Tardif: Les Facecies de Poge, traduction du 'Liber facetiarum' de Poggio Bracciolini*. Geneva: Droz, 2003. Pp. 315.

The editors of this fifteenth-c. translation realize that Poggio's facetiae (printed 1474) were a great success in Italy as well as in France, especially in Tardif's translation (1492). Poggio (1380–1459) was one of the most colorful and versatile of the Italian humanists, and the *Liber Facetiarum* was the first volume of its kind to be published in Europe. In this collection of two hundred and seventy-three items — jests, bons mots, puns, and humorous anecdotes — the expansive Arab-Italian *novella* can be seen turning into the swift *facezia*. However, Tardif's French *facecies* seemed to be different enough in style from their source text to contribute to French narrative literature all by themselves, as this translation is visibly aimed at his nation's readers. In general, early modern *translations* took certain liberties with their source texts, as we have shown in the case of Sebastian Brant's *Ship of Fools* (1494): certain works were deemed worthy of being transmitted into another language primarily because of their subject matter, but were not necessarily faithful to the original (see the introduction to my edition of Pierre Rivière's *La Nef des folz du monde* [1497], 2 vols. [Ann Arbor: UMI, 1977]).

Duval and Hériché-Pradeau's edition contains 115 facetiae (of a total of 273 tales), most of which tell a salacious story ended by a moral lesson or proverb. Duval's introduction of fifty-two pages is a valuable key to Tardif's (autonomous) work, the latter being an adaptation of the *facetiae* that meets the French readers' horizon of expectations — in Duval's opinion. Some modern critics consider Tardif a pedant with a lack of humor and his work a misogynous degradation of the original version, while Duval seems to prove that the text is the result of rewriting Poggio intentionally in view of the moral and social backgrounds of target readers (14).

For Poggio, the stories were to distract the readership above all, written as they were in an elegant style (*urbanitas*), obscene only when they castigated human stupidity. Tardif, in contrast, chose these 115 tales because they contained moral themes or attitudes which led this *translator* to embroider upon specific points. Under Tardif's pen, Poggio's sexual impudicity was indeed turned into witty allusions and images: lust, for Tardif, was one of the capital sins — not a subject of comedy, according to Duval. Guillaume addressed the French king (Charles VIII) and the nobility, and if a nobleman showed ignorance in a story, this fact remained without comment or was blamed on the man's subordinates. When something happened in the distant past, Tardif spoke of *Gallia* rather than France; once the text passed the Alps, it thus entered a new cultural universe, Duval and Hériché-Pradeau continued.

In fact, Tardif changed the narrative structure decisively: what was expressed as direct discourse in Poggio became now indirect speech which introduced causality into the narrative, thus motivating intentions and rendering actions as credible. Yet sometimes the moral endings of Tardif's adaptations seemed oddly out of place. Thus, in story # V, we witness the wedding night of an *uneven* couple (young wife/old husband), where intercourse is coupled with sodomy, apparently by the man's stupidity. The (hasty) moral ending simply remarks that this circumstance shows how men become fools in the hand of women and that a fool can be persuaded by anything (or anyone). The editors, however, did not question this ending for its possible play with the readers, tongue-in-cheek; in other words, they may not have recognized Tardif's stylistic finesse, and the same is true for stories X, LXXI, and LXXII. To reinforce this playfulness, Tardif quotes St. Bernard, Pseudo-Cato, or a proverb, following a referencing habit of both medieval and humanist authors. If the reviewer is correct, the readers of this edition may come to the same conclusion.

Edelgard E. DuBruck, Marygrove College

Findlen, Paula, Michelle M. Fontaine, and Duane J. Osheim, ed. *Beyond Florence: The Contours of Medieval and Early Modern Italy*. Stanford: Stanford University Press, 2003. Pp. 324, nine maps & figures.

If one looks for a comprehensive publication that both represents and exemplifies the major directions which historical research of Pre- and Post-Reformation Italy has been following lately, *Beyond Florence: The Contours of Medieval and Early Modern Italy* is one of the best such publications. Originating from a conference at Stanford University in 1998, the collection includes revised and expanded papers written by senior and junior scholars, all of whom have been inspired by the teaching and guidance of William M. Bowsky.

The first two articles (Part I), by Gene Brucker and Paula Findlen, are the veritable introductions of the book, as they survey the ever-growing studies on Florence and evaluate these sources' impact on past and recent scholarship. The last study of this collection, by Randolph Starn, may be perceived as the conclusion (and, to some extent, a review) of the entire volume, since it reveals implications of leaving Florence behind, in a manner of speaking, and concentrating on what he (and Elena Fasano Guarini) see as the periphery (239). All the other fourteen essays form the bulk of this collection honoring Bowsky's work on Italian history; the studies edited here explore diverse historical issues associated with towns and regions across the Italian peninsula, including known cities such as Rome (or rather the Papal State), Venice, Naples, Bologna, Orvieto, and Siena, as well as less frequently investigated, if not completely overlooked, places such as the Mugello (in Tuscany), Lucca, Modena, and Fabriano (in the March of Ancona).

Of the amazing array of subjects examined in the present collection, the role that religion played in public and private life not only in medieval but also in Renaissance and Baroque Italy receives the most attention here. For example, Cynthia Polecritti scrutinizes the many ways in which Bernardino da Siena (1380–1444) tried to teach, convince, chide, and encourage his listeners who gathered in the squares and churches of Siena (and Florence). Moreover, Robert Cooper examines the interrelationship between the Silvestrine monastery and Fabriano during the thirteenth century, concluding that Silvestrine presence sacralized urban space.

Robert Davis introduces readers to the German and English clerics who stopped in Venice on their way to the Holy Land (c.1380–1530s), intent on touching and kissing local relics such as the bodies of Saints Mark, Zacharias, Lucy, and Marina, among many others. Roberto Bizzocchi's conviction that the Church's fundamental presence in [Italian] secular society was beyond questioning, as Starn reminds us (238), is certainly one of the underlying concerns of *Beyond Florence*. Even articles which appear in sections of the book devoted to such themes as city and countryside (Part II), law and society (Part III), and topographies of power (Part IV), present readers with instances of and observations on the inseparability between most aspects of Italian history and Catholicism. Thus, Robert Brentano's conclusion that fourteenth-c. Italians identified themselves by place (72) is drawn from his study of itinerant Franciscan friars and, in particular, Salimbene of Parma, who lived in and wrote about Pisa as well as other cities. Similarly, Thomas Dandelet's revelation that Spain financed the rebuilding of early Baroque Rome is supported by his analysis of the economic benefits shared by Pope

Pius IV (and the Papal State) and King Philip II of Spain after the middle of the sixteenth century.

Among the essays which focus exclusively on the secular facet of Italian society, most fascinating is Carol Lansing's detailed examination of poor women in Bologna who, having no dowries, had to be content with common-law marriages and who on other occasions were deemed prostitutes and exiled from the city. Another interesting article shedding light on legal processes is the one by Laurie Nussdorfer who, guided by the manual of the Roman lawyer Prospero Farinacci (written from 1581 until 1614), enumerates and studies the crimes committed by notaries.

The fact that each paper focuses on a singular phenomenon in Pre- and Post-Reformation Italy does not mean that the panoramic and often vivid picture that the articles as a whole provide us is neglected. Several studies reinforce each other's arguments to indicate that some aspects of medieval and early modern Italian societies were quite similar. For instance, when Polecritti recounts that San Bernardino once promised the members of his captive audience that he would show them the devil himself and succeeded in assembling a considerable crowd (147), she prepares us, as it were, for Jennifer Selwyn, a later contributor, who writes that in order to attract people in Naples and the Italian South, Jesuits often preached in squares in which acrobats were simultaneously performing (172). Likewise, when David Foote surveys the reactions of the Orvieto commune to the arrival of the new foreign lord, Cardinal Gil Albornoz (appointed by the Avignon papacy in 1354), Foote gets us ready, so to speak, for Michelle Fontaine's upcoming examination of the changes occurring in the community and public life of Modena when Cesare I d'Este made the city the center of his Duchy (1598).

The studies are the products of distinct viewpoints and approaches, a common and expected characteristic of anthologies such as the present one, and each of the articles demonstrates a different methodology. Although many analyses focus on one area, a few, including Maureen Miller's comparative treatment of centers of ecclesiastical and communal power throughout central and northern Italy, provide us with glimpses about broader parts of the Italian peninsula.

This review would not be complete had it not considered, or at least mentioned, some of the ideas penned by Starn at the end of the publication. While these points are complex and thought-provoking, they sometimes leave the readers with conflicting views which may prove confusing. For instance, while Starn seems to deplore the absence (in this book and earlier collections of essays) of signature themes having long characterized Florentine Renaissance studies (233), he reiterates Brucker's statement made in the first article; namely, that "rumors of the demise of a dynamic and productive Florentine historiography are greatly exaggerated" (234). One of the questions with which we may be left when reading Starn's afterword is whether he believes that such studies as those included in this anthology represent "more and more research in the margins" which is likely "to lead to ... trivia" (235); or whether he agrees with Findlen who stated in the second essay that "polycentrism and the interdisciplinary read that goes with it are ... the most hopeful signs of the future" (ibid.).

Yael Even, University of Missouri/St. Louis

Hope, Geoffroy, éd. *Le Violier des histoires rommaines*. Geneva: Droz, 2002. Pp. xxvi; 675.

Le *Violier* (Bouquet) résulte de la traduction, vers 1521, d'un choix de 151 des quelques 181 textes de l'anthologie des *Gesta Romanorum*, qui, elle, remonte au XIVe siècle (MS Innsbruck, cod. lat. 310, daté de 1342). Le succès des *Gesta* attesté par de nombreux imprimés au XVe siècle (p. xii) — 1472 exemplaires à Utrecht, 1473 à Cologne, 1499 à Paris (et la Bibliographie, p. 619, en relève quatre autres) — suggère que l'œuvre avait déjà connu, avant sa traduction en français, du succès, autant comme ouvrage de lecture que comme instrument de prédication (xii). Ce statut équivoque du *Violier* — à la fois, œuvre de prêche et texte de recréation — ressort de sa facture. Prenons le premier mot du titre, *violier*: il désigne bien sûr un bouquet de belles fleurs-textes; mais le mot devait bien aussi évoquer le *violeur* [violator] pour les lecteurs de la génération de Clément Marot; et puis, que faire des *histoires rommaines*? Si la plupart des récits se placent sous le nom rassurant d'un grand de l'antiquité (aussi bien troyen que bysantin que romain), les récits que ces mots du titre coiffent n'ont en général rien d'antique ni de romain. Ce florilège de textes très divers (maximes, isopets, fabliaux, bestaires, contes), semble pourtant tirer son *unité* de la *moralisation* qui suit généralement le récit et dans laquelle on nous fait apprendre inlassablement que l'histoire précédente ne raconte rien de plus ni de moins que le conflit entre Dieu et le monde avec l'âme, avec *ton âme*, lecteur, en enjeu. Presque toujours, le titre du récit entre dans la même intention *spirituelle*. Or, en fait, c'est l'inceste (textes 13, 79, 126), l'adultère (3, 66, 80), la vengeance (113, 117), la ruse (21, 27, 95), la férocité (48, 123), et les mutilations du corps (28, 44, 47) qui constituent des sujets de choix de ces beaux récits. En somme, tout se passe ici comme si l'éditeur/auteur visa à déguiser sous une épaisse couche de théologie normalisante des récits libres. Mais l'acheteur/lecteur avisé du *Violier* pouvait de la sorte s'offrir le plaisir de lire en toute tranquillité des histoires *réalistes* sous les yeux mêmes des censeurs. L'invention était belle; elle annonce une pratique pareille chez les dames de la cour un siècle plus tard: "Les dames élégantes, au temps d'Henri IV, allaient jusqu'à faire relier les oeuvres de Nervèze [Antoine de, vers 1576–1614/15] sous forme de livres d'heures afin de pouvoir les emporter sans scandale à l'église" (Antoine Adam éd., *Romanciers du XVIIe siècle* [Paris: Gallimard, 1962]: 7).

Pour le texte (1–459) de son édition du *Violier,* Hope transcrit avec soin la traduction que l'imprimeur/éditeur Jean de la Garde fit faire en 1521 des *Gesta* (Bibliothèque de l'Arsenal, fol. H.920); l'éditeur relève dans ses notes en bas des pages des variantes prises des deux autres éditions du XVIe siècle: 1525 (Philippe le Noir, avec quelques petites modifications linguistiques et stylistiques); 1529 (Denis Janot). Depuis ces oeuvres, il n'y avait eu qu'une autre édition avant celle de Hope: celle de 1858 procurée par Gustave Brunet pour la Bibliothèque elzévirienne et que l'on peut aujourd'hui consulter sous forme de texte numérisé à l'internet: www.bnf.fr (gallica).

Les notes (461–618) où l'éditeur relève en grand détail les antécédents et les suivants des *histoires* rendront de grands services aux lecteurs, surtout aux folkloristes. Dans l'impossibilité de contrôler en détail la masse d'informations fournie par l'éditeur, nous avons noté une omission: pour le texte le plus long du recueil, le # 126 (354–94), qui rapporte une version du *Roman d'Apollonius de Tyr,* il manque dans les notes une référence à l'importante édition de cet excellent roman d'aventures par Michel Zink (Paris: Union Générale d'Éditions, 1982 [voir p. 315]).

La Bibliographie (619–34) est très fournie. Une critique mineure: l'ordre suivi par nom d'éditeur et non pas par auteur/titre pour les "éditions d'autres textes" en rend la consultation plus difficile que nécessaire. Sous la rubrique "Illustrations," se trouvent bien reproduits (641–61) vingt des quarante-huit feuillets historiés de l'imprimé de Jean de la Garde. La plupart de ces gravures proviennent des *Fantaisies de Mere Sote* (1516) de Pierre Gringore: on peut actuellement consulter une reproduction de cette édition sur "Gallica" du site internet de la Bibliothèque Nationale (voir au-dessus).

Quant au "Petit Glossaire" (663–75), il est en effet plutôt minimal. Au cours d'une lecture non systématique nous avons relevé une vingtaine de termes qui auraient pu y figurer: *confabuloit* (113) [*confabuler=s'entretenir familièrement avec quelqu'un*]; *contrir, se* (102) [*se repentir*]; *discertation* (318) [*exposition?*]; *fas* (33) [*faste*]; *fielle* (387*)* [texte corrompu: erreur sans doute pour *fille*; voir le texte du *Roman d'Apollonius de Tyr* (1982)*,* 144]; *garruler* (p. 105) [*parler beaucoup*]; *guynase* (362–63*)* [*gymnase*]; *hameau* (243) [ajouter un renvoi à *claveau*]; *impitié* (355) [*méchanceté*]; *ladresse* (350) [*femme attaquée de la lèpre*]; *margarite* (418) [*perle?*]; *macter, se* (67) [*s'immoler*]; *natalices* (383) [*natales*]; *nefas* (33) [*interdiction?*]; *nidifie[r]* (110)[*nicher*]; *[se] procurant* (316) [*s'occupant de*]; *reht* (56) [erreur de lecture pour *reth* = rets]; *saisa* (284) [erreur pour *saisi?*]; *superbité* (27) [*superbe; parole orgueilleuse*]; *utilitez* (360) [*profit matériel*].

George T. Diller, University of Florida

Jankrift, Kay Peter. *Krankheit und Heilkunde im Mittelalter.* Darmstadt: Wissenschaftliche Buchgesellschaft, 2003. Pp. ix; 148.

This volume forms part of the series "Geschichte kompakt," which covers various aspects of history, from antiquity to modern times. As stated in the introduction to the series, "the interested, teachers and learners, demand . . . reliable information which concentrates on complex . . . concepts and presents them in a readable manner" (my translation). In many respects the series is similar to the French *Que sais-je?,* but the format is more expansive. The research on sickness and medicine in the Middle Ages was done by Jankrift, who received his habilitation in 2002 and now does research in the Institute for the History of Medicine (Robert Bosch Foundation); he specializes in the late Middle Ages and emphasizes the social role of the science of healing.

In the first chapter the author describes the various written and material sources for the study of medical history, including osteoarcheology, while the next section deals with the theoretical underpinnings of medieval medicine. Jankrift begins here with the theories ascribed to Hippocrates and Galen, and their reception in the post-classical Christian world; he stresses the role played by magic and mentions Muslim scholars. Monastic medicine prior to the twelfth and thirteenth centuries (before the Church prohibited that clergy practice medicine and especially surgery) is contained in chapter three. Jankrift explains that generally monks were skilled in healing and mentions in particular their reliance on medicinal plants grown in herb gardens. Here, he also points out the medical significance of the Abbess Hildegard von Bingen (1098–1179), Germany's first female physician.

The following chapter is devoted to the development of medical education in the universities, starting with Salerno and continuing in Bologna, Montpellier, Padua, and Paris (all these facts covered in two pages). The next twenty-five pages discuss the social aspects of medicine and the manner in which patients were treated in public hospitals and leprosaria, starting with trends reigning during the crusades. The last chapter is the longest, forming almost one half of the book and treating "the great medical threats to medieval society": bubonic plague, leprosy, and other epidemics. The reader will consider this part as the most valuable, because the author gives abundant details and frequently quotes original sources in German translation.

Furthermore, the book contains three pages of extracts from archives in contemporary German, pages which may be of scant use to those who did not study *Mittelhochdeutsch.* The five-page selected bibliography reflects mainly German scholarship. Thus, the work will not be usable by the American readership at large and, incidentally, scholars in the field may find it too primitive; most students would not be able to profit from this short outline unless they had sufficient German.

Leonardas V. Gerulaitis, Oakland University

Séris, Émilie. *Les Étoiles de Némesis: La rhétorique de la mémoire dans la poésie d'Ange Politien (1454–1494)*. Geneva: Droz, 2002. Pp. 494; illus.

The Florentine author, translator, and scholar Poliziano opens his best-known poem, the "Stanze per la giostra" (stanzas for the joust won by Giuliano de' Medici), with a confession that his poetic song is engendered by a yearning to ensure that "fortune, death, or time may not carry off great names and uniquely eminent deeds" (my translation). Nemesis — who, in Poliziano's description, bears a diadem of stars, read by Séris as shining images of memory itself — is given by the author a central role of remembrance in Poliziano's literary oeuvre. Acutely aware of the power of word and image to defeat death and forgetfulness, Poliziano is concerned with the art of memory, Séris convincingly contends, for three mutually reinforcing reasons: the value placed by newly appreciated classical authors on preserving their exemplary lives and works, the stated desire of his well-born patrons for immortality, and his own personal agenda for lasting fame. However, Séris concentrates less on the *why* than the *how*: the rhetorical techniques and symbols Poliziano employs to structure his works and maximize their utility as *aides-mémoire*. She identifies the wide range of antique sources on which he drew both for underlying methods — mainly the works of Cicero and Quintilian — and for specific references or tropes.

Séris develops this straightforward theme of Renaissance mnemonics (in the tradition of Frances Yates) through a series of variations, each a case study of some scenario drawn from ancient, biblical, or medieval texts. Her survey is divided into three parts, devoted to major functions or forms of memory — political, ethical, and literary; each section is further subdivided into three units detailing specific memory-images, from Orpheus to the Adoration of the Magi. According to classical rhetoric, an author is expected, first, to invent vivid visual descriptions of the subjects to be recalled, and then to help a reader hold these images in the "mind's eye" by arraying them at specific sites in an orderly spatial panorama, from which they can be easily summoned to mind (e.g., Arcadia; the Underworld). Séris parses some two dozen of Poliziano's "places of memory" (*lieux de mémoire*), both their debts to classical tradition and their relevance to contemporary concerns.

An integral and valuable element of Séris's book is its close attention to visual images. Poliziano was deeply involved with the arts, writing ecphrases of imagined works and advising artists on iconography; not surprisingly, his mnemonic system was, like its classical prototypes, profoundly bound up with the sense of sight. In Séris's terms, "the goal of the art of memory is to place before the eyes things whose memory we wish to conserve" (p. 19, my translation); in other words, in the now common topos, *ut pictura poesis* — poetry is like painting. She draws connections, some more convincing than others, between texts by Poliziano and images by contemporary artists. In part one of the book, devoted to the cult of princes, she examines Poliziano's poems celebrating the Medici in relation to Botticelli and Gozzoli, and she notes parallels between the Florentine's drama *Orfeo*, written for the Gonzaga rulers of Mantua, and images by their court artist Mantegna. In the third section, Séris proposes Poliziano's writings as possible sources for Raphael's later Roman frescoes. While the author deserves credit for stretching beyond her primary textual expertise, she does not avoid minor errors: Uccello illustrated the battle of San Romano, not San Gimignano (76); the date 1480 is decades too early to speculate about a stage "proscenium" (152).

In its structure and reasoning, Séris's work is perhaps too influenced by the very mnemonic systems it studies, tending like them (and like dissertations) toward the overschematic, overstated, and overlong. While its threes-within-threes structure is easy to follow (and usefully recapitulated in a final five-page grid and index), the system is too tidy by half: most of the nine subtopics embrace precisely three further concepts. Séris never met a possible source, parallel, or overtone she did not like, and quotes them all at length, in Latin or Italian and smooth French translations. Discussing Raphael's fresco of Parnassus, she devotes ten pages (365-75) to the crowns and lyres adorning its painted poets, even though both attributes are utterly conventional.

Part two, treating ethical memory, offers an example of these interlocked weaknesses; among the paintings discussed here is Botticelli's allegory long called *Pallas and the Centaur*; though she cites the standard English catalogue, Séris takes no note of Lightbown's reinterpretation of the heroine as Camilla, proposing instead a strained parallel to verses in Poliziano's "Stanze" describing Venus and Cupid. At this point the book begins to lose its way in a welter of sometimes minor examples, and the connecting thread of memory grows increasingly attenuated: little evidence is adduced that these images were *intended* as mnemonic, rather than merely *resembling* memory places, and frequent slippages occur from suggesting an idea to treating it as proven. In view of the plethora of sources and endless recycling of motifs, where she sees meaningful correspondences and conscious structures, it is possible to see merely coincidences and formulas. Notwithstanding her active imagination, the conclusion of this part, like much of what follows, is disappointingly dry, limited to restatement without further synthesis; her failure to mention Poliziano's homosexuality skews her reading of *Orfeo*, whose ending pivots on the hero's turn from women to men.

Book Reviews 215

Such reservations aside, on its own terms this is a workmanlike, if not ambitious, study, offering a clear thesis. However, a book of this heft raises a final question about its intended audience: why put out such an exhaustive tome in the usual few thousand copies read by as few specialists? Like other such works, it would be ten times more useful at one tenth the length. Converted into a suggestive and readable essay mapping out Poliziano's belief in poetry's importance for cultural memory, the principal techniques the Italian deployed to serve that function, and a representative sampling of visual and verbal sources, the book might offer students a helpful introduction and scholars a thoughtful *aide-mémoire*. In fact, Séris's concise "general conclusion" could well provide the skeleton for such a condensation (her detailed source material might be made available as an on-line appendix).

James M. Saslow, City University of New York

Wolfegg, Christoph Graf zu Waldburg. *Venus and Mars: The World of the Medieval Housebook*. Munich: Prestel, 1998. Pp. 115.

The invention of printing opened new spaces of expression and graphic representation to artists; *reality*, until the mid-fifteenth century to be found in the margins and illuminations of manuscripts, after the advent of printing came to assume center-position in illustrated editions (see Jan Białostocki, *L'Art du XVe siècle* [Paris: Librairie Générale Française, 1993], 212–13). Ever since the seventeenth century, the fifteenth-c. *Housebook* has been safeguarded and studied: the bibliography lists more than 200 entries. The book is a manual for the household of a knight's castle north of the Black Forest and covers a variety of subjects: warfare and defense; soap making; jousting and courtship, remedies against constipation, household implements, the art of memory, and astrology — all primarily secular themes.

The unknown artist of the dry-point engravings (by which images are drawn directly on the printing plate by a sharp stylus) is called "Housebook Master" or "Master of the Amsterdam Cabinet" (which location exhibits the Master's other works), and his dates are c.1470–1500. All prints and drawings were collected at Wolfegg Castle during the period of 1604–72, but since interior evidence relates to events which happened during the fifteenth century, this manual reflects life during the late Middle Ages.

The Housebook Master stood head and shoulders above most of his contemporaries in draftsmanship by embracing with sensitivity princes, priests, prostitutes, peasants, soldiers, prisoners, and even babies at play. He observed human character, not without reflecting his own sense of humor. The book is a delicate artifact (of sixty-three parchment leaves bound in flexible leather) and consequently rarely shown even in Germany. This reviewer had a chance to study it and to acquire Christoph von Wolfegg's lovely presentation in English at the National Gallery (Washington), where the book was exhibited for a short time early in 1999. The texts were written by two scribes in South German language with a sprinkling of Italian expressions (the latter for business-related matters).

The title page shows "the Artistes," skilled public performers clad in red and green tights, evidently taken from an engraving by Master E. S. (fl. 1450–67, Upper Rhine) and resembling figures on playing cards. In the background, two castles are visible, one more palatial than the other, showing the transition from Romanesque to Renaissance style (the reviewer). "The Art of Memory," an auxiliary to rhetoric, comprises only three pages in Latin and is the cornerstone of the entire manuscript: memory is faulty, but this book is to keep its owner from forgetting many items and functions necessary for the maintenance of a household.

The chapter on "The Children of the Planets" bears the late-medieval conviction that the macrocosm reflects the microcosm (and vice versa), namely, that humankind, characterized and distinguished in Hippocratic ways (the four-humor theory), is related to the planets and constellations at the moment of one's birth. Astrology was linked to astronomy, and the Church interwove astrological with Christian teachings. An imbalance of humors in a person was thought to cause diseases.

On the etching called "Saturn and His Children," Saturn is an old man with a crutch, and his offspring are vicious, dry, cold, and envious people; they shovel dirt, dig graves, and end up as criminals. "Jupiter's Children," in contrast, are blessed by Fortune, well-mannered, refined aristocrats, or they are judges, scholars, and jurists. This etching shows target-shooting, a stag-hunt (with falcon), and a perfect young couple on horseback. The illustration of Mars is *not* devoted to chivalry but presents defenseless villagers and a pilgrim roughed up and killed by soldiers (the Housebook Master was probably a bourgeois). Sol, the sun, under the sign of Leo, gives his children piety and joy; they listen to concerts and enjoy outdoor activities (some resemble the artistes on the title page). Venus, also on horseback, has her backside to us (*Frau Welt?*) and is accompanied by Libra and Taurus. The etching shows different kinds of eroticism: on the bottom (right front) we see "proper" lovemaking, while on the left there is bathhouse frolicking, and, set back, intercourse within bushes, and again artistes.

Mercury (Gemini and Virgo) seems serious, with many craftsmen (goldsmiths, painters, sculptors, organbuilders, and teachers) — all indoors, with some individuals at a meal; perspective is attempted but remains faulty. Luna, with consummate refinement, resembles a Botticelli figure on horseback; yet, the moon engenders people difficult to govern, among others millers, fishermen, and a fowler (dubious reputation). Our explanation for the array of people in these astrological etchings is that we may trace here an early attempt at psychological characterization, to be of help to a domestic steward in dealing with the persons of his surroundings (the reviewer). Some figures stem from Blockbooks.

The next seven drawings depict genre scenes. "Chivalrous Life" shows warlike jousts, a castle with a bathhouse, tournaments, the tilt, the hunt, and love, "pursuit of lesser game," and a knight. The castle is surrounded by a moat, but the life shown on the terrace may be fictitious: the lovely etching is probably the result of bourgeois imagination (the reviewer). Both sexes bathe together fired by wine, and the column on the left might nowadays be considered phallic. In the following illustration, a fortified city is shown in the background (with a gate), resembling the Jerusalem of several Netherlandish paintings (the reviewer). Here, everyday life is visible: duck hunting, fishing, a pilgrim in front of a chapel, women laundering in a river or moat.

Tournaments were prestigious and costly affairs, the basic requirement being aristocratic rank. The riders are armed to the point of immobility, and the horses' foreheads are also protected, while the shields carry ingenious devices or initials — straightforward names are avoided. As etching # 29 shows, a large audience was expected. There may be an influence here from the *Walther Codex* (Augsburg), but the exact dates of it and the *Housebook* are not known. A tilt is produced on figure 32: a joust between two riders with lances, and with warriors as the only spectators. Here, battle armour is more flexible (than that of tournaments) but also increases vulnerability; this joust could be staged ad hoc in a camp and is less costly than a tournament; music accompanies the proceedings, as it does during most of the *Housebook* activities.

"The Noble Hunt" is staged in the forefront of etching 33, while the villagers and their lives occupy the background (quite differently from arrangements in the *Très Riches Heures du Duc de Berry* — the reviewer). The hunt is for the noblest species: the stag; the knights' ladies sit behind the hunters on steeds. In the distance we see "the bent figure of a peasant who, having broken out in sweat from plowing, is pulling his smock off over his head" (60). Farther back, a gallows and a wheel (of torture?) are visible, watched by four crows expecting a meal.

"In Pursuit of Lesser Game," etching 34, shows common women hunting men! Plenty of allusions to lust and procreation have been made here, such as a stork on a chimney, a trapped peasant hanging by one leg from a tree (reminding one, however, of Goya!), and women at windows, signalling to attract men. Yet, this drawing remains a riddle: not all parts of it can be explained. "The Obscene Garden of Love," the final drawing in this gathering, is located in an enclosed garden (such as that of the *Roman de la Rose*), partially based on an etching by Master E. S. Here, the color is subdued: commoners of both sexes frolic at a meal, and two planks allow crossing a brook in order to reach an oversize waterwheel (alluding to the subsequent technical drawings of household implements). Large cliffs are visible — as a prelude to figure 44 (mining). We admire the interior cross-references of the Master's book.

The chapter on "Household Remedies" contains numerous recipes, encoded in Hebrew letters: the treatment of wounds, internal medicine (e.g., laxatives, cures for diarrhea, hemorrhoids, and the plague); also, methods for hardening iron, dyeing fabric, and two recipes for cooking. Then, we discover the first spinning wheel ever drawn (taking the place of the distaff), and further on, the scenes change to mining (a lovely illumination in bright colors, followed by detailed sketches on how to extract silver and copper from ore). Smelting recipes with tables of weights for gold conclude this gathering.

"The Technology of War" shows scaling equipment (here, not without humor, three males reach a girl up in a tower by different rope arrangements); an army on the march and an encampment, a battle wagon with chassis, a handmill with pin gear, a gun cart, and gun wagon. This second (very practical) part of the *Housebook* presents tools in clear array (even if sometimes the perspective is not quite correct). Generally in this book, courtly ideals have technology as a counterpoint; the original owner's name will probably be never found, but obviously, his choice of (a single) artist was brilliant. Nevertheless, the debate about "the Housebook Master is far from over" (109); it seems that he was familiar with the so-called international style and Dutch painting.

Edelgard E. DuBruck, Marygrove College